IMAGES
of America

NORTH FORK VALLEY

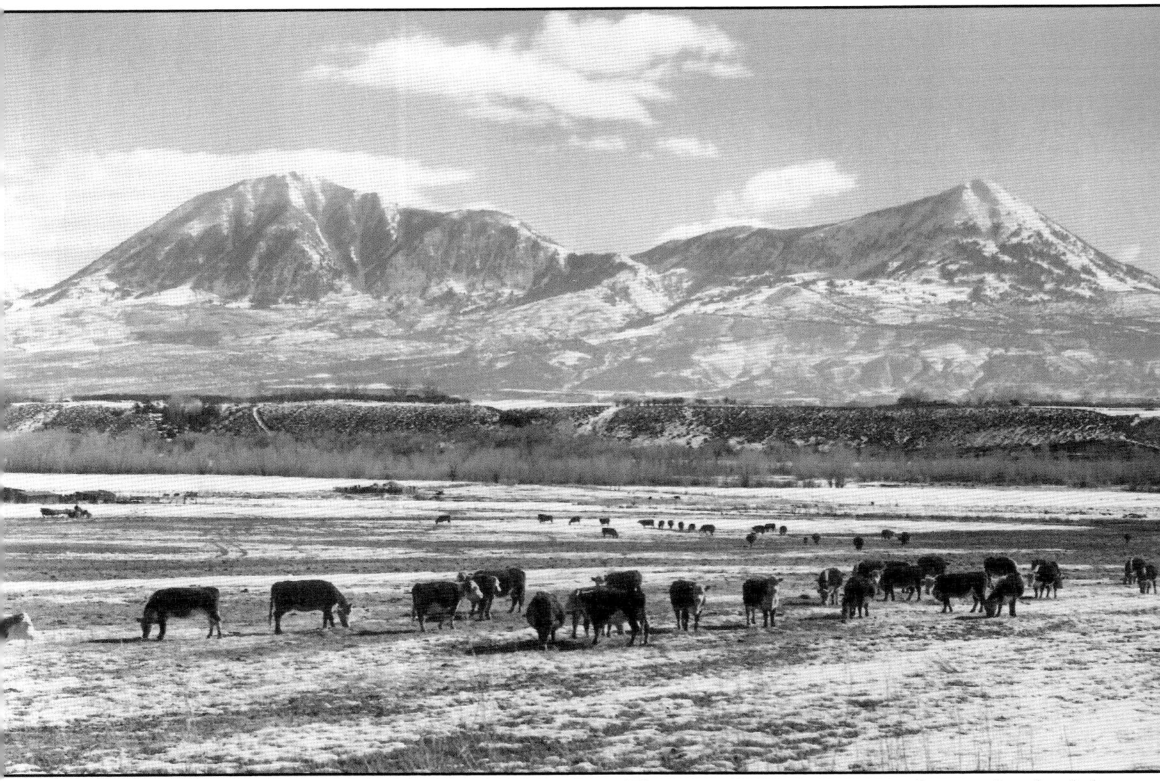

Mount Lamborn and Land's End Mountain. These two mountains provide a perfect backdrop for North Fork cattle. Ever changing, these mountains shelter fertile fields and orchards. In yesteryear, the meandering North Fork of the Gunnison River deposited rich silt in the river bottom, enticing settlers to stake their claims in this agricultural paradise. (Hotchkiss-Crawford Historical Society.)

On the Cover. By 1908, W.S. Edwards was called "Photographer Edwards." Almost all of the photographs in the Paonia chapter and a few in other chapters were taken by him. Pictured on a lawn is a packing crew from the early Nelson Brothers Packing Shed. They must have changed clothes for the photograph, as handling peaches was a hot, fuzzy, and dirty endeavor. (W.S. Edwards photograph, North Fork Historical Society.)

IMAGES
of America

NORTH FORK VALLEY

Kathy Addams McKee and Claudia Sutliff King

ARCADIA
PUBLISHING

ISBN 978-0-7385-9584-5

Published by Arcadia Publishing
Charleston, South Carolina

Printed in the United States of America

Library of Congress Control Number: 2012941057

For all general information, please contact Arcadia Publishing:
Telephone 843-853-2070
Fax 843-853-0044
E-mail sales@arcadiapublishing.com
For customer service and orders:
Toll-Free 1-888-313-2665

Visit us on the Internet at www.arcadiapublishing.com

To the founders of this beautiful valley, the museums for preserving its history, and the people who make it a wonderful place to live

Contents

Acknowledgments		6
Introduction		7
1.	Hotchkiss	9
2.	Lazear	39
3.	Crawford and Surrounding Areas	51
4.	Paonia	73
5.	Bowie	105
6.	Somerset and Nearby Mines	115

ACKNOWLEDGMENTS

The North Fork Valley needed a book on its history, and the museum in Hotchkiss asked its book committee to see how this could be done. Arcadia Publishing was the best way to accomplish this. We gathered photographs from our museums and other private collections and obtained information from oral histories, family history files, newspaper research, and other publications. We went from fearing that we would never have enough photographs to having too many. It was hard to choose which photographs to use. There were so many wonderful ones, and we were limited on the number we could use.

Words could never show my gratitude to my husband, Bill, for his patience with me through this whole process and to my daughter, Tara, for her support. Inez Pottorff gets credit for telling me that I could do this book and for keeping my spirits high when I was frustrated. Thanks go to other members of the book committee—Marilyn Tate, Dennis Turner, Karen Martin, and Joan Queen—for their support and photographs. Bud Bowie and Bill Bear shared interesting mining information and photographs. Appreciation goes to Chuck Farmer for "leading the way." Special thanks go to Claudia King for her help and positive support. Lastly, a thank-you goes to my ancestors, who decided to make this valley a home for many generations to come.

—Kathy McKee

My appreciation goes to residents of the North Fork Valley who made this such a great place to live. A special thank-you goes to Kathy McKee for scanning the photographs. The images from the North Fork Historical Society supplied by museum curator Judy Livingston were remarkable. My appreciation goes to historian Louise Sanders (1921–2012) for her helpful suggestions. Thanks also go to Myrna Hunten Pierson, Bill Palmer Sr., and Ralph Audin Jr. for mining information. Historical documents *Coal Mining of the North Fork* by Mabel Livingston, *The Formative Years* by Wilson Rockwell, and Wally Eubank's *Resumes of Items in the Paonia Newspapers* were invaluable.

—Claudia King

Hotchkiss-Crawford Historical Society (HCHS), North Fork Historical Society (NFHS), and Delta County Historical Society (DCHS) provided many photographs.

INTRODUCTION

Over a century ago, a wild river ran along the western slope of Colorado and joined the raging Gunnison River at the mouth of the precipitous Black Canyon. At its narrowest point, the Black Canyon gorge falls to 1,700 feet, and the wild river continues on to Delta, where it meets the Uncompahgre River, which brings cold melted snow from the breathtaking San Juan Mountains. After a trip through Dominguez and Escalante Canyons, the river arrives at Grand Junction, merging with the mighty Colorado River on its untamed journey to the Pacific Ocean. The name of this river is the North Fork of the Gunnison.

In the late summer of 1881, when the river was lowest, the Utes made their sad trek to the reservation in Utah. This opened the valley to settlement. Even before the Utes were removed, quite a few white men had entered the valley. One was George Duke. The following is from a 1923 letter to his daughter:

> Will [Duke] and I were camping on Crystal Creek. E. T. Hotchkiss (1832–1900) brought S. A. Wade, Sam Angevine (gunman), Bill Clarke and Dave Platt to our camp on Crystal Creek. They stayed all night with us, and we all pulled out for the North Fork country on August 30, 1881. Hotchkiss and I went ahead of the wagon . . . to cut trail. . . . We followed the old Indian trail as near as we could. . . . We cut cedars out through about where Crawford is. . . . Then we followed down and west of the ridge south of Hotchkiss along the Olson Valley until we came to the North Fork.

The Hotchkiss ranch remains to this day at the same location of the original claim. George Duke took a ranch up the river from the Hotchkiss claim, and Will Duke's claim was south of the river. Originally, Samuel Wade and William "Bill" Clarke had staked claims near Hotchkiss. When these claims were jumped, they went farther up the North Fork Valley to the Paonia area. Wade's claim lay below current Grand Avenue, while Clarke's property encompassed most of the present town of Paonia. Sam Angevine located at an Indian cornfield near the later Chinn Ranch.

The river bottom was very fertile and looked promising for agriculture. Young fruit trees were brought by wagon across Black Mesa in the winter of 1882, and thus began the fruit industry in the valley. The exceptional fruit won awards as far away as the 1893 World's Fair in Chicago. To support the wide variety of fruit—apricots, cherries, pears, peaches, plums, and apples—many ditches and canals began to honeycomb the valley. The most significant of these was the 32-mile-long Fire Mountain Canal, providing irrigation water from the North Fork River near Somerset to Paonia and Hotchkiss orchards. Another important canal was the 21-mile Overland Ditch, which expanded irrigated land to the mesas above the river. From 1882 to 1912, fruit became increasingly important. The climate, fertile soil, and lack of pests fueled optimism.

In 1902, a second event opened the valley to settlement. It was the narrow-gauge Denver & Rio Grande Railroad. The iron horse provided transportation for people, produce, and, more importantly, a link to markets for coal discovered in Bowie and Somerset. Coal proved to be abundant and low in sulfur content, becoming the dominant economic force in the second half of the 20th century.

The mining towns of Bowie and Somerset developed. The Somerset area became more connected to Paonia and less dependent upon the Indian trail to Crested Butte. Mining had its good times and bad times. Many miners farmed to supplement their incomes.

Crops played an important role in the area. Because of its location on the railroad, the agricultural community of Lazear grew. Crawford crops and livestock benefited from water from the early Gould Reservoir and the Crawford Reservoir, constructed in 1963. Both Crawford and Hotchkiss were especially suited for cattle and sheep. However, at first there was a running conflict between cattlemen and sheep ranchers, sometimes erupting in armed confrontations.

Two significant events, the completion of McClure Pass in 1946 and the construction of the Paonia Reservoir in 1962, had great impact upon the area. Even as early as 1920, McClure Pass was a dream because this road provided a means to transport agricultural products and livestock from the valley. The connection to Glenwood Springs was celebrated in July 1947, when a huge crowd gathered at the top of the pass for hot dogs, beer, and camaraderie. Representatives from the Paonia Chamber of Commerce and Glenwood Chamber of Commerce shook hands to cement the relationship.

The Paonia Reservoir was a Bureau of Reclamation project that brought life to the valley by providing water to crops and livestock. Today, the thriving farms and vineyards are a testimony to the importance of this project. Recreational opportunities, such as camping, boating, and water-skiing, in a stunning setting framed by majestic mountains are an added bonus.

In 2012, the main communities are Hotchkiss, Paonia, and Crawford. Each town has its own special events: Hotchkiss hosts Sheep Dog Trials in May and Delta County Fair in August, Paonia celebrates July Fourth Cherry Days and Harvest Festival in September, and Crawford emphasizes small-town traditions with Pioneer Days in June.

Needle Rock, Black Canyon, and Grand Mesa are popular destinations for visitors coming to the area. Just as it was for the early settlers, new residents and tourists are mesmerized by the fertile North Fork River Valley sheltered by Mount Lamborn.

One

Hotchkiss

George Duke and Enos Hotchkiss sat on a hill on the west side of the present town, in an area where the cemetery is now. They were making sure there were no Indians in the area. Enos looked down below, pointed to an area, and announced, "This is where I want to live." That place is still there today, as are living descendants of Hotchkiss.

These two men, though they were not alone, shaped the area into one of prominence and fortitude. Water projects, telephone lines, stores, ranches, organizations, and banks are ventures of which they had a part.

George was the first postmaster of Hotchkiss. Of course, the town had to have a name, so George just put down the name of his old friend, Hotchkiss. Enos, on the other hand, had another name in mind, but it was too late.

Enos Hotchkiss died in January 1900. The town of Hotchkiss was incorporated just months after his death.

The best example of the Hotchkiss community working together was on the construction of Memorial Hall, starting in the late 1940s. It was built to provide a place for community gatherings and would later house the library as well. Fundraising for the construction started out with a few donations and other activities such as the Kowboy Karnival. Soon, everyone took part in the fundraising, and money was never borrowed for construction of the building. People of all ages worked together to make a dream come true. An added attraction was a roller-skating rink, and it became a favorite place for the young and old to have fun. Enos Hotchkiss and George Duke would have been proud.

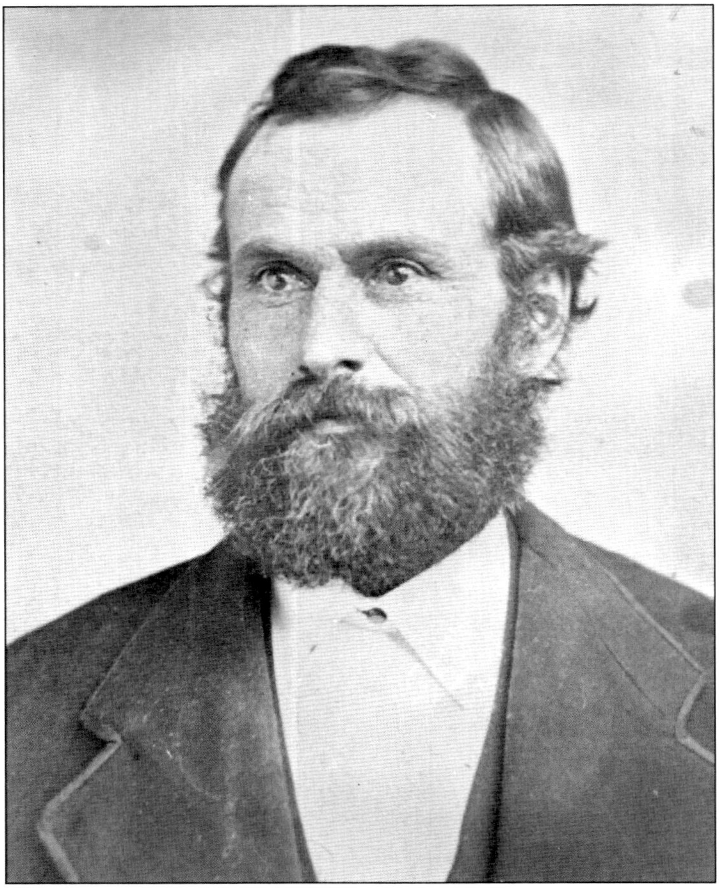

Enos T. Hotchkiss. After arriving in Colorado in 1859 with his brother Preston, Enos traveled to the Saguache area. A true entrepreneur, Enos was a prospector, rancher, an owner of a sawmill and a gristmill, a postmaster, and a justice of the peace, to name a few. He married Elizabeth McIntyre Cowen and then scouted the North Fork area in 1879. (HCHS.)

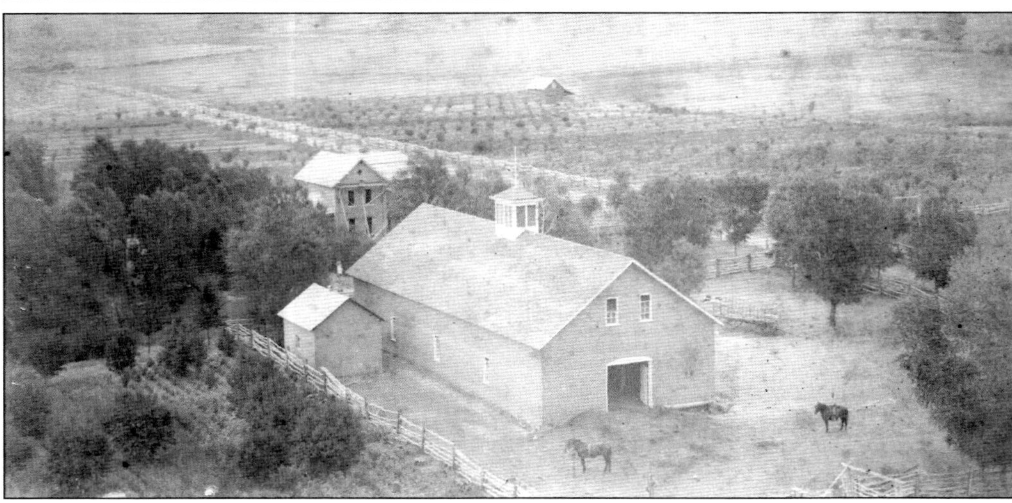

The Home Place. Enos Hotchkiss's son Monette paid $200 for 160 acres in 1884. In 1888, he received a patent and sold it to Enos for $800. In 1886, the brick barn was completed and a celebration was held there. There was also an unofficial fair to celebrate harvest time. In 1889, the house was built with brick from Montrose, Colorado. (Mary Hotchkiss Farmer.)

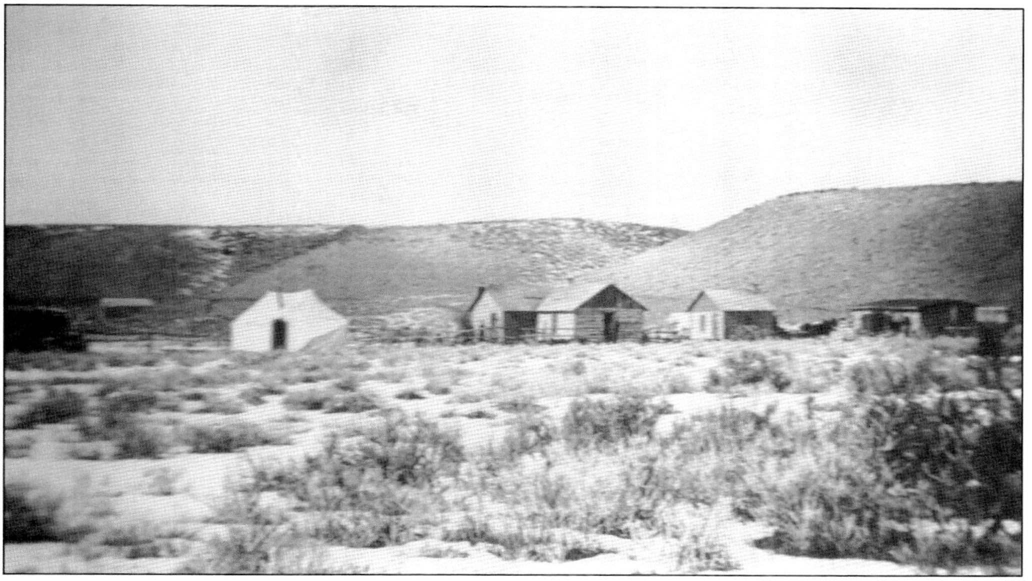

George H. Duke. George and his brother William came to Colorado from Illinois. They were hired to deliver horses to Pueblo, Colorado, for Enos Hotchkiss. When they arrived, Hotchkiss wanted them to accompany him on his trip to the North Fork area with promises of securing land through the Preemption Act. George's land was mostly comprised of the present town of Hotchkiss. His first house was a log cabin (above), but in 1896, he moved into a Victorian house on Duke Hill (below). George had many accomplishments, which included becoming the first postmaster, mayor, and county assessor. He was a promoter of the Fire Mountain Canal, financial provider for the construction of the Overland Reservoir, inventor of many items, and owner of a general store/bank. (Both, HCHS.)

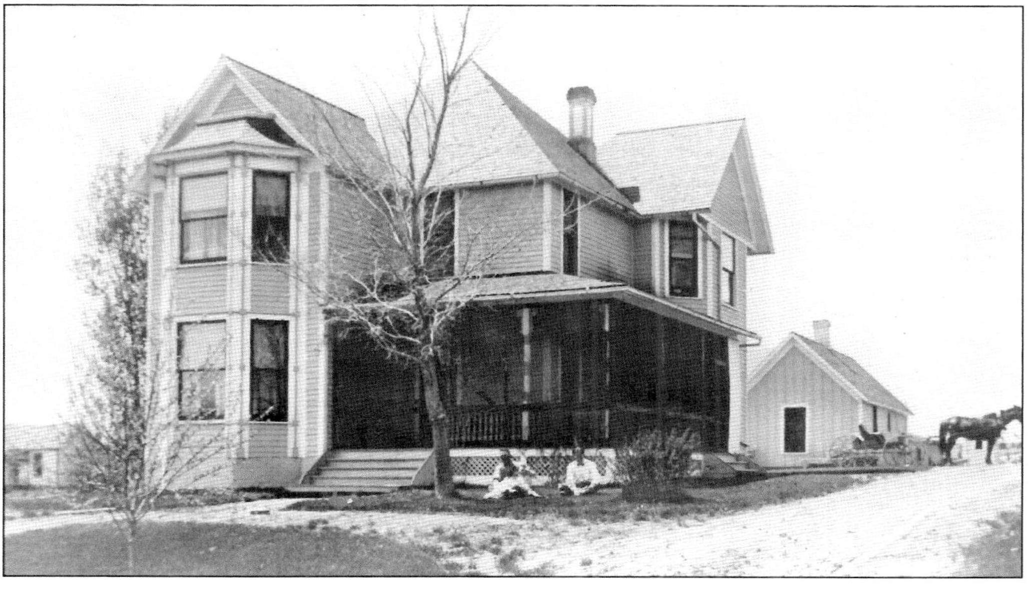

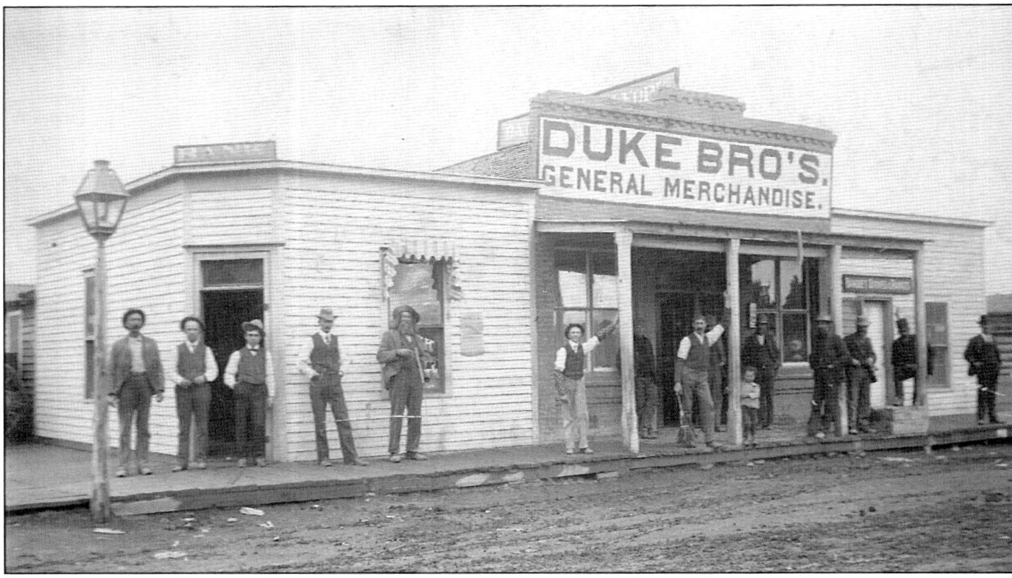

Duke Brothers General Merchandise and the Bank of North Fork. In 1886, the store opened and grossed over $70,000 annually. The three Duke brothers and Fred Simonds sold groceries, clothing, hats, boots, shoes, agricultural implements, buggies, and so on. It stood on the present site of Memorial Hall. The location was moved as it grew larger and in 1907 became Duke-Deutsch and Scott Company. When there was a fire, the owners bought out another general store, Stockham Brothers, to get merchandise again. In 1908, it became the Duke-Hanson Mercantile Company. In the 1950s, it was sold to the Hotchkiss Elks Club. The Bank of North Fork was established in 1893 by the Duke Brothers and Samuel Hartman after an attempted robbery at the store. Later, the bank moved to a stone, two-story building across from the "big store." (Both, HCHS.)

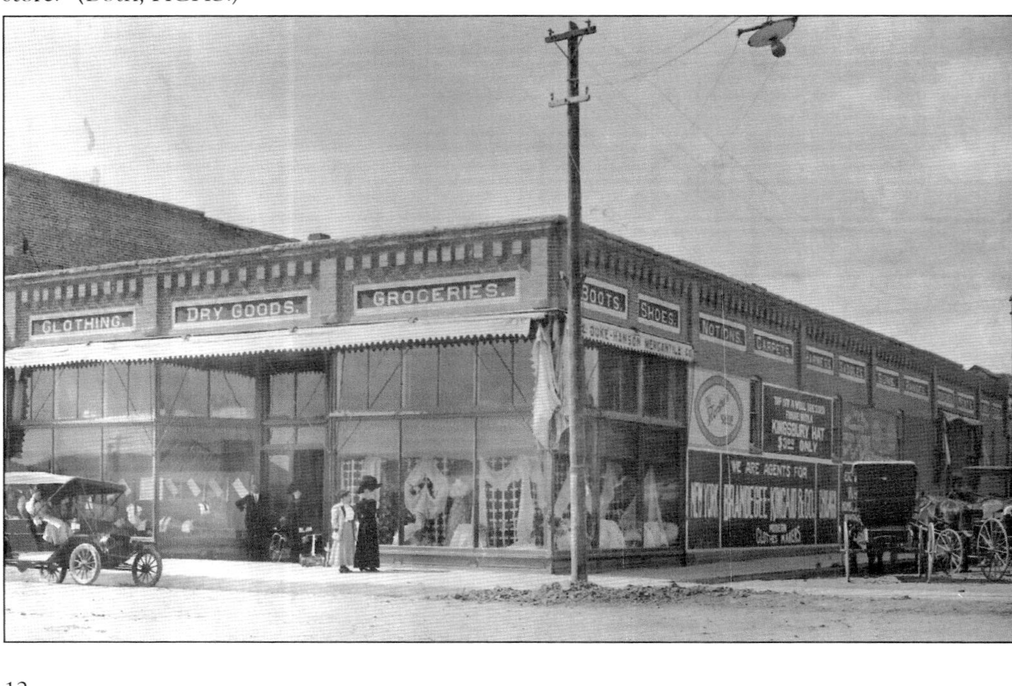

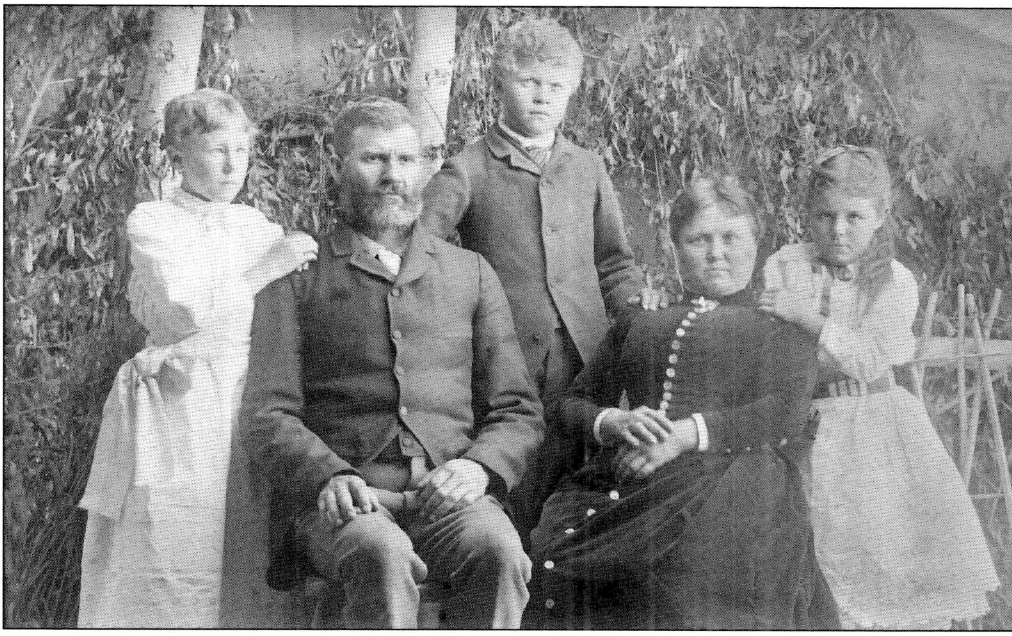

First Nuclear Family. The Swendt family—consisting of David, Ada, and their children, Mary Ella, Gary, and Cora—came to Hotchkiss in 1882 and was the first family to live here. David was a blacksmith, and he got a land patent on about 40 acres in 1890. He had a two-room log home with his blacksmith shop nearby. Daughter Cora married Robert Ashbaugh, and Ada lived with them around 1900, while David went to Cotopaxi, Colorado, for work. While in Hotchkiss, he sold land to the school district for $1 for the first brick school to be built. This school was built in 1887. In 1898, a two-story addition on the south side was added. On the east was a tower that had a school bell. (Both, HCHS.)

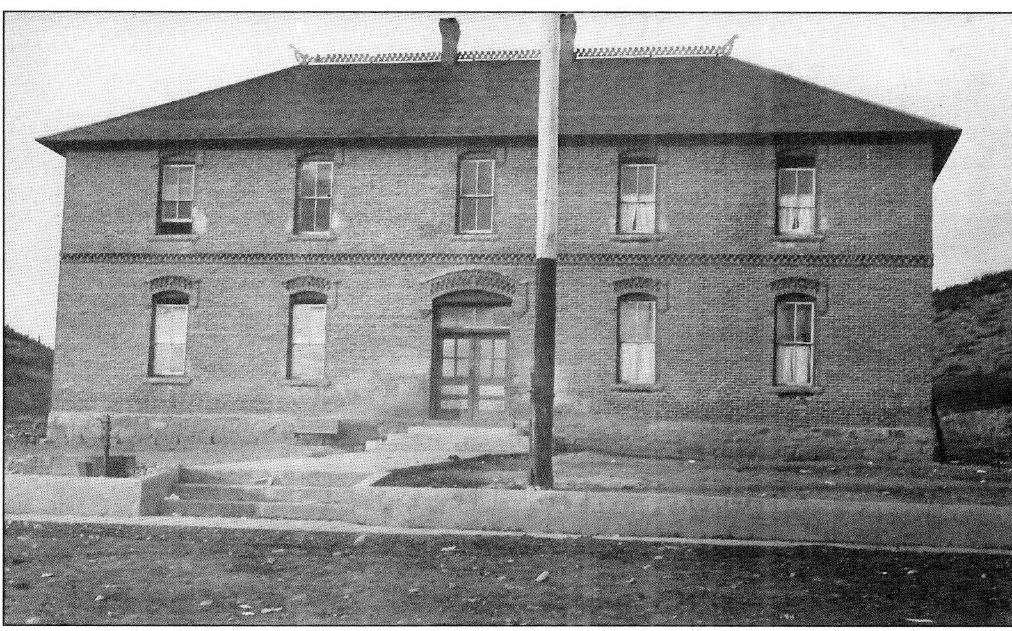

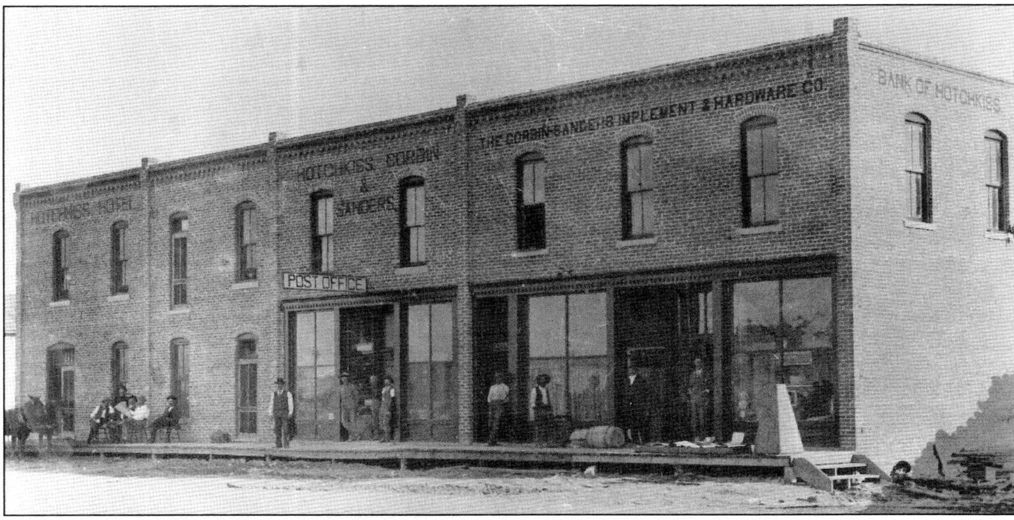

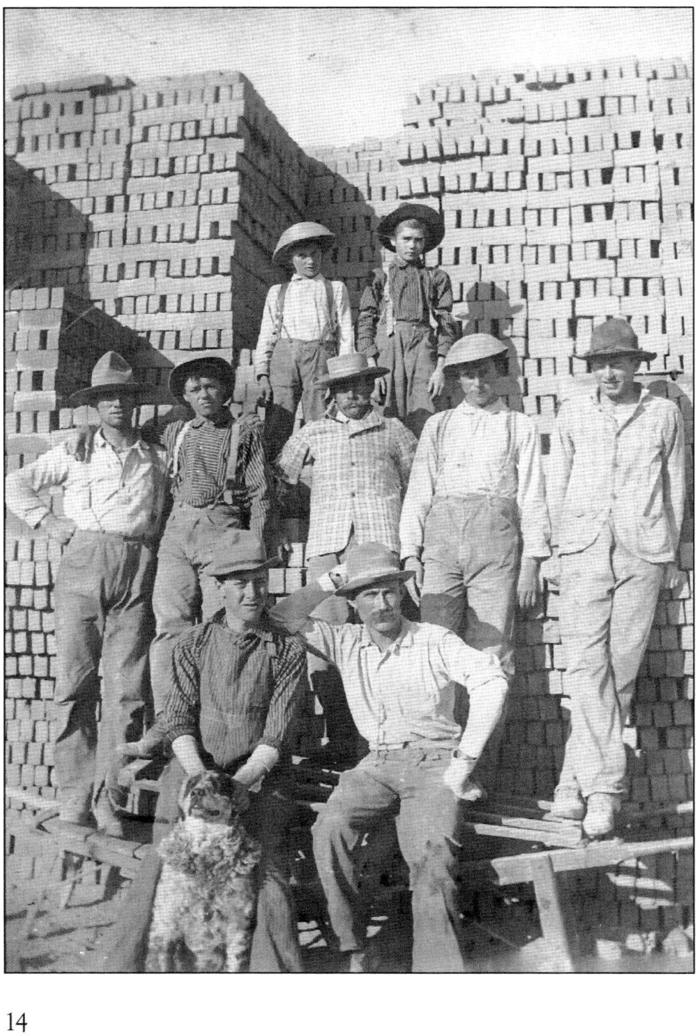

HOTCHKISS BLOCK. Built in 1897, this building had a post office, the Corbin-Sanders Implement and Hardware Company, the Bank of Hotchkiss, and a hotel. Later, the telephone company occupied the space where the bank was. Most of the building is still standing and has businesses and a restaurant, as well as apartments upstairs. (HCHS.)

SHERMAN BRICKYARD. The brick used in the Hotchkiss block came from this brickyard. Located where the present fairgrounds are, it was run by Carl and Alvin Sherman, nephews of Enos Hotchkiss. The bricks were made from clay (which is prevalent in the soil), sand from the river, and possibly straw or other binding material. The mix was poured into a wooden mold until formed and placed in a kiln or sun-baked. (HCHS.)

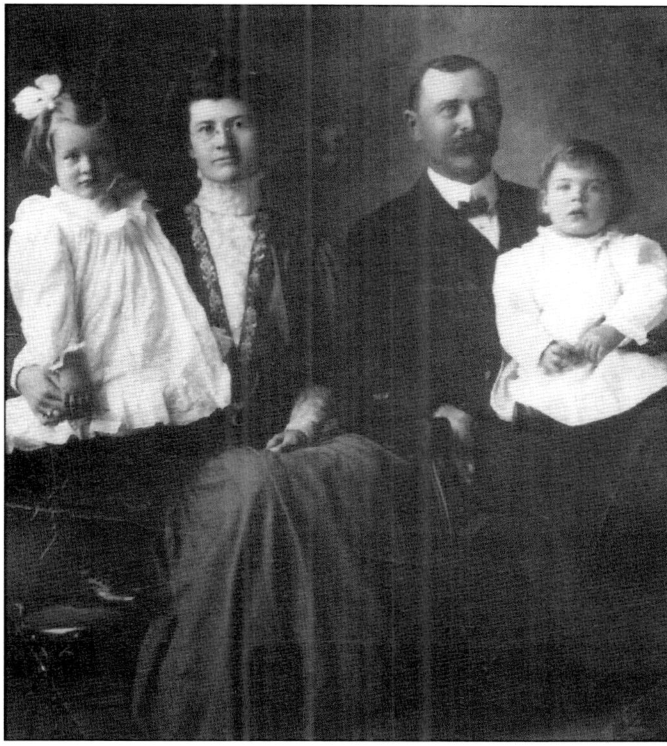

JOHN EDWARD HANSON. Born in Denmark, Hanson came to America at the age of four. After attending schools in Michigan and Chicago, he headed west in 1884. He came to Hotchkiss to see a friend, Joseph Reich, and partnered up with him on a stage line that ran a mail route. After moving back to Lake City, Hanson's wife died suddenly, and he turned to gambling. (HCHS.)

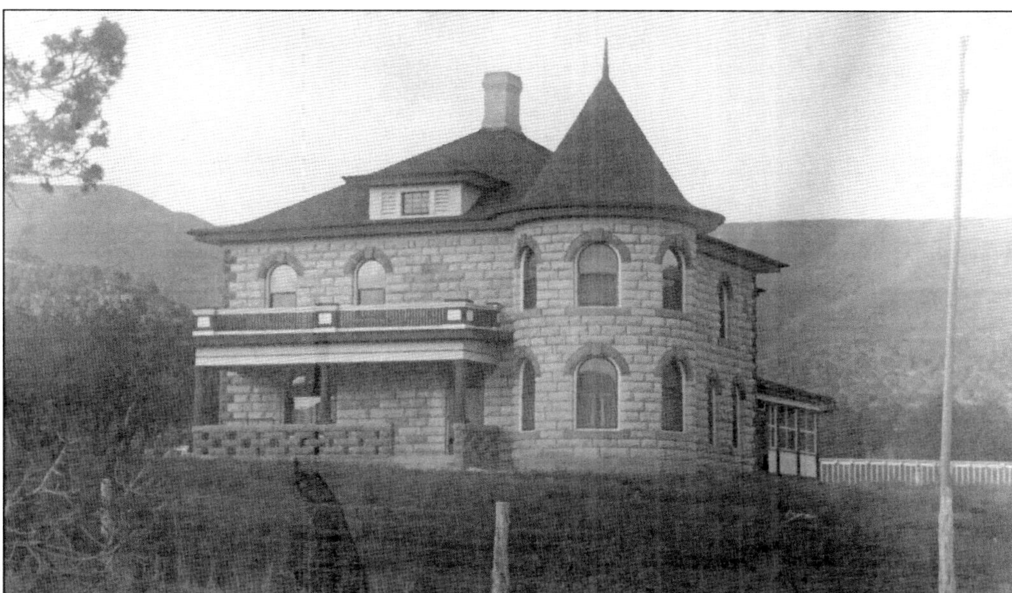

HANSON CASTLE. Hanson returned to Hotchkiss and bought land, later owning the mesa named after him. He continued the Farmer's Ditch, ran cattle, organized the First National Bank, and, in 1902, married Marcia Skinner. After many real estate sales, he hired the Sherman Brothers to cut rocks from his property up Leroux Creek for the castle to be built in 1909. It still is there today, although it has been remodeled many times over the years. (HCHS.)

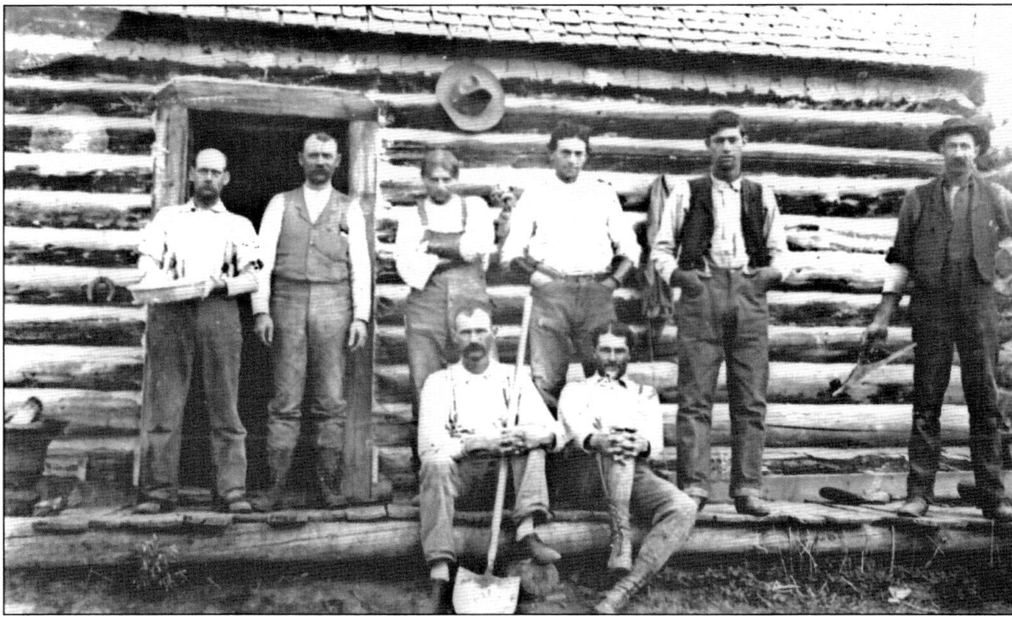

Men at Cabin, c. 1900. After a hard day, these men are gathering at a cabin. Ed Hanson was buying land up Leroux Creek (north of Hotchkiss). Standing, from left to right, are Lyman Reich, J. Edward Hanson, two unidentified men, Joe Reich, and Elmer Thompson, who helped build the Hanson barn. The men seated in front are unidentified. (HCHS.)

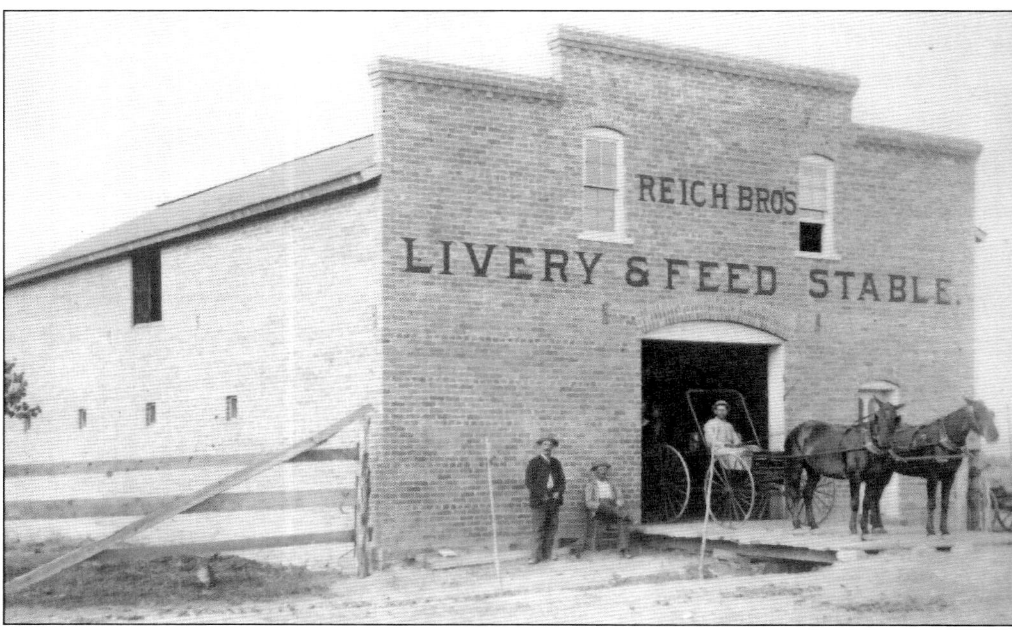

Reich Brothers. The livery was built after Ed Hanson's friend, Joseph Reich, who had the first small general store in town, suddenly left his family and went to California. Reich's sons ran the business, and his wife, Elizabeth, remained without her husband. (HCHS.)

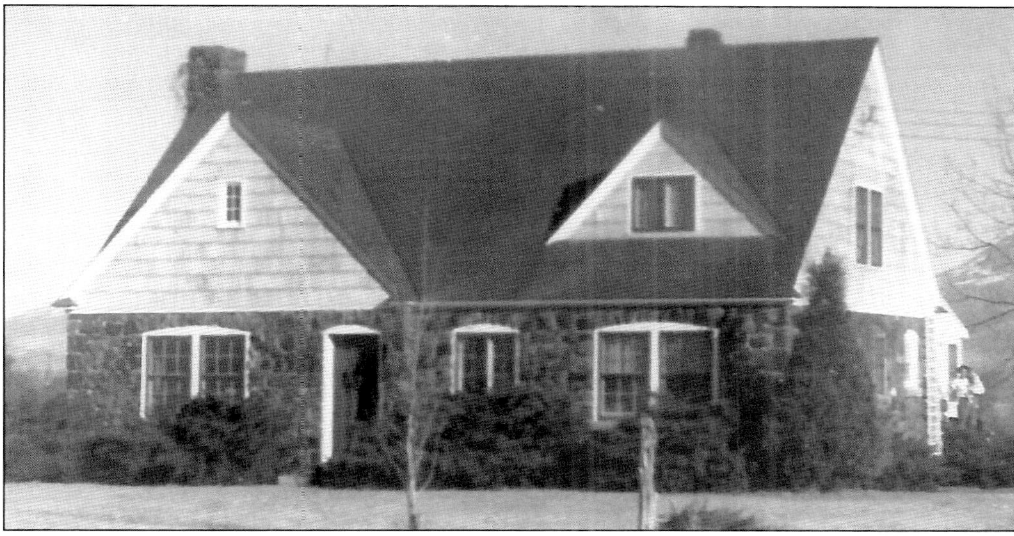

Plenty of Rocks. The outside of the Swisher house on the lower end of Rogers Mesa was built with rocks common to the area. William Coutts, a native of Scotland, moved to Colorado in 1921 as a stonemason. Besides this house, he built other structures with rock, including the Methodist church, the archway to the fairgrounds, and the entrance to the cemetery. (Joan Queen.)

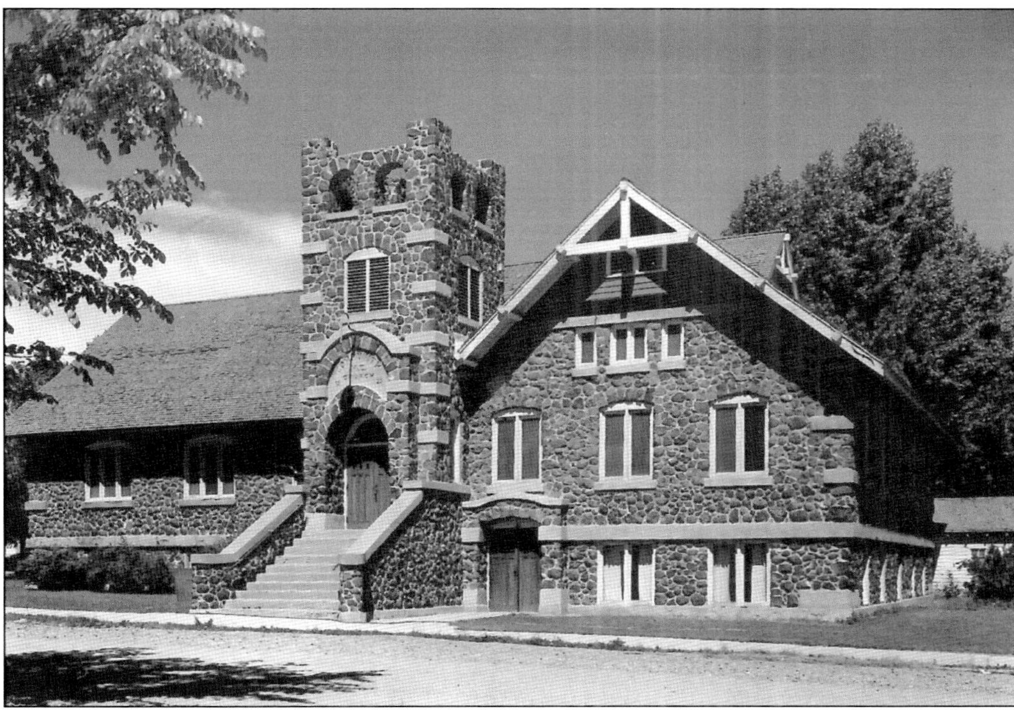

Methodist Church. In 1898, the first Methodist church was dedicated. Then in the late 1920s, a new church was planned. Brick from the old church was used in the inner wall of this volcanic stone church. In 1926, William Coutts worked with another mason, Charles Hurst, and they built the stone church, which is still in use today. Project superintendent was P.G. Stewart. (HCHS.)

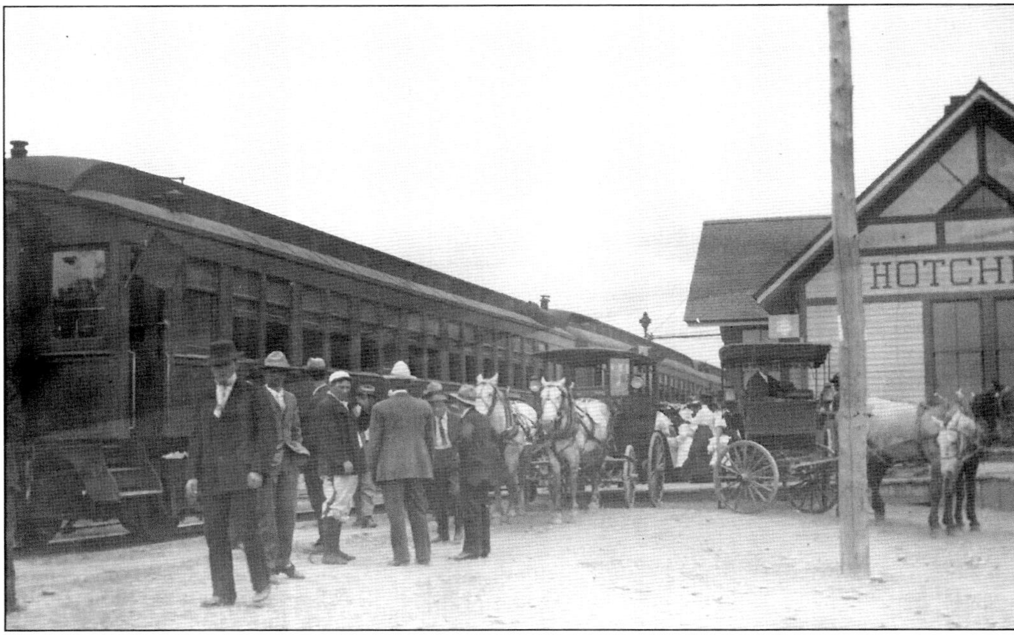

HOTCHKISS DEPOT. The train came to Hotchkiss in 1902. Railroad Day featured a band, speeches, and other festivities. Buggies transported people to and from town. In 1909, the depot safe was blown up. Three men were caught and sentenced to 25 years in prison. The depot closed and, in 1969, was moved to the Blue Mesa Dam area. (HCHS.)

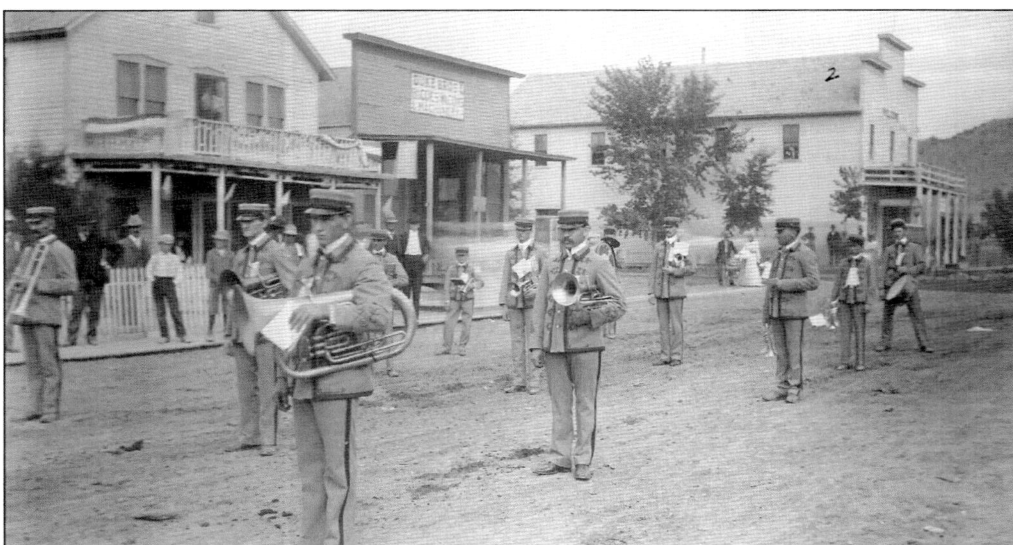

THE BAND. Playing for many special events such as Railroad Day, band members Jim Bainard (a mayor of Hotchkiss in 1913) and Pete Grier (salesman for a general store) march down the street. Railroad Day also had speeches, horse races, and a typical, western rodeo. The Grier Hotel is in the background, next the Duke store that sold wagons, buggies, and machinery. Niles Hall is on the right. (HCHS.)

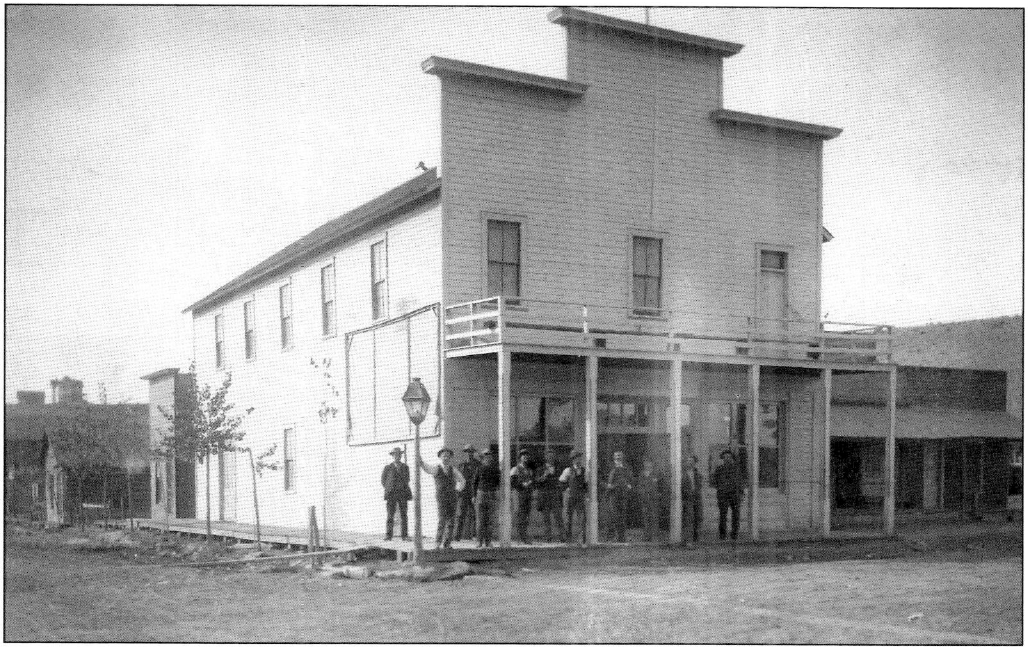

NILES HALL. Built from 1895 to 1896, this building would host many events in town. On the lower floor was Barrow Pharmacy. The upstairs had classrooms and an auditorium. In 1896, when nine men started a Masonic lodge, they met at Niles Hall. George Duke's house can be seen on the hill behind it. Trees have been planted along the street. (HCHS.)

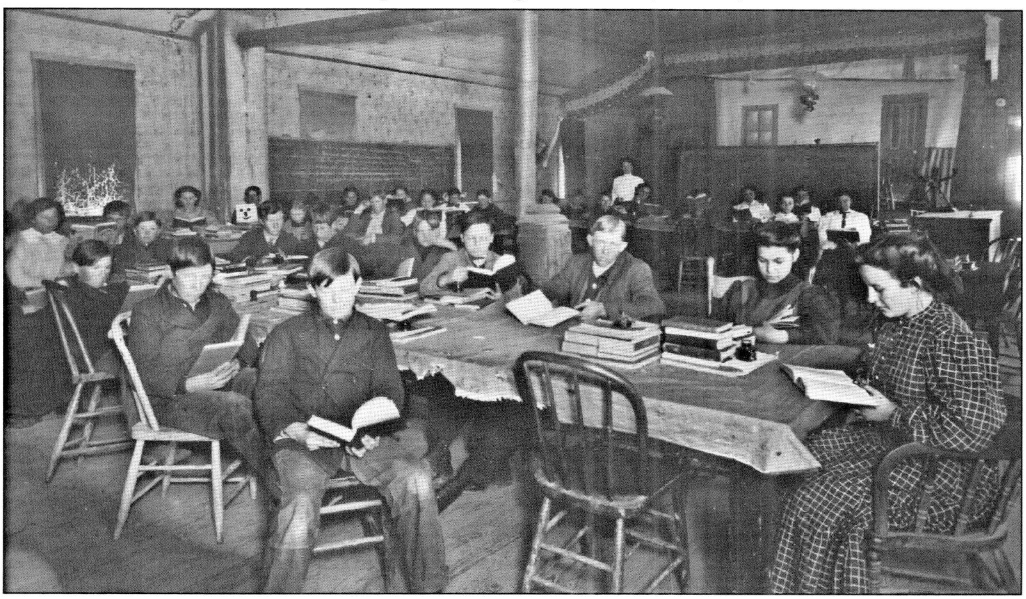

SCHOOLROOM IN NILES HALL. The seventh and eighth grades were held in this room in 1910. Jessie Duke Fields is the teacher. Jessie was a sister of the Duke brothers—Edward, George, and William. Besides teaching, she was postmistress from 1911 to 1915. She took care of her ailing mother, and upon Mary Duke's passing, Jessie accompanied the body on the train back to Illinois for burial. (HCHS.)

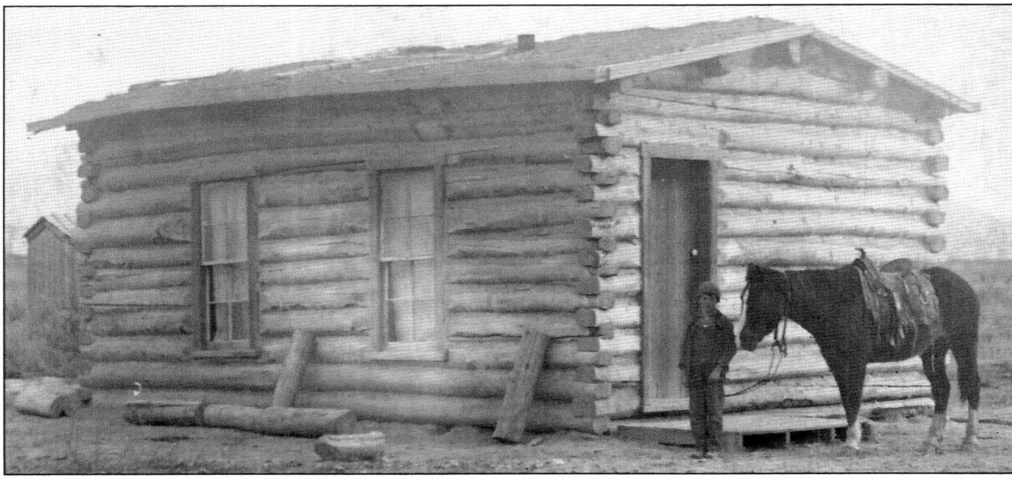

OLD RURAL SCHOOL. East of Hotchkiss, the Cottonwood School was built in 1885. Many children had to ride their horses to school as they lived far away, and there was no other means of transportation. In 1895, the school was moved a half mile north of this location. It was torn down when the new school was built. (HCHS.)

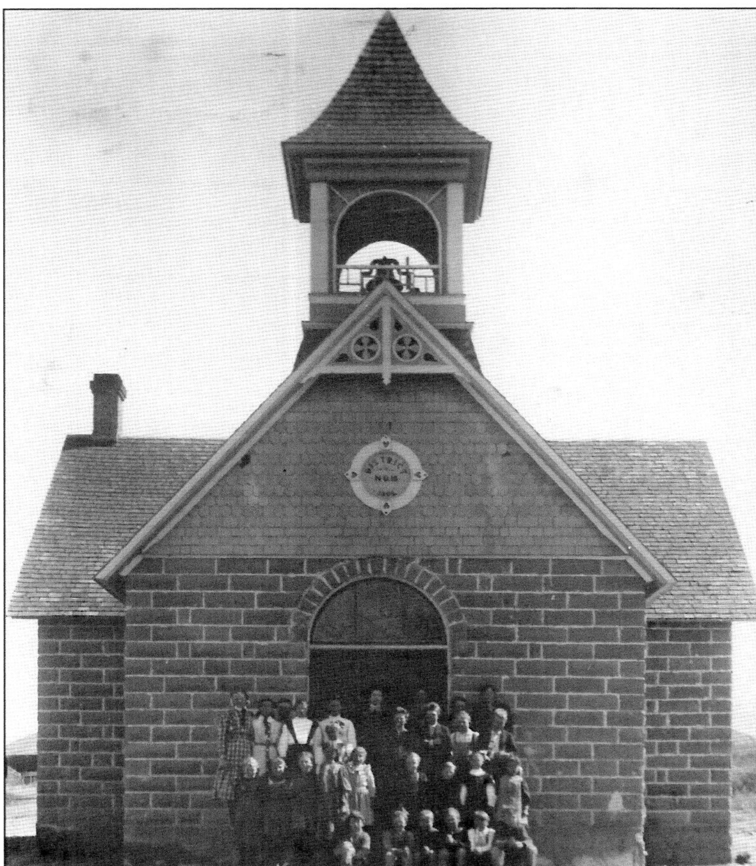

NEW COTTONWOOD SCHOOL. This new Cottonwood School was built in 1906 and was made of concrete bricks. This school was closed when District 15 consolidated into District 25. Larson and Roady advertised in 1909 that they had moved their concrete block machine into the basement of the Hotchkiss Block building so they could work in the cooler weather without danger of frost. (HCHS.)

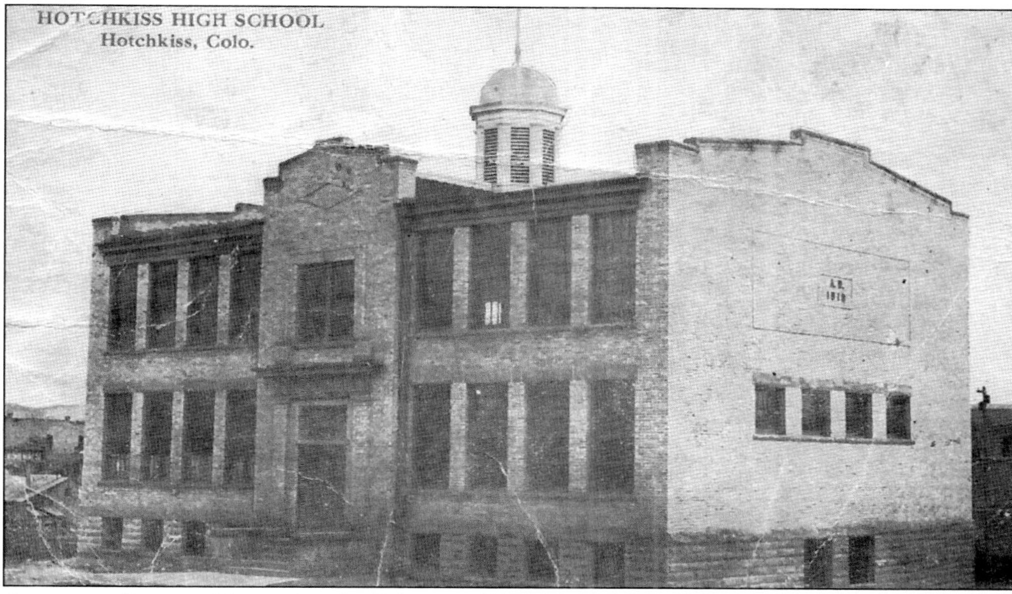

ANOTHER SCHOOL BUILT. In the February 25, 1910, *North Fork Times*, there is an architect's drawing of the new school to be built. N.H. Rogers was the contractor. The cost was estimated at $13,720 without a heating system. This building was completed in 1910. Years later, the school was turned into an apartment building. In 1925, a new high school was started, which cost $100,000. (HCHS.)

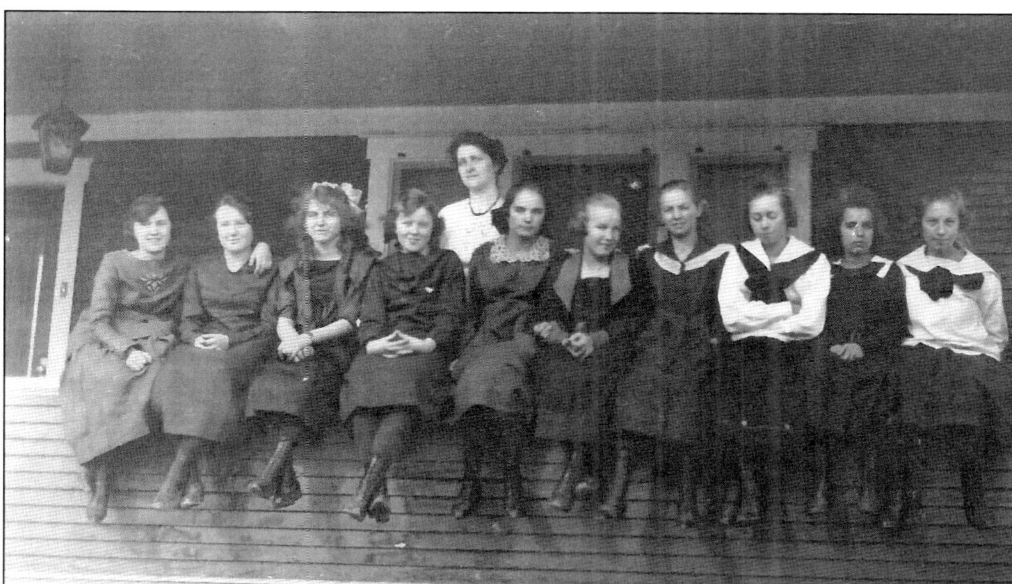

HOME ECONOMICS, 1920. A group of girls was instructed in home economics by Clara Wilson, an eighth-grade teacher. Clara gave her free time to teach the fundamentals of cooking as an extracurricular activity. At the end of the school year, the girls prepared and served a formal dinner at her home; the girls had never attended such an event. (HCHS.)

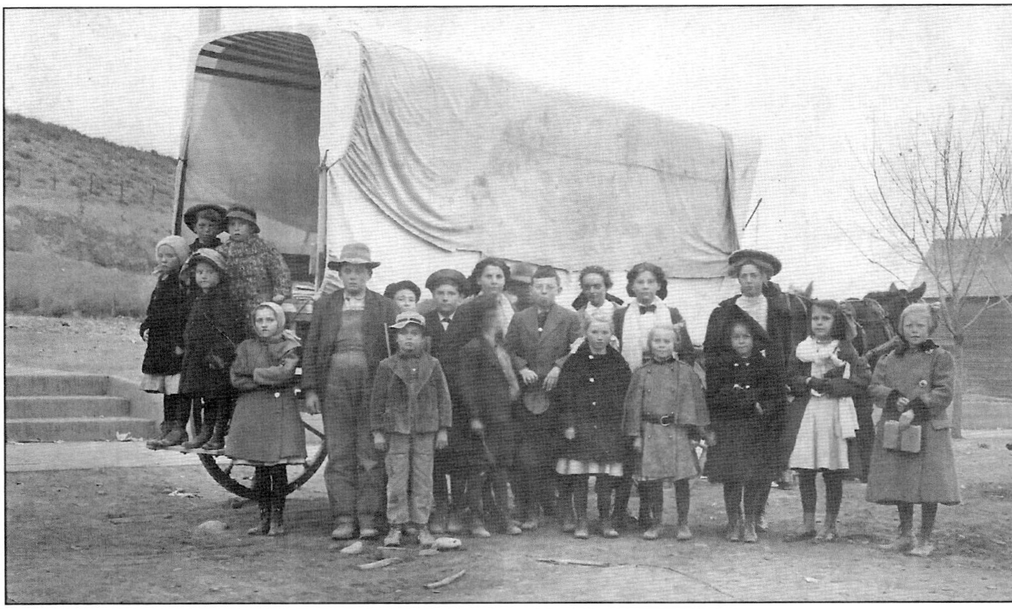

From Horse-Powered to Gas-Powered. This wagon had flaps in the front and back that were shut in bad weather. The "bus" was for the Hanson–Powell Mesa area to get the children to school in Hotchkiss in 1911. In 1922, the school bus was a gas-powered vehicle and was on the lower end of Rogers Mesa, west of Hotchkiss when it ran off the road and rolled on its side. It took a horse, still used in spite of those gas-powered vehicles, to help pull the bus upright. (Both, HCHS.)

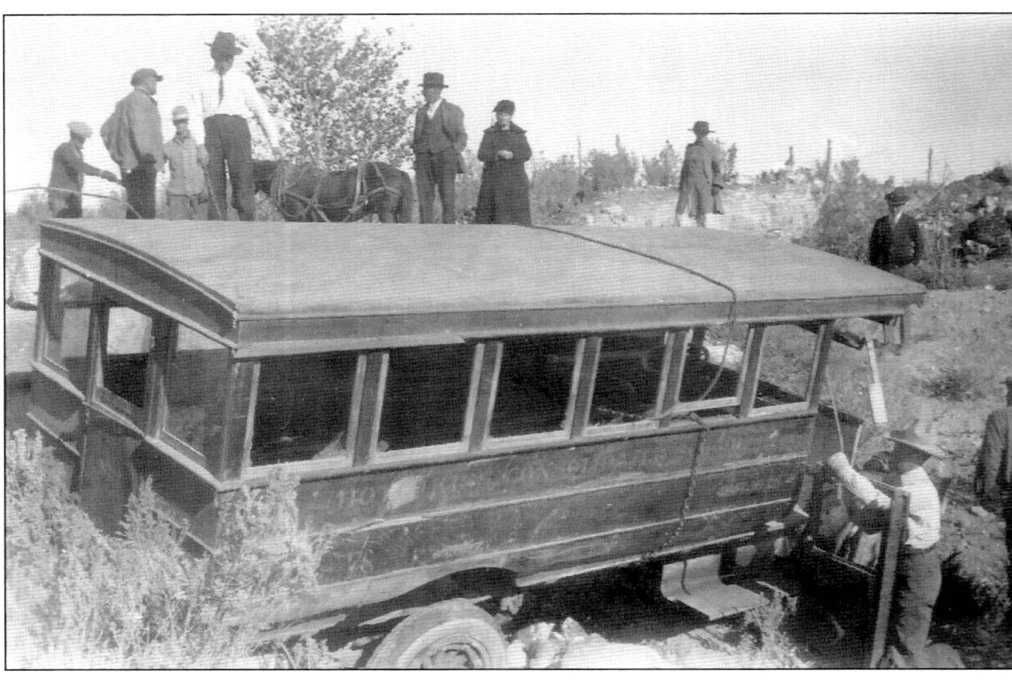

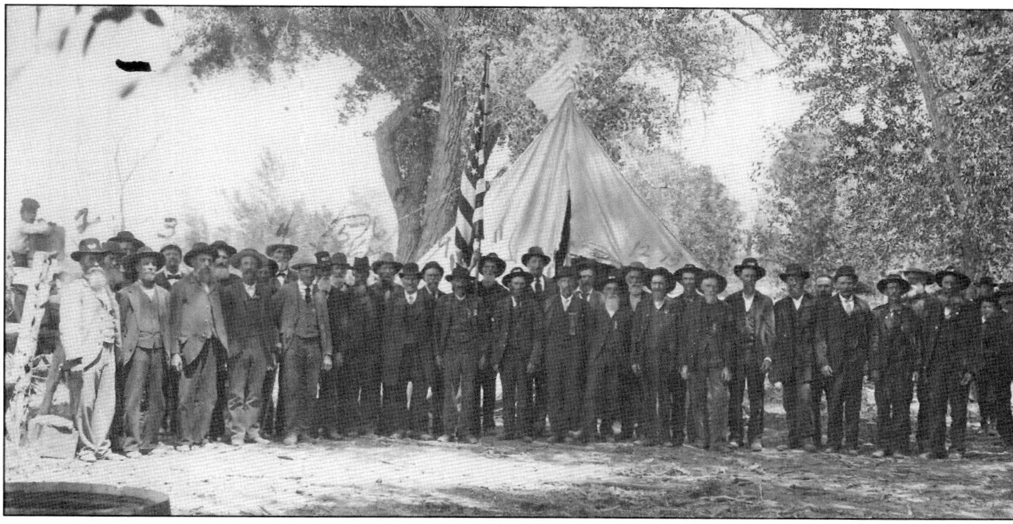

North Fork GAR. In 1884, the North Fork post held an encampment. The Grand Army of the Republic was an organization made up of Union veterans. The first post was in Decatur, Illinois. In 1866, there were only 12 members nationwide; in 1890, there were 400,000 members. The last member nationally died in 1956 at the age of 109. The organization had three main purposes for its members: fraternity, charity, and loyalty—to each other, their families, and their community. In August 1909, Amos Reynolds went to Salt Lake City, Utah. Z.F. Rawson went as mascot and tolerated the trip, even though he was 90 years old. There was also a women's auxiliary called the Ladies' Relief Corps, and Hotchkiss had a branch. (Both, HCHS.)

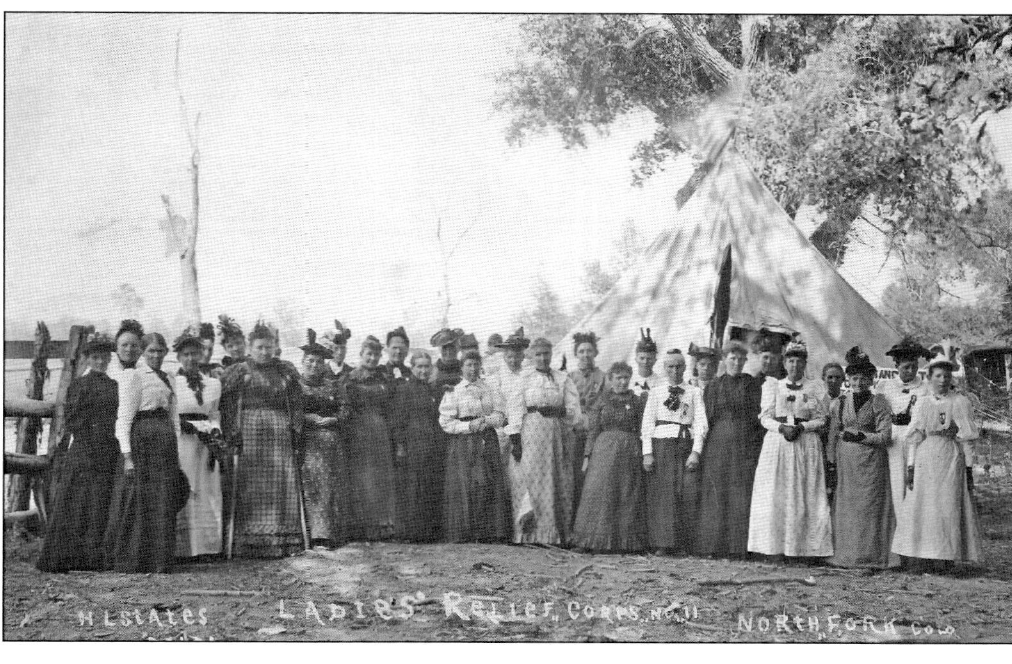

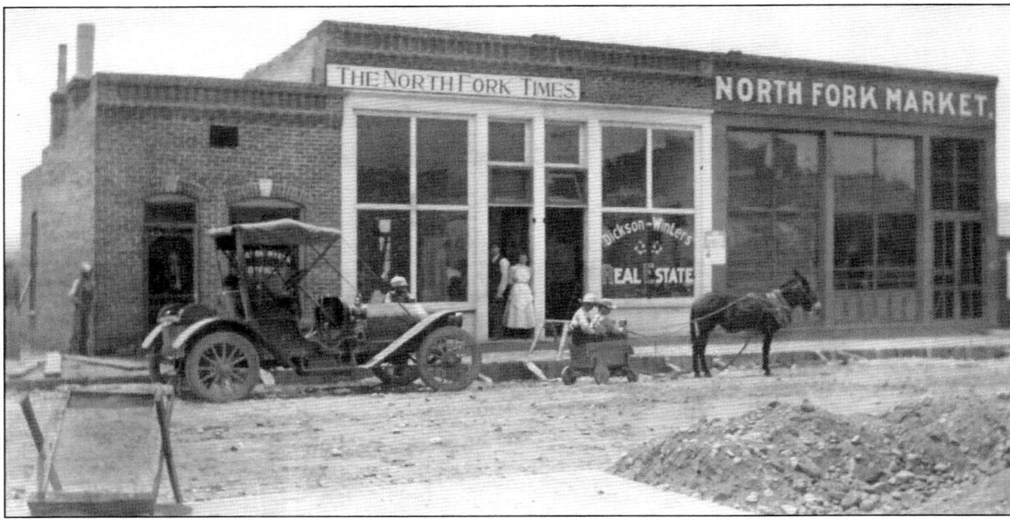

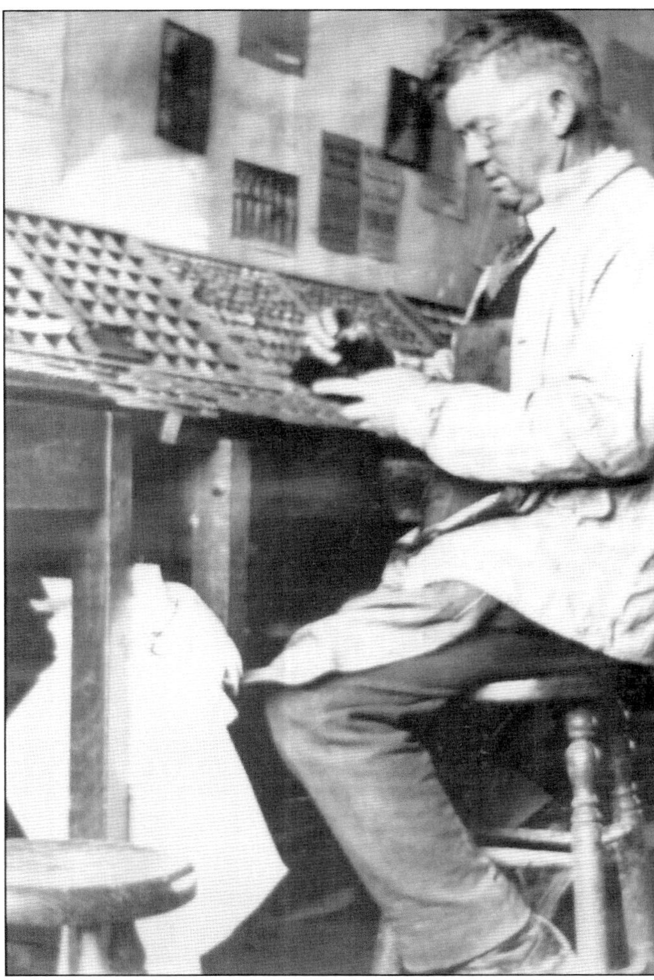

CONCRETE SIDEWALKS. In 1909, Hotchkiss finally began to replace the boardwalks and dirt paths with sidewalks. This group of businesses includes, from left to right, Dr. Myers office, the *North Fork Times* newspaper office, the real estate office of Dickson and Winters, and the North Fork Market. Along with the workers are two children playing as if they are helping, with a donkey pulling them along. (HCHS.)

EDITOR OF THE *NORTH FORK TIMES*. Thomas Blackwell, editor of the *North Folk Times*, was a charter member of the Knights of Pythias, police magistrate, justice of the peace, state representative, and a member of the businessmen's association that was responsible for promoting the valley. (HCHS.)

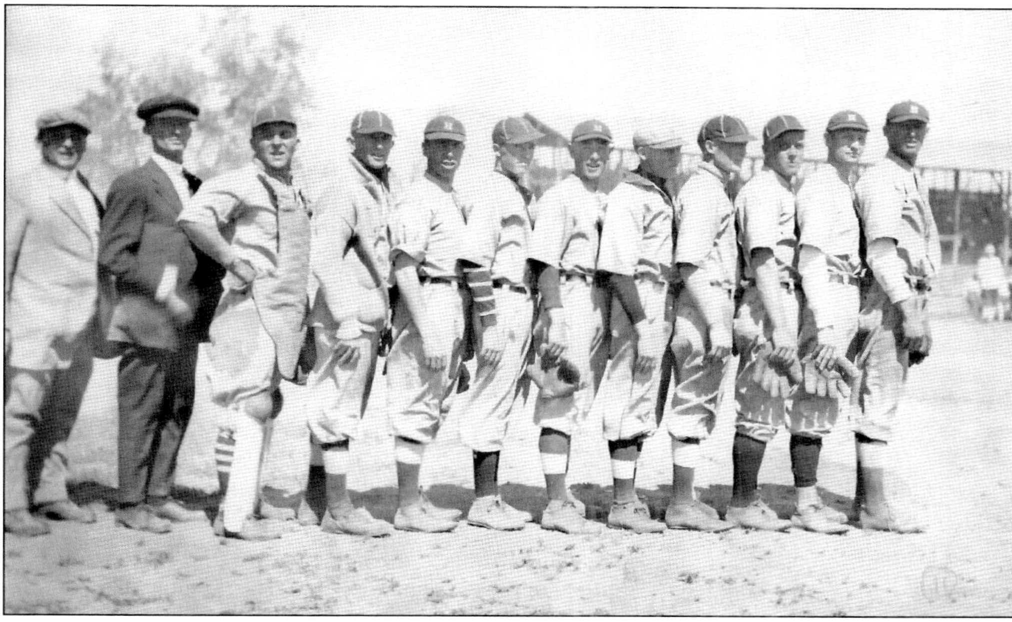

Baseball to Banking. While working in California for a telephone company, Harry Addams met Melvin Wade and Simon Fisher. They told him on his way back home to Illinois to stop in the North Fork Valley and work in the fruit crop the fall of 1910. After discovering Addams was also a baseball player, Walt Thomas found him a job in the First National Bank. Above, Addams is second from the right in this photograph of the 1915 Hotchkiss baseball team. After a short move to Paonia, he returned to purchase the Bank of the North Fork, below, with Albert Smith, C. Bowen, H.B. Fetz, O.G. Taylor, and H.A. Duke in 1921. The bank became the North Fork State Bank and was incorporated. Addams was a banker for 63 years and never lost his love of baseball. (Both, HCHS.)

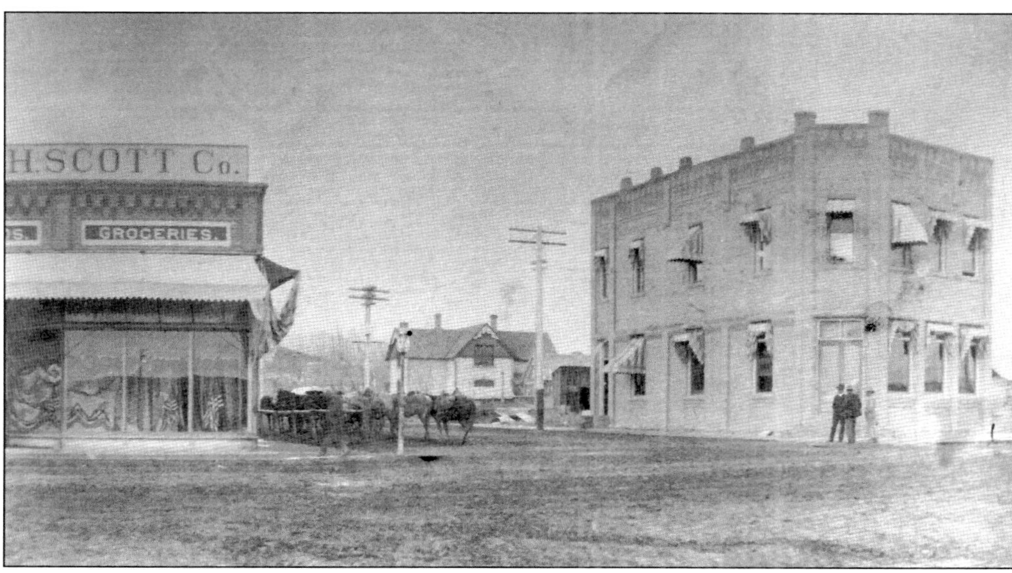

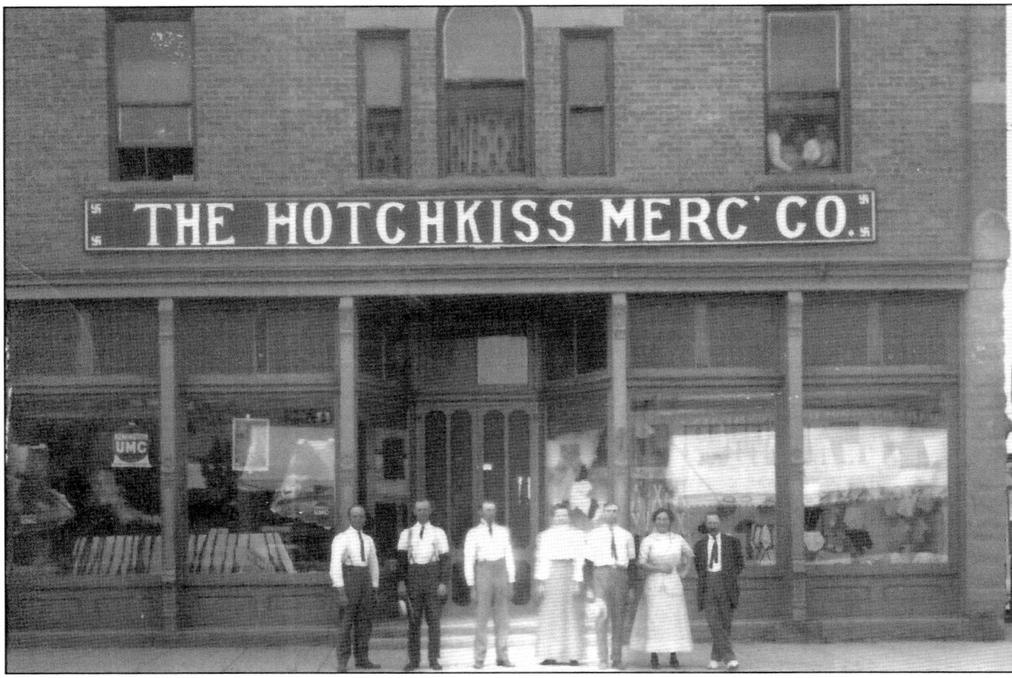

THE HOTCHKISS MERCANTILE. In 1909, A.D. Garrett, George Roller, and N.B. Cool formed this company. A 10-year lease was signed in the Hotchkiss Block building formerly occupied by Stockham Brothers. The store carried general merchandise and bought and sold real estate, houses, cattle, and farming implements. One of the first advertisements to lure people in was to promote giving away a Heney buggy with rubber tires. The inside of the store was well stocked with canned goods, fresh fruit, and a variety of products. George Roller was the manager and, in 1911, built a house on the hill overlooking the town. He soon saw a need for steps leading up the hill and had wooden ones built for people to climb, but they were torn down in the 1960s. He became quite the businessman, later buying a huge ranch and raising prizewinning sheep. (Both, HCHS.)

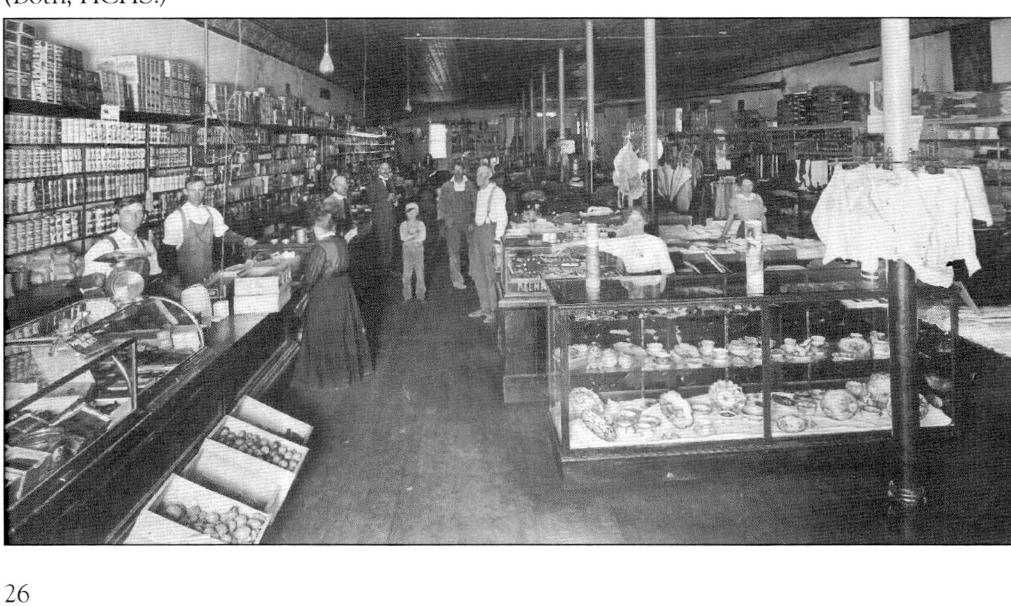

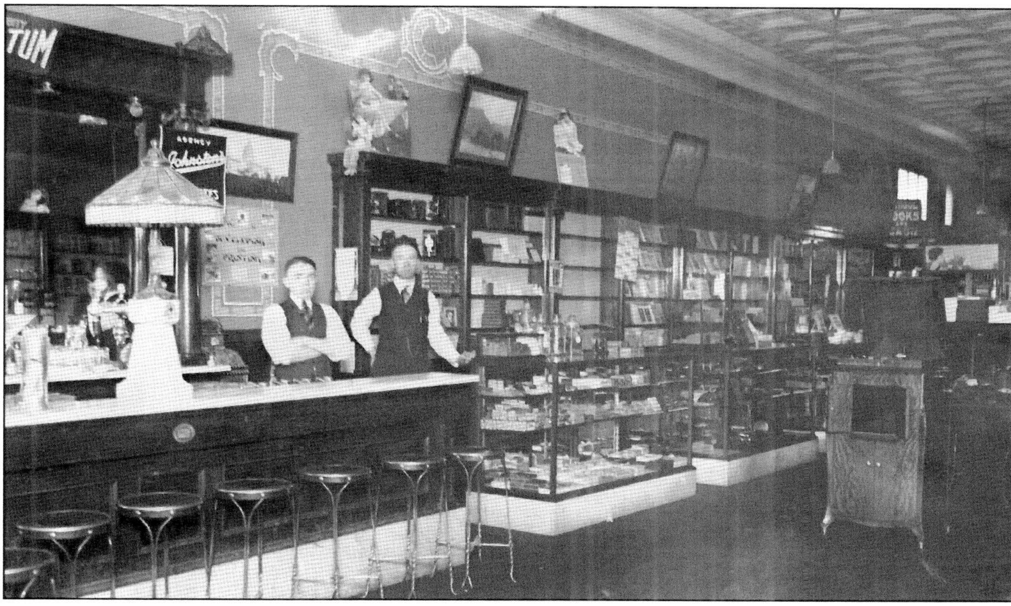

ROBERTSON DRUG STORE. Sometimes, the druggist was also the physician, and Hotchkiss always had at least one doctor, usually more. In 1909, this drugstore was incorporated, with John W. Robertson, D.W. Thomas, Edgar L. Williams, James T. Myers, and Edward P. Barrow as directors. Robertson was the former owner of City Drug Store. (HCHS.)

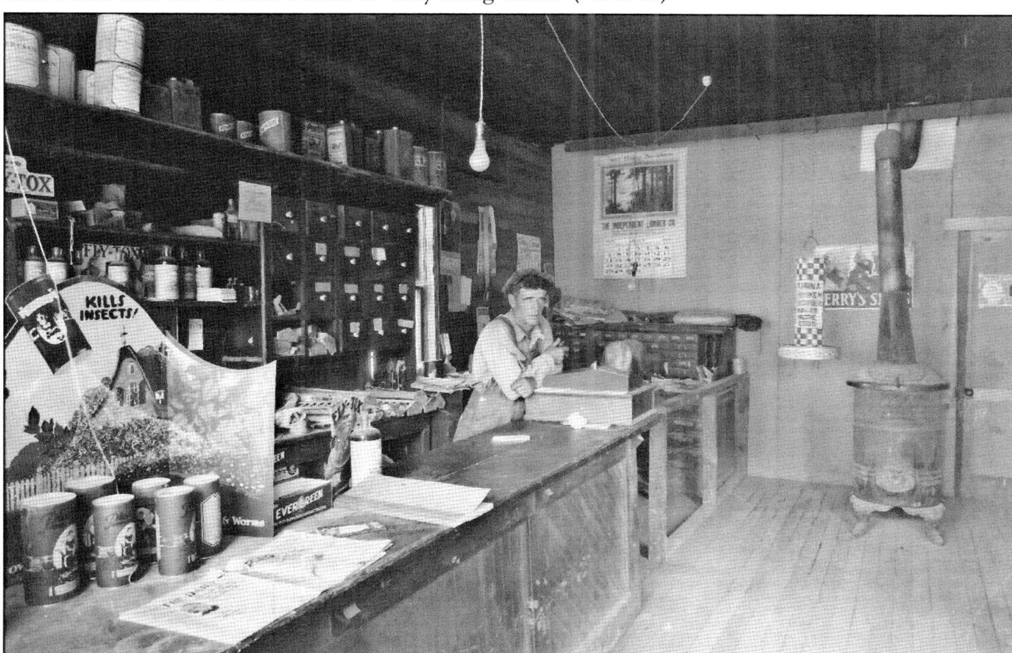

DAGUE'S FEED STORE. In 1929, Grover Andrews tended this business. The feed store was a cash buyer of poultry and eggs. It also bought and sold corn, wheat, oats, and hay. The sign on the wall states that Purina Chicken Chowder makes more eggs. Some pretty potent products are for sale, like Fly-tox, Evergreen Poisonous Insecticide, and Kow Kare. (HCHS.)

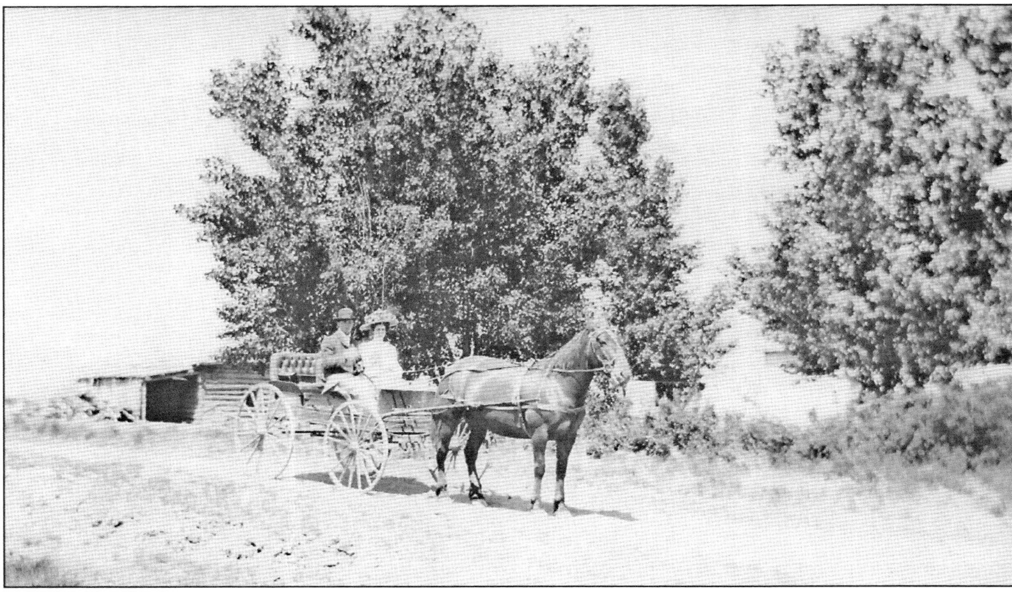

The Bishops. In 1908, Joe and Mable Bishop began their married life farming on Rogers Mesa. Joe needed to find a way to unload his fruit before it spoiled. He began traveling to Delta to the rail center, where buyers gathered to bid on fruit. Traveling at night when it was cooler was a necessity, as it was a long dusty trip on the alkali road. (HCHS.)

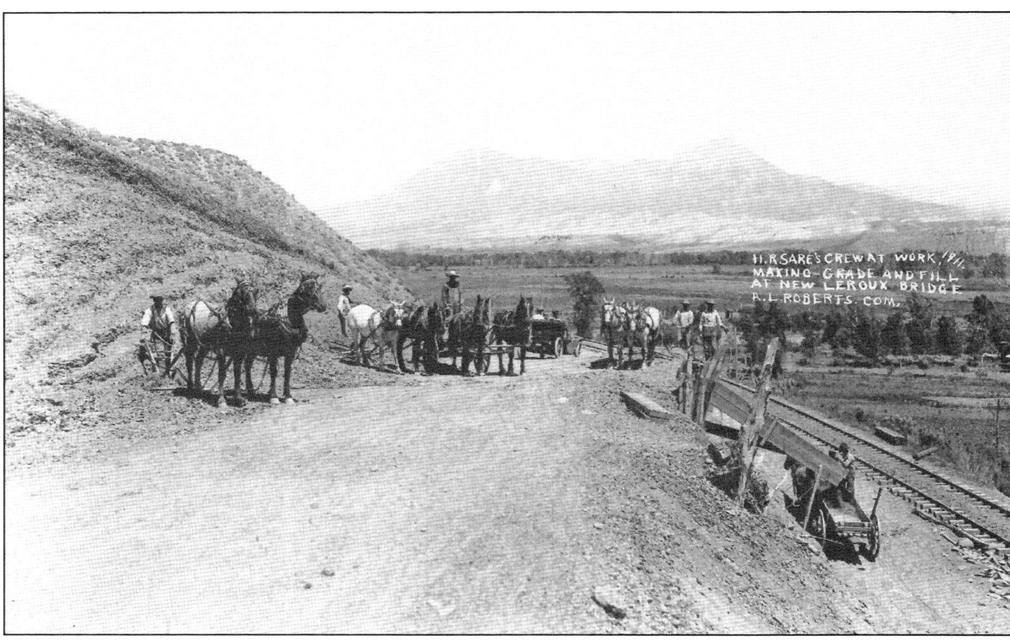

The Road to Hotchkiss. Today, this is considered the back road, but it was once a main way to get into town from Rogers Mesa. The new bridge appears on the other side of the railroad tracks, and this road crew is fine-tuning the road. Note the valley ahead leading to Mount Lamborn on the left and Land's End on the right. (HCHS.)

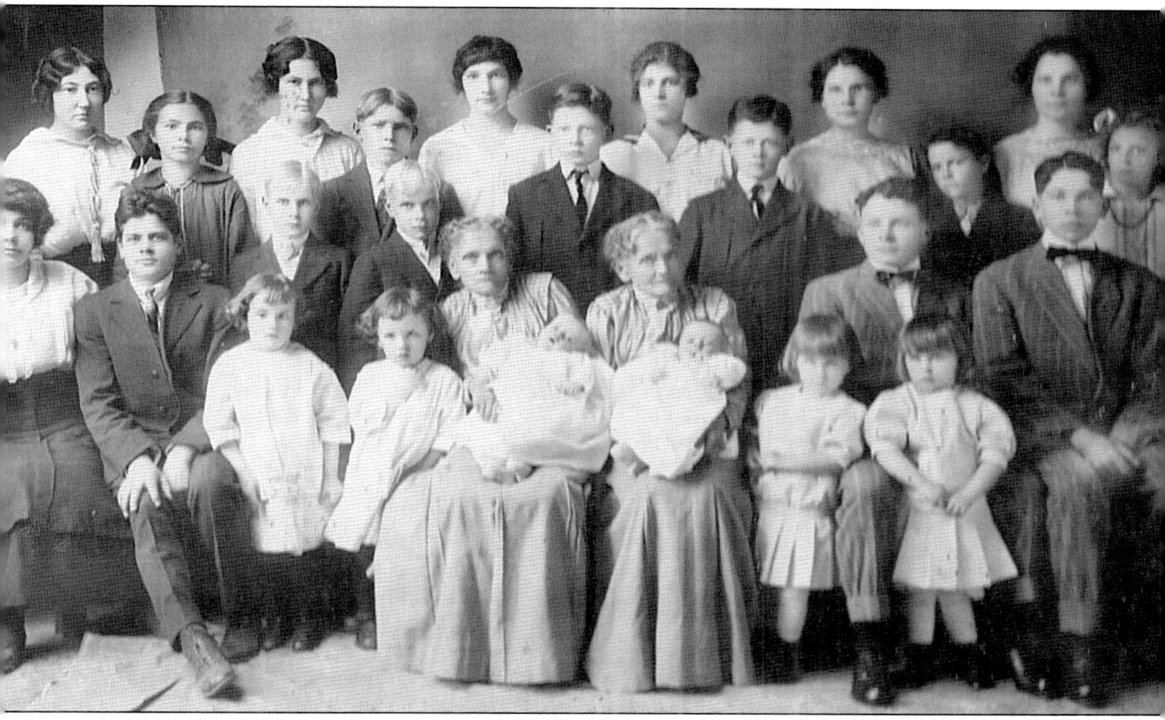

The Twins, 1915. Thirteen sets of twins living in Hotchkiss are pictured here. Because there was not a panoramic camera, five more pairs could not get in the photograph. There was a grand total of 18 sets of twins in the town at the time. The eldest pictured here are close to 82 years old. The twins, from left to right, are (first row) Anna and Thomas Addleman, Frances and Frank Willoughby, Martha Willoughby (grandmother to twins) and Mary M. Doughty holding Maxine Lea and Erma Loraine Edwards, Velma and Alma Grier, and Edward and Frederick Theobold; (second row) Osa and Lee Snyder, Hubert and Hunley Thomas, Vinton and Thomas Blackwell, and Oliver and Ola Johnson; (third row) Ruth and Genevieve White, Ruth and Helen Kehr, and Fay and Fern Wooley. A local saying was, "Hotchkiss raises peaches and twins." (HCHS.)

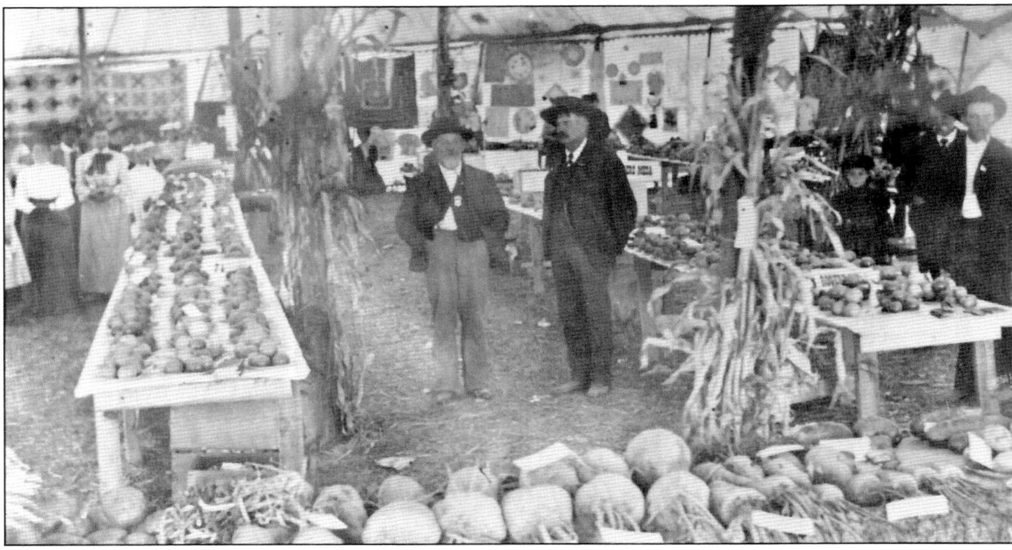

Fair Time, Early 1900s. The first fair at the Hotchkiss Park was held in 1905. It included horse races for entertainment. The displays were shown in a tent that included fruits, vegetables, grains, and handiwork. The train offered reduced rates for those coming from out of town. (HCHS.)

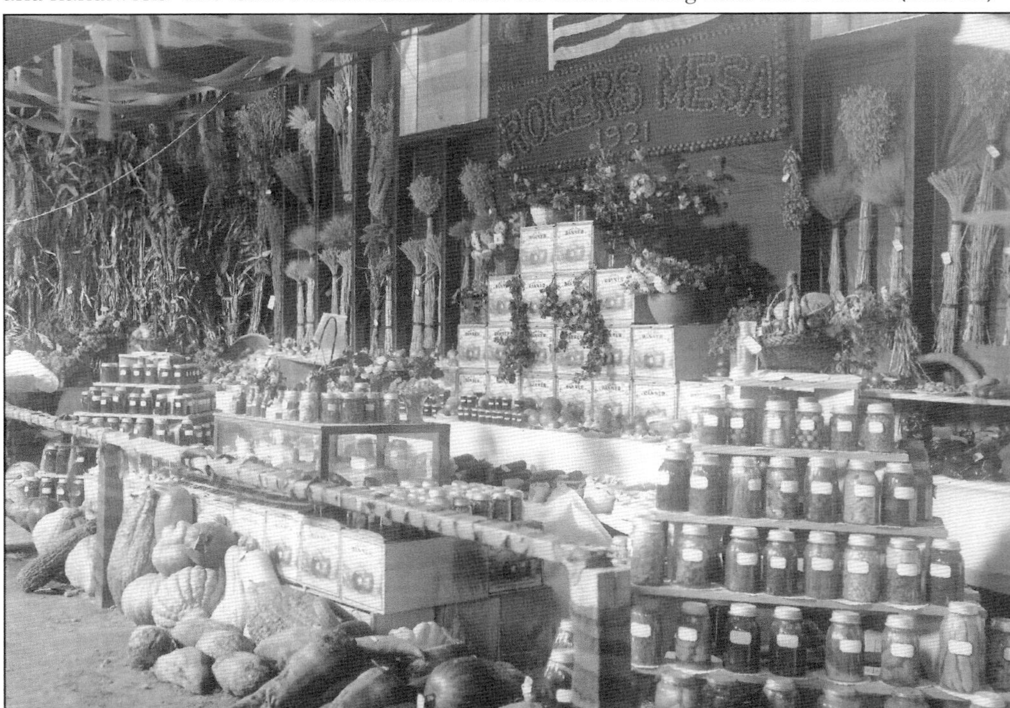

Rogers Mesa Exhibit, 1921. The object of this fair was to promote patriotism, production, and preparedness. The first-place community booth received $75. The first day was Entry Day, followed by Farmer's Day and Delta Day; Dairy and Children's Day was the last day. George Roller was the general superintendent. An addition to the grandstand, a new building for agricultural exhibits, and playground apparatus were new items. (HCHS.)

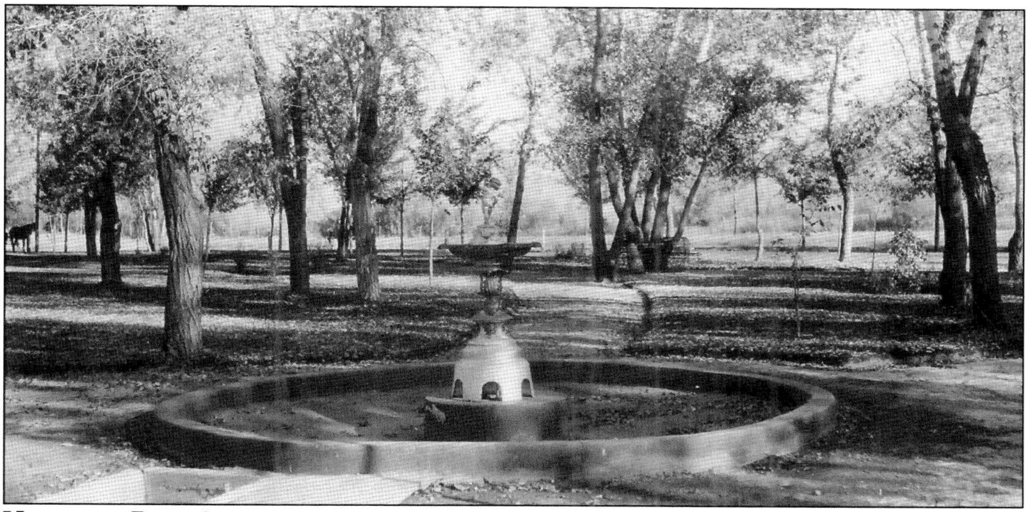

Hotchkiss Park. In 1909, work began to clean up the park area to make it appealing for visitors. Dredging the marsh, building a dam, making a lake, reseeding the grass, and buying rowboats and Peking ducks added to the renovation. There was a fountain in the center of the park and a pathway called Lover's Lane. (HCHS.)

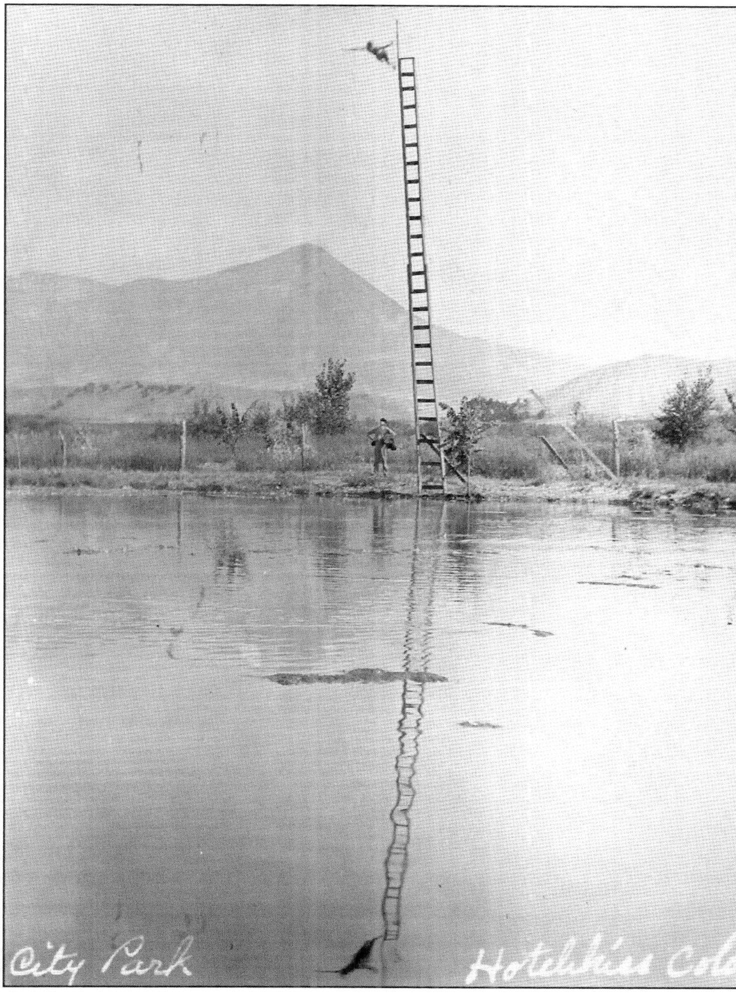

The Lagoon. When the lagoon was added south of the grandstands, the lake was an attraction for rowing, relaxing, and spectator events, such as this high-dive act. (HCHS.)

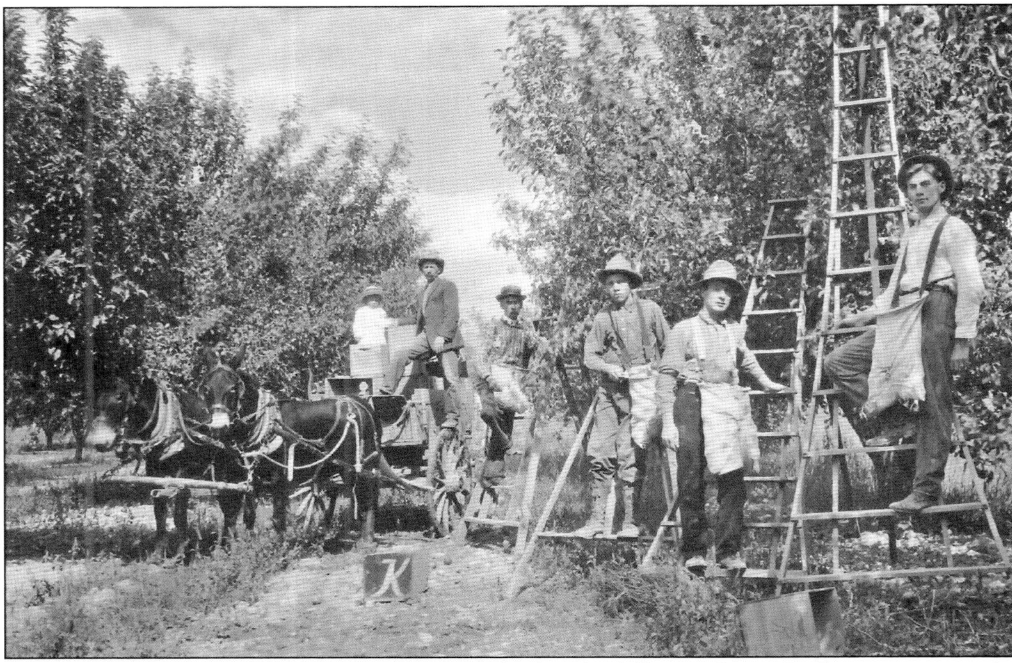

HARVEST TIME. The apples were ready to be picked in the fall once the nights began to get cooler. Tall wooden ladders, picking bags to wear, and a wagon to haul the boxes of apples were needed. A peach crop could grow and prosper all season, but one afternoon hailstorm could ruin the crop. If apples were exposed to freezing temperatures, they could not survive. In the spring, when blossoms appeared on the trees, below-freezing temperatures would stop trees from even setting fruit. George Duke sold smudge pots in the Duke store. They would be set out to burn under the trees to keep the air around the tree safe from frost. P.G. Slatten's crew (below) set up a sorting and packing area near the orchard. Slatten had started as a hired hand, then bought 40 acres and produced some fine fruit. Boxes were made at sawmills or special venues. (Both, HCHS.)

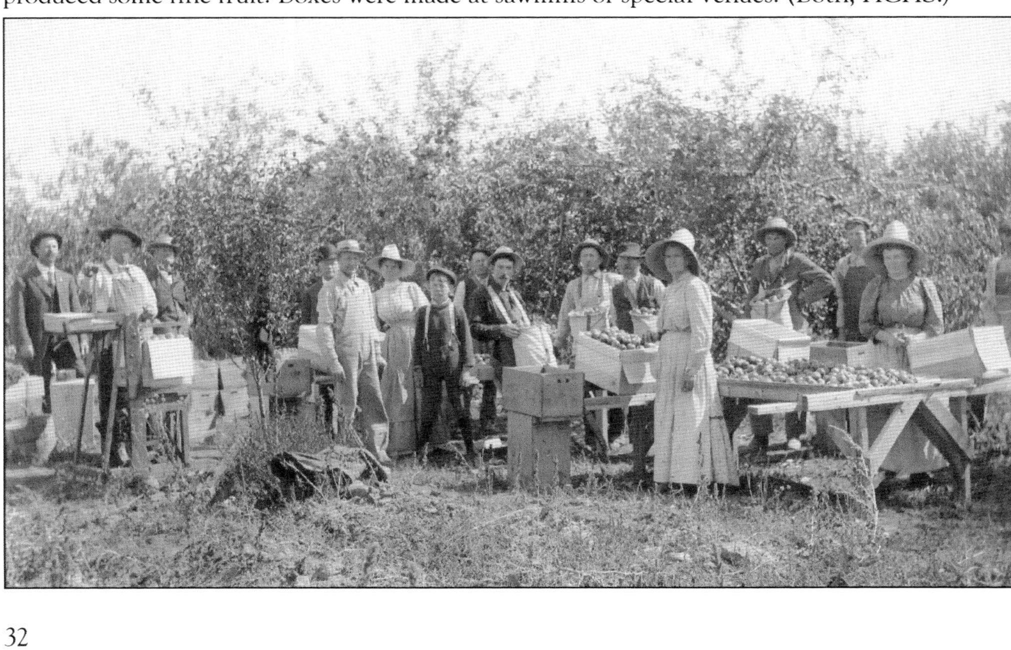

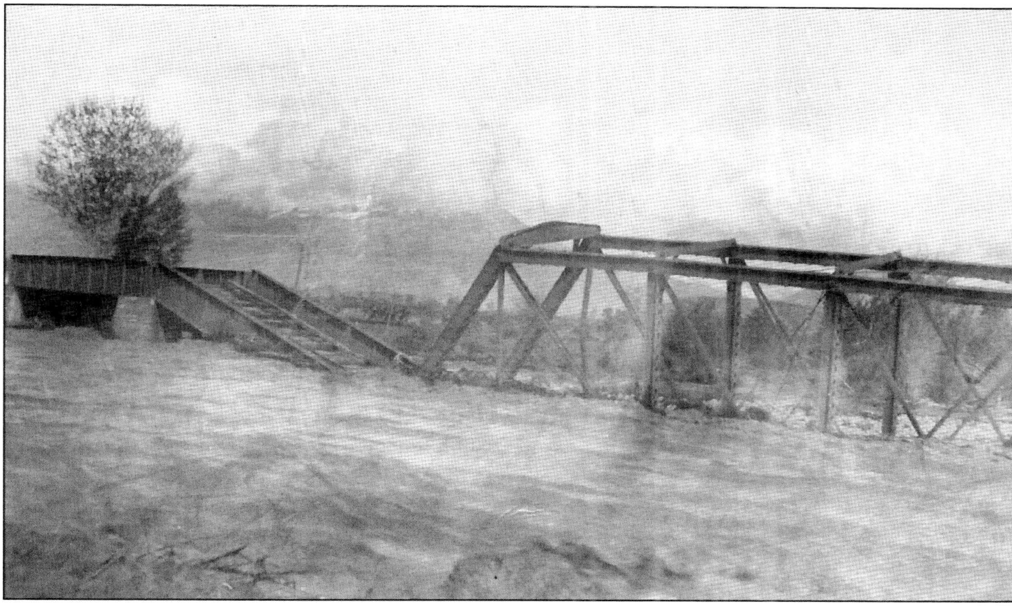

The North Fork River Goes Wild. As the snow melts in the spring, the river races wildly downstream. In 1920, this train bridge collapsed under the torrent of water. Earlier, the solution to get people across the river in this area was to use a ferry. In 1884, it was operated by J. E. Fobare. There was a 16-foot boat tied to a pulley, which stretched across the river on a cable. (HCHS.)

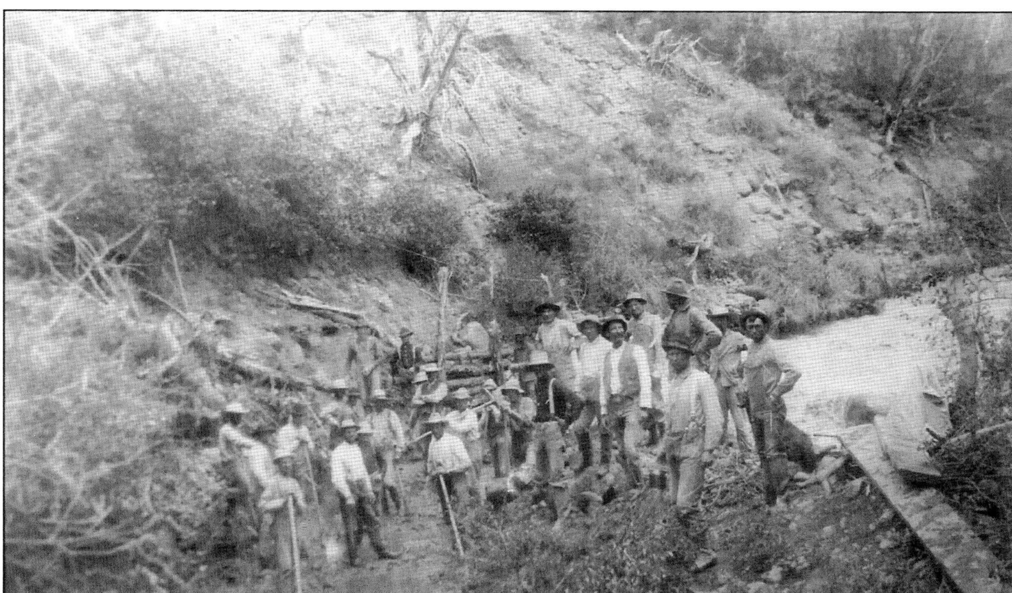

Importance of Water. Without regular water, crops would fail. The answer was to divert water from the reservoirs and natural sources in the mountains. One such effort was getting Leroux Creek water to areas in the valley around Hotchkiss. This involved the use of shovels, picks, and hard work. (HCHS.)

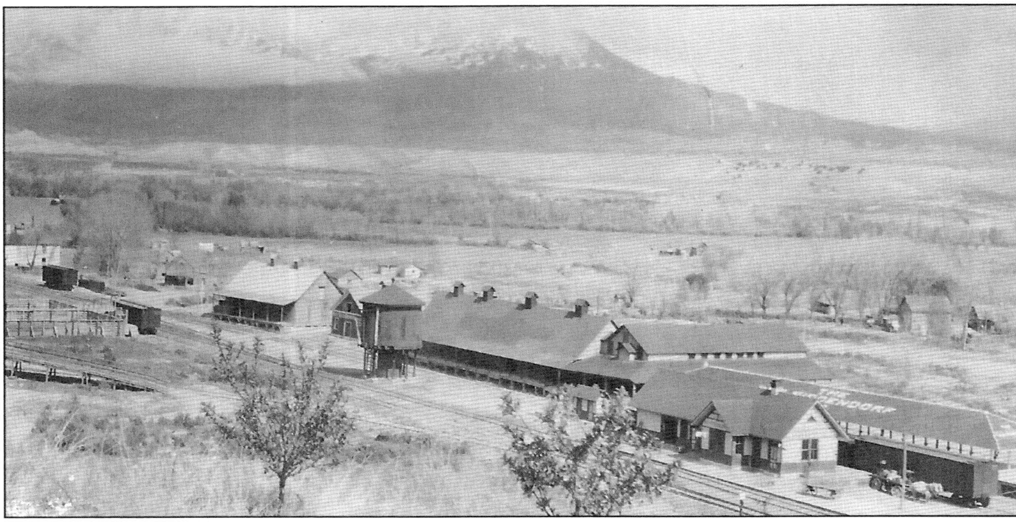

THE DEPOT AREA. This area of the little town boasted the most activity. The train stopped at the depot before heading up the valley. There were fruit-packing sheds, like the Middendorf, that put the fruit into cars seasonally. Also, the stockyard loaded livestock for shipping. A beet tipple dumped sugar beets into railroad cars at one time. Just to the east of this area was the evaporator and cider mill, built in 1906. J. Walter Lee, a teacher, devised a plan to buy the evaporator and combine it with a power plant and cannery around 1908. Adam Seager became the manager of the Hotchkiss Packing and Power Company. (Both, HCHS.)

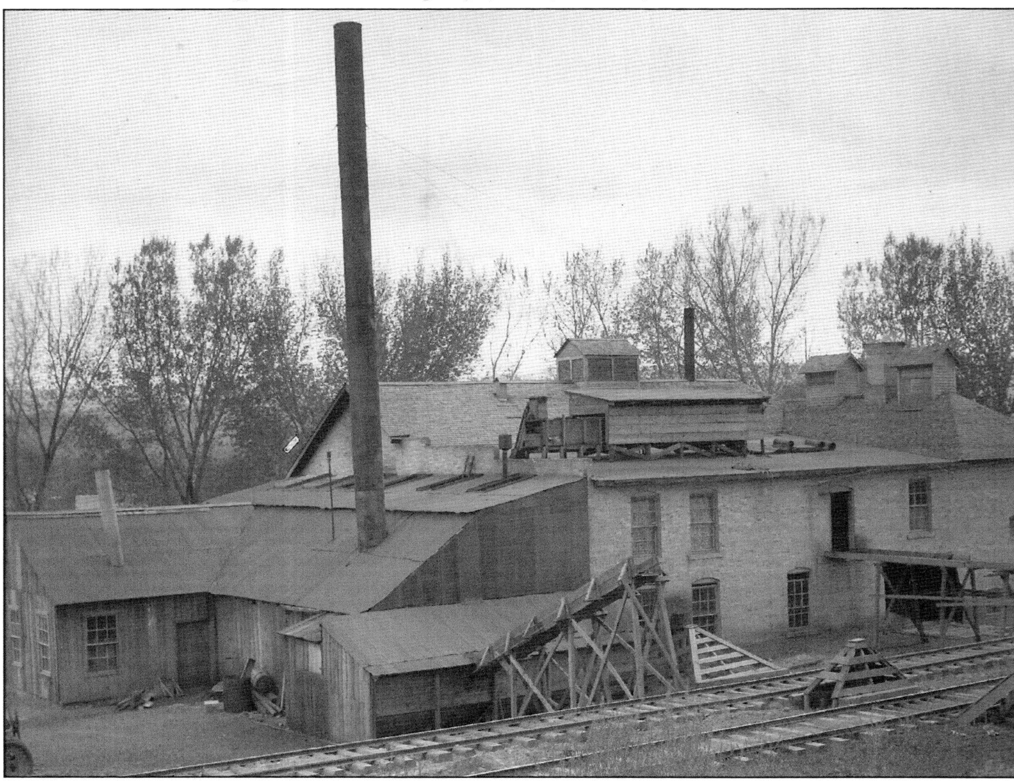

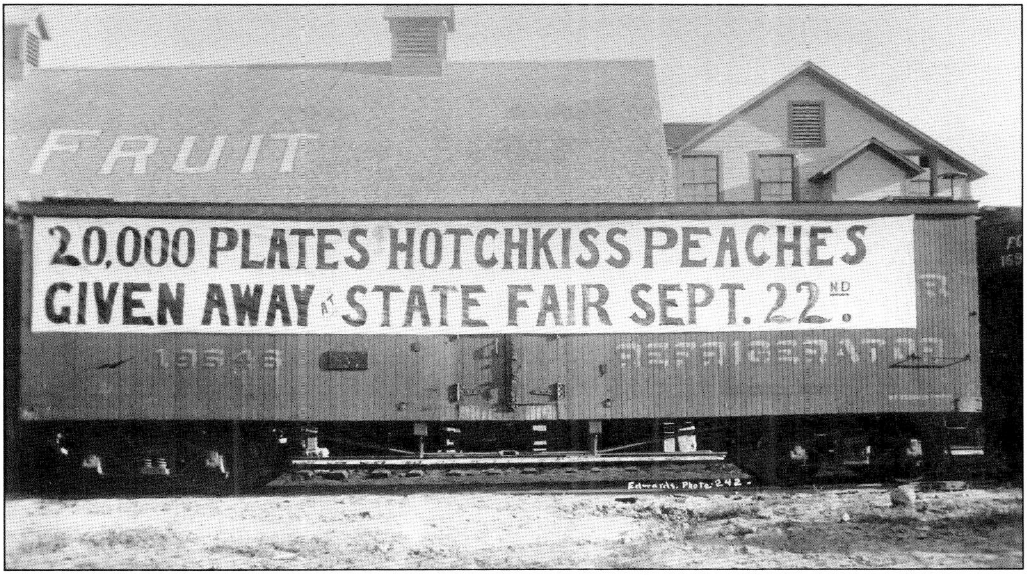

PEACHES GIVEN AWAY, 1909. Above, a banner advertising that Hotchkiss is giving away 20,000 plates of peaches at the state fair on September 22 is strung on a train. Graded "extra fancy," they were to be presented to President Taft on his visit. When the peaches arrived in Pueblo, Colorado, they were not in good shape, and only 400 boxes were considered suitable to use. Mildred Barlow presented President Taft with a prize box of peaches and told him where they came from. He replied that he would think of Hotchkiss whenever he ate one. During his stroll though the exhibit building, he stopped at the Duke Brother's display and took a bite out of a peach. Delta County had more first prizes than any other county in the state. Fruit displayed was not sold but was instead sent to orphanages. (Both, HCHS.)

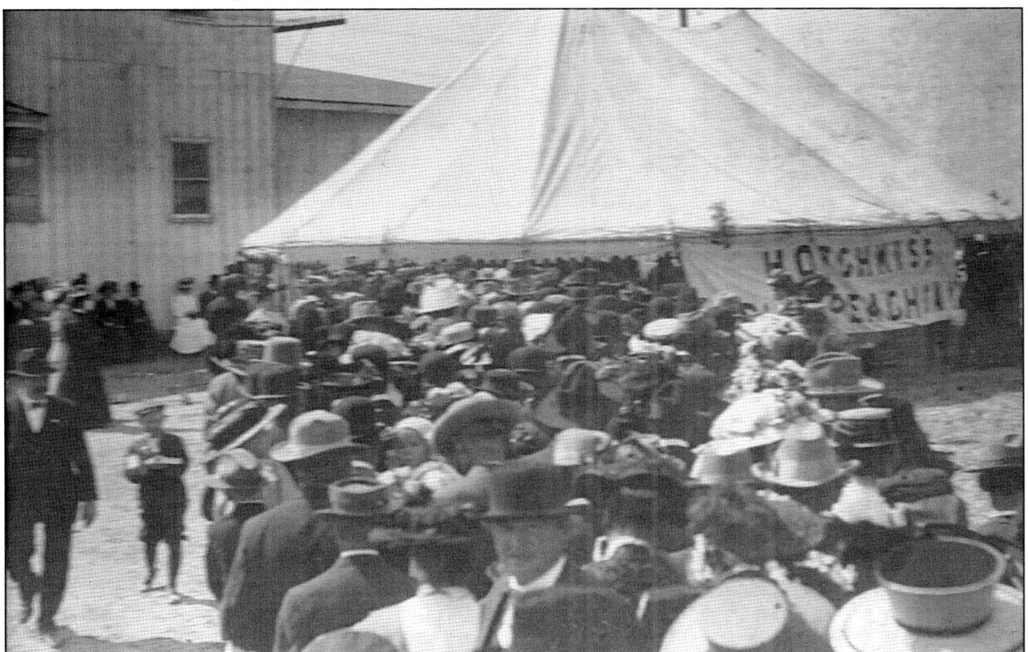

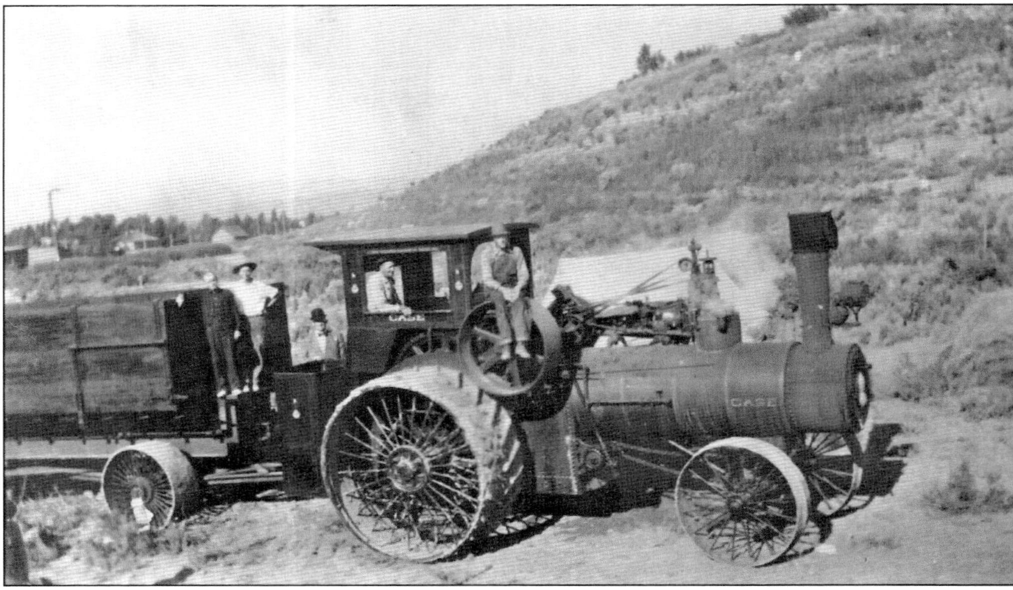

North Fork Coal Company. In 1911, James Pearce devised a way get coal. His plan involved a Case traction engine to haul the coal to the railroad, cars with iron wheels, and a new road. But poor management and a road with slides and seepage caused the dream to fizzle. (HCHS.)

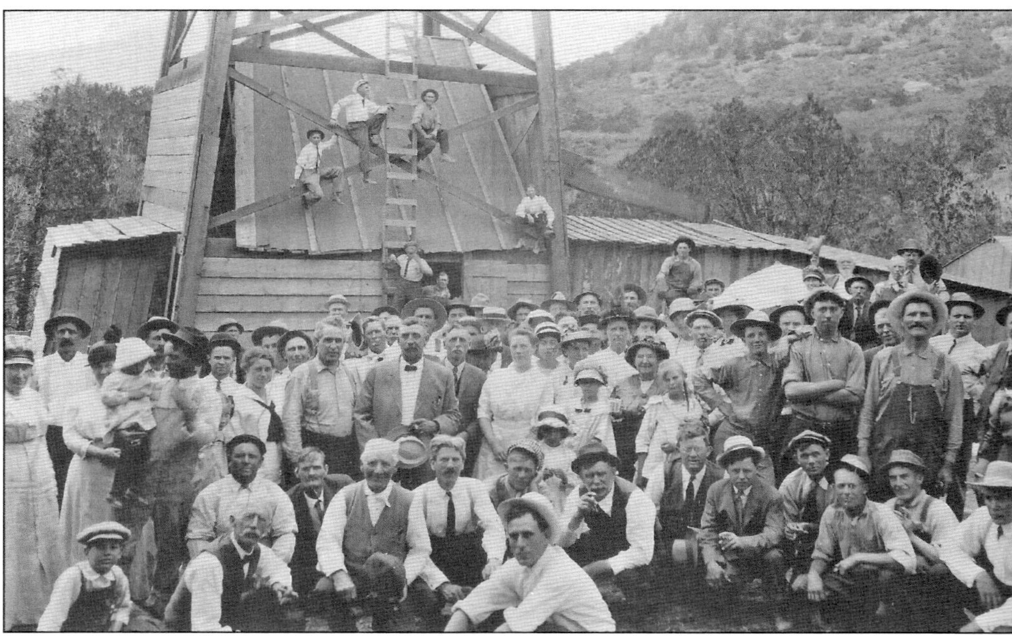

Finding Oil. In 1915, enthusiastic people incorporated the Hotchkiss Oil and Gas Company for the purpose of putting down a well down at least 3,000 feet, five miles north of Hotchkiss. Many invested money in this project. The oil-drilling plant needed five railroad cars to haul it. After many months, no oil was ever found and the high cost forced drilling to end. (HCHS.)

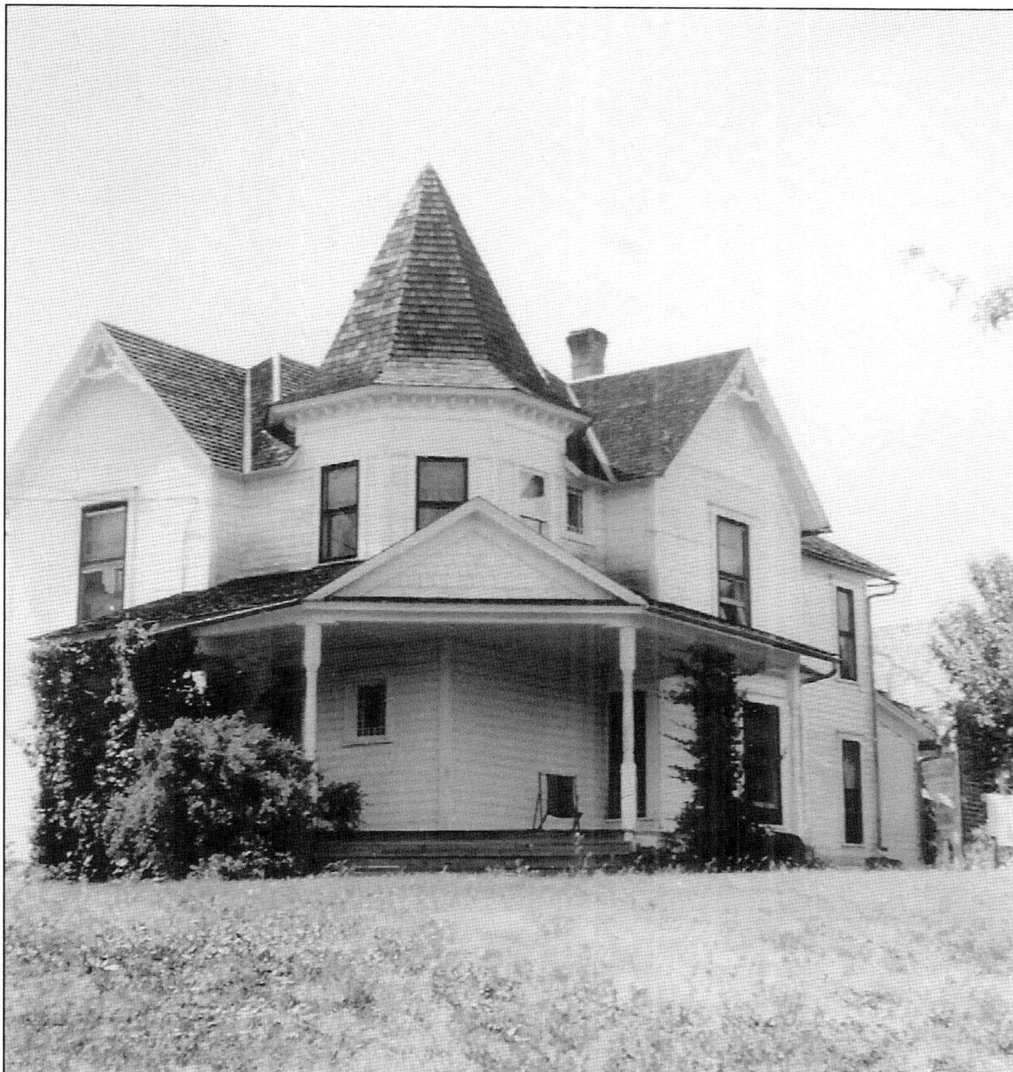

HARTMAN HOSPITAL. A house was built on Duke Hill in 1902. In 1939, A.H. Gould bought the house, named after Sam Hartman. With the assistance of Dr. Dugan, the hospital opened. The 11-bed hospital contained five rooms upstairs, used for sterilization, operations, obstetrics, and a recovery ward for the more seriously ill patients. Downstairs was a kitchen, waiting room, three rooms for patients, and a large pantry. Employees did all the laundry on a back porch. Patients paid $7 a day for a single room or $5 for a double room. Most employees were paid around $1 a day. One registered nurse and two or three nurse's aids were on duty. During World War II, it became a community project, with local citizens donating chickens, eggs, beef, vegetables, and wild game. Dugan went to the Army, but the hospital retained the services of Dr. Weiker, who studied in Germany. After coming to America, he obtained his medical license. The hospital closed in 1949 with the opening of the Delta Memorial Hospital. (HCHS.)

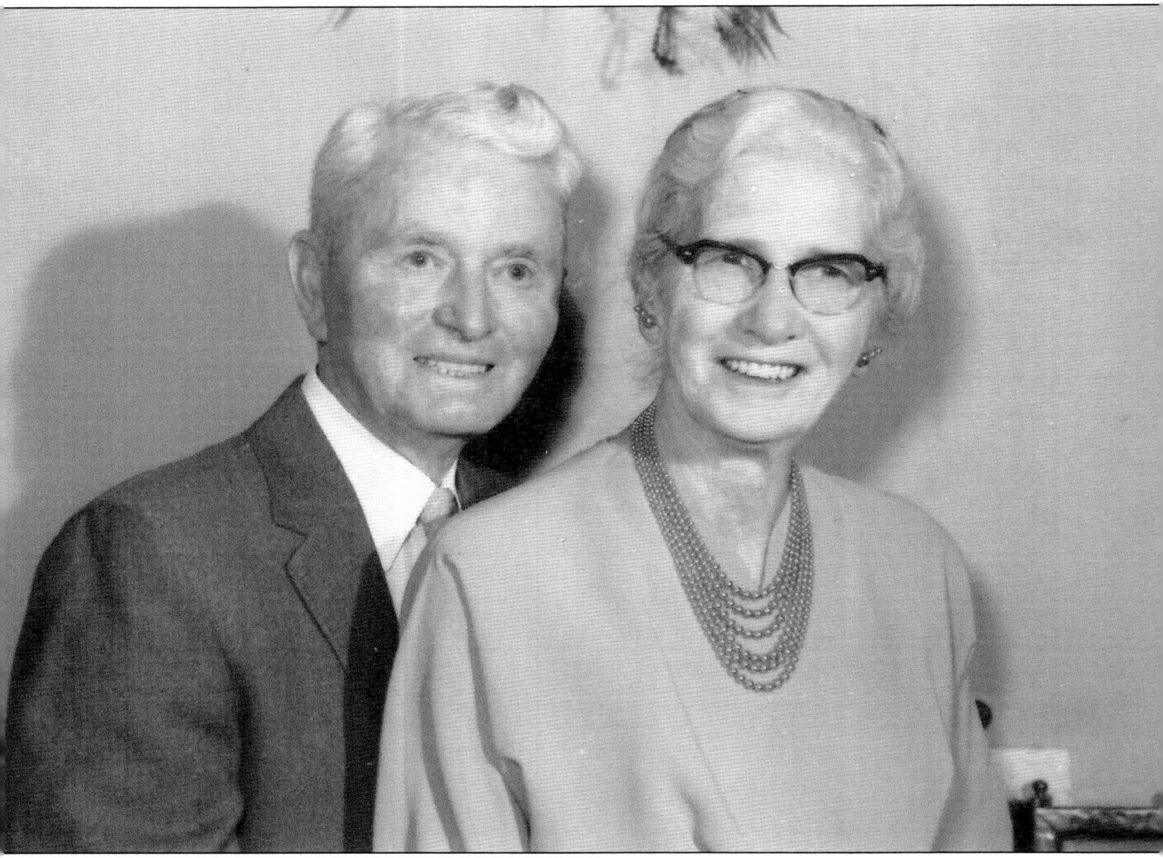

The Copelands. Dr. Claude and Leila Copeland are a prime example of people who contributed to the community. Starting his practice in 1904, Dr. Copeland served in the medical field in World Wars I and II and in the Civilian Conservation Corps camps. He always smoked cigars and never had a nurse in his office. He undressed at night, putting the clothes on a chair in the order that he took them off, so that he could dress quickly if needed. The Copelands collected many Indian artifacts, which were donated to the Hotchkiss museum. Leila was born in 1889 in Hotchkiss. She and others began the process of planning to build a community center. She was on the Memorial Hall congress and served as president from 1951 to 1968. Most will remember her as being in charge of the roller-skating at Memorial Hall. Importantly, Leila raised funds for the Memorial Hall that is still in use today. (HCHS.)

Two

LAZEAR

Lazear is located about five miles west of Hotchkiss on Rogers Mesa. It was necessary for the residents of the mesa to have a place to buy groceries, get supplies, and have a post office, but the area was never incorporated.

The original homestead was obtained by John Ashbaugh, who later sold 40 acres to James B. Lazear, who then sold the land to a group of men for a packing shed. It opened in 1908. Not having to haul fruit to Hotchkiss was handy, because fruit was proving to be a lucrative business.

In 1909, Bennett Stone platted the town and named it after Lazear. Stone also published a brochure to lure settlers to the area, promising mineral springs, coal at $1.50 a ton, an orchard of 10 acres that would support a family, and irrigation. The brochure also said there was a fine packinghouse and a supply company for the fruit farmer. It stated the need for hotels, newspapers, and blacksmith shops.

At one time, there was even a cheese factory. Cheese was left out for the public to sample in the general store, and children sampled cheese all day long. One man, Royden Girling, is responsible for many avenues of prosperity in this community. His partners through the years were his brothers Robert and Ralph, Louis Owens, and Tom Coutts.

A.E. Busey married Sadie Allen, and they lived in the Lazear area from 1904 until their passings. He had a general store and was in business with Wilson Allen for seven years. He also ran the Lazear Post Office and delivered mail by horse and buggy. A busy man, Busey also had an orchard and a slaughterhouse and was a beekeeper.

This small, struggling town has remained a pleasant place to live, just as the founders dreamed it would be. Misfortunes include the closing of the railroad depot, numerous fires, and a declining economy.

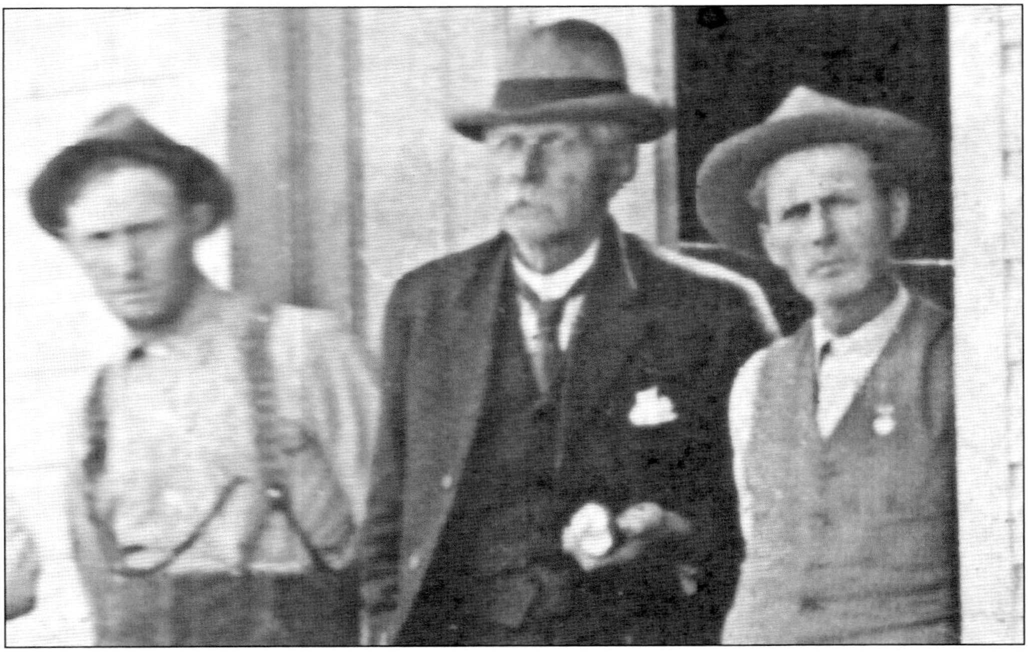

IMPORTANT MEN OF LAZEAR. James Lazear (center), from Pennsylvania, was appointed a national bank examiner for western states, including Colorado. He became connected with Central National Bank and was a financial backer for properties in western Colorado. In 1910, a post office was opened, and the town was named after him. Royden Girling (below, right) came to this valley in 1911, after his parents bought a fruit farm on Rogers Mesa. In 1920, Royden bought the Lazear Mercantile Store from A.E. Busey and became postmaster. In 1923, the Girling brothers bought a store across the street, which was a better building. In 1929, a longtime employee, Tom Coutts (below, left), became a partner, and the store became Girling and Coutts. After Royden retired as postmaster in 1953, Tom became postmaster and later bought out his partner. The store became Coutts and Company. (Both, HCHS.)

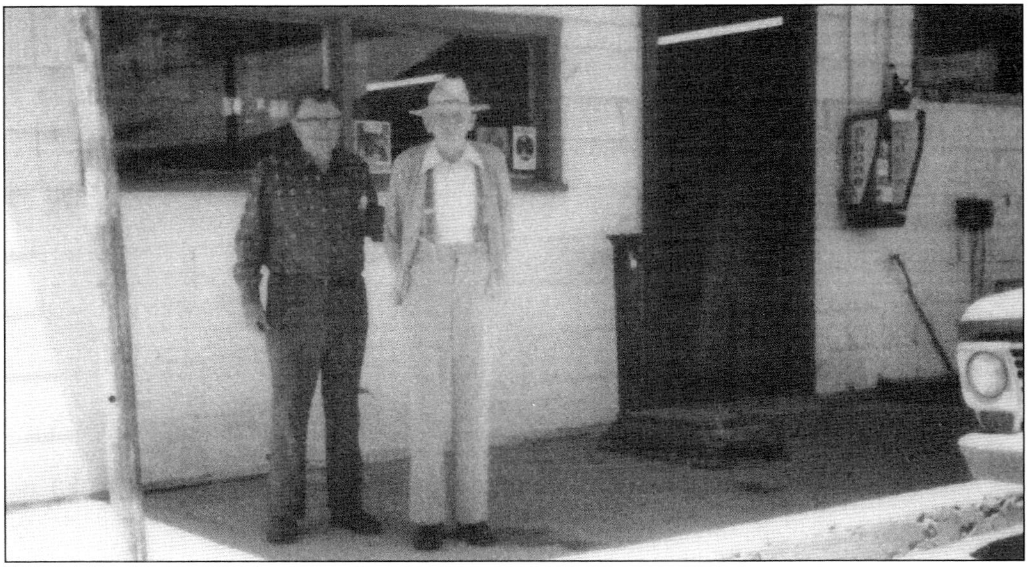

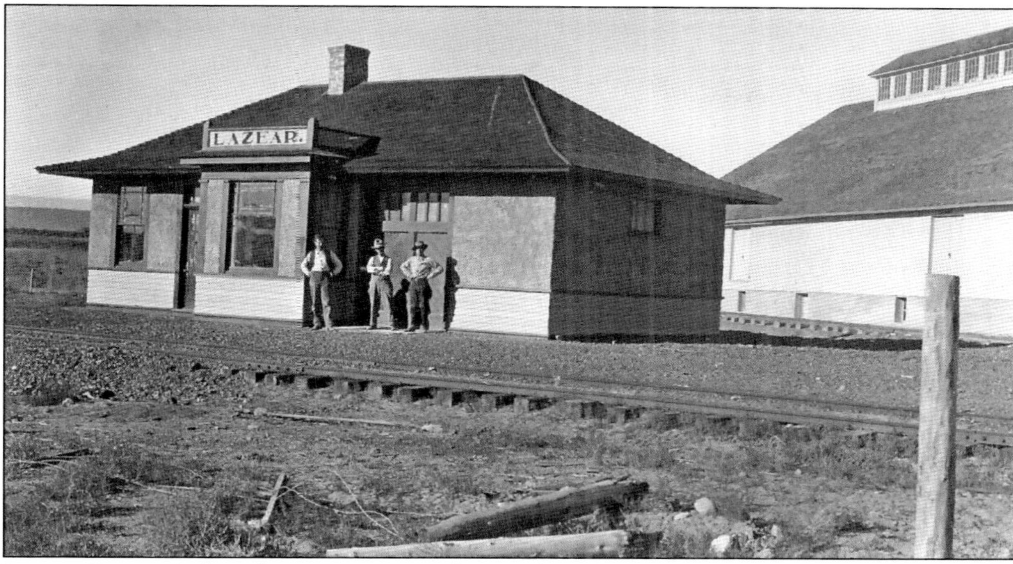

LAZEAR DEPOT. When the train came up the North Fork Valley to Hotchkiss in 1902, people on Rogers Mesa did not like hauling their fruit to town. With the new packing shed, it was thought that a depot in Lazear would benefit the farmers by having a train stop there and pick up their fruit. It was short-lived, however, for reasons unknown. (HCHS.)

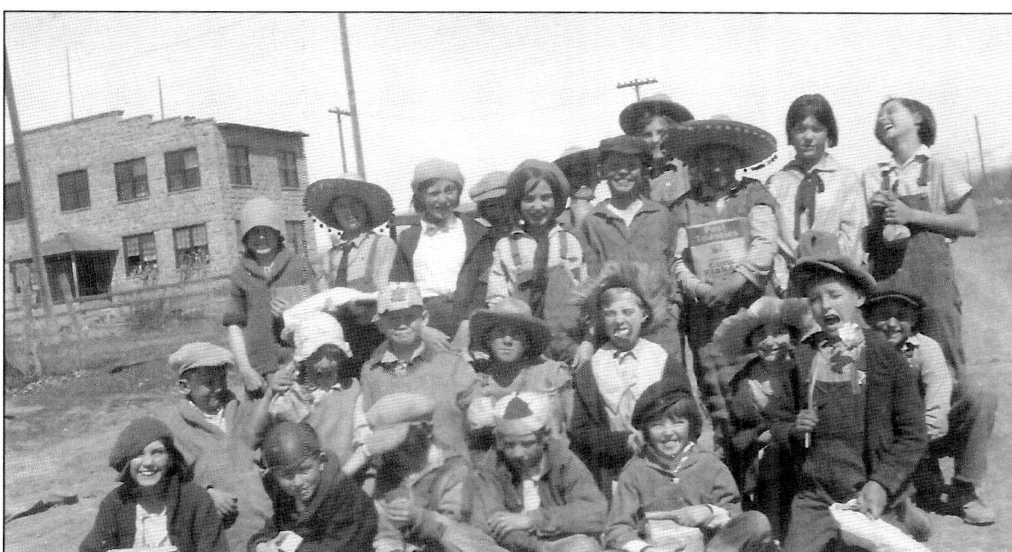

LAZEAR SCHOOL, 1929. In 1911, a bond election was held for a school building for $4,000. The school was made of cut stone quarried one mile away. It was equipped with a Smith heating plant. In 1917, the Red Cross used one upper room. In 1929, this group of students is going on a hike to the river that day. In 1989, the school was torn down in one day. (HCHS.)

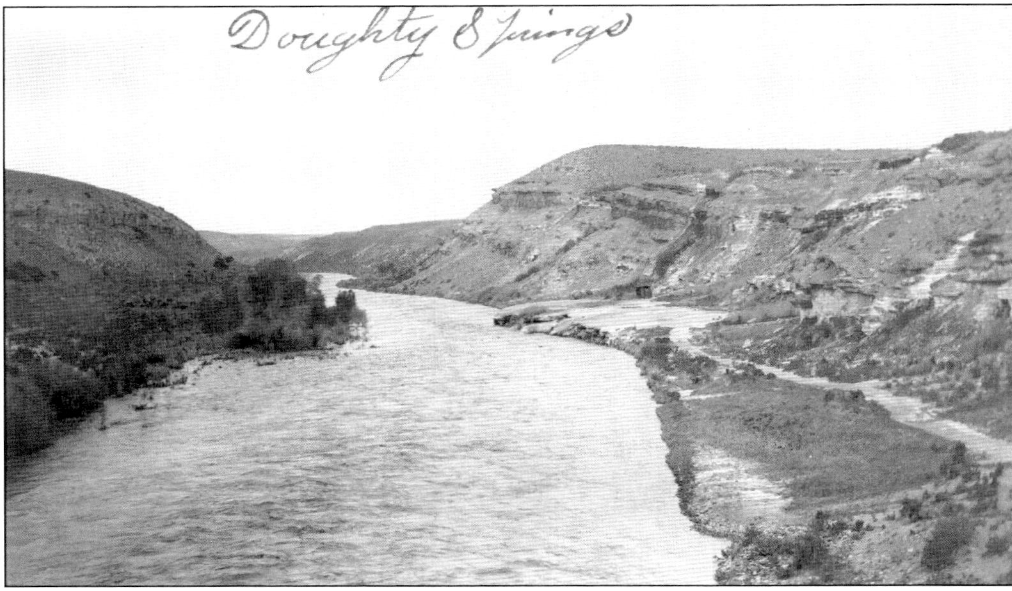

Doughty Springs. In 1891, John Doughty homesteaded at the lower end of Rogers Mesa in an area called Doughty Mesa. Below this mesa were springs also named after the Doughty family. They were beneficial for those suffering from rheumatism, weak stomach, liver and kidney troubles, and skin diseases. Many from the Lazear area made trips to the springs armed with anything to gather water on a regular basis. The water was said to have a peculiar taste. John planned to erect a hotel with bathhouses and to ship the special water; however, the springs quit producing, and his dream died. They had a bluish-green cast except for one, which would deposit a black substance. Lore has it that Indian artifacts were found in the deepest pool. (Both, DCHS.)

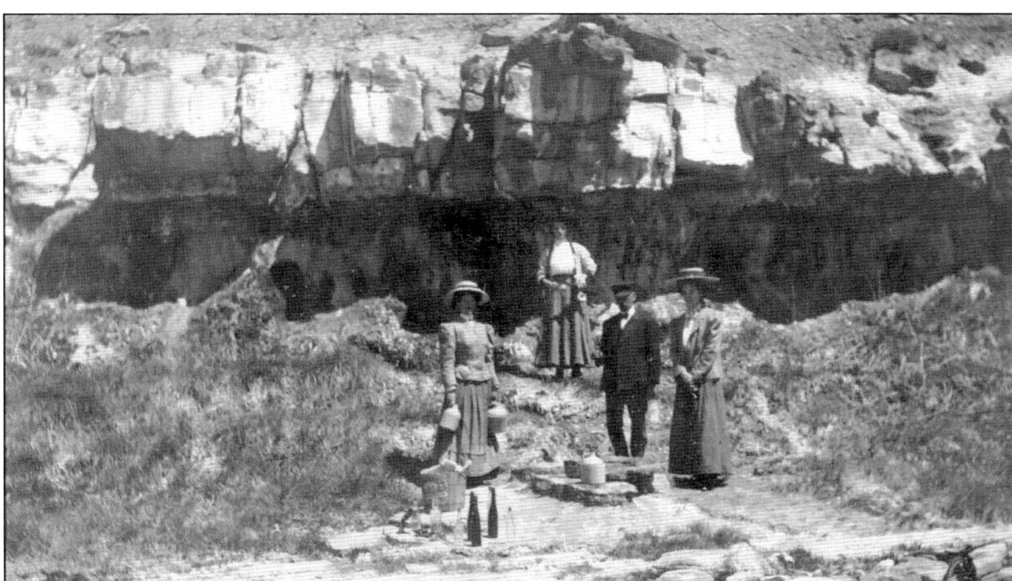

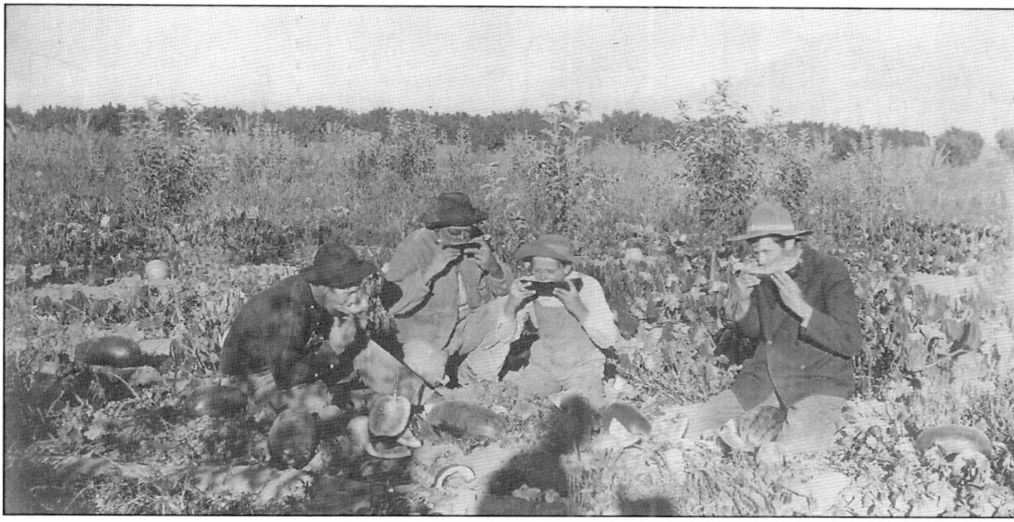

Thomas Jamison and the Slack Family. Jamison was originally from New York, but he came west in 1910, after being stricken with the white plague. He lived with the Perry Slack family near Lazear. During his stay, the family showed Jamison the region, and he took photographs portraying the area at that time. Years later, the photographs were sent to the museum in Hotchkiss. The photograph above shows Jamison (far right) feasting on fresh watermelon. Perry came to Lazear from Texas after marrying Carrie Greenwood. They had three children—Amy, Arthur, and Ellis. Perry helped organize the Lazear Church and was a good farmer. In the photograph below, the family is also shown having a picnic in the "Dobies" with Jamison. Unfortunately, he lost his battle with tuberculosis; he is buried in Hotchkiss. (Both, HCHS.)

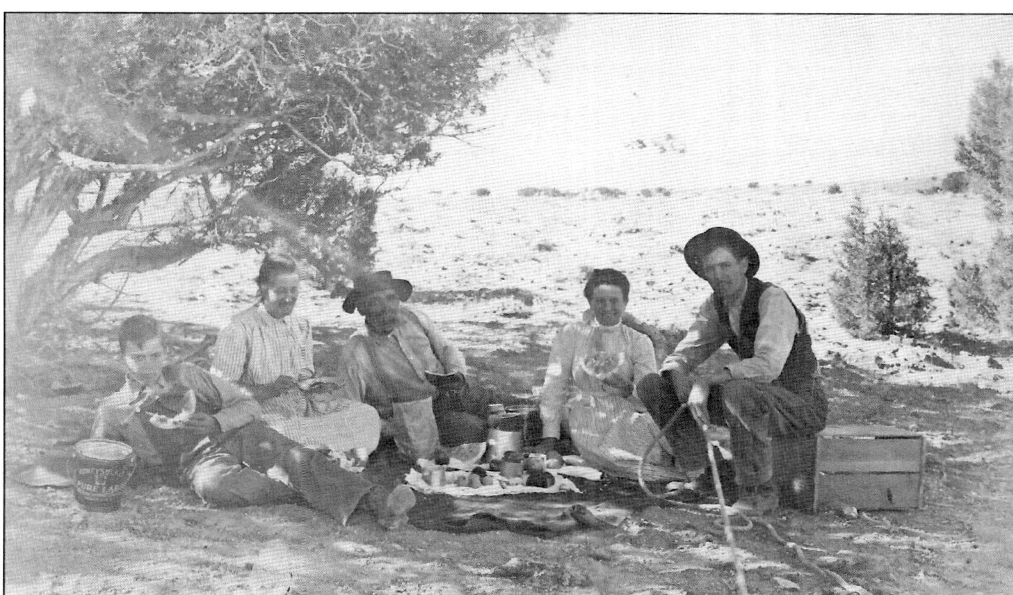

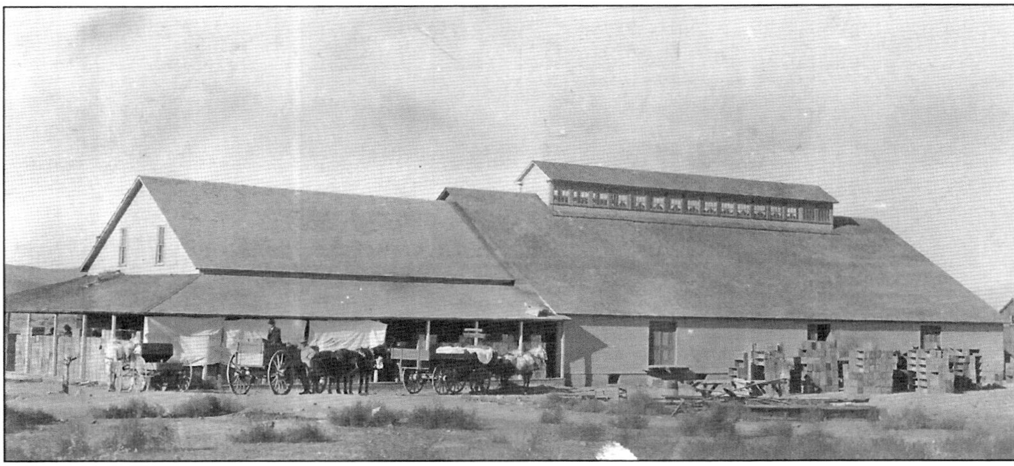

Rogers Mesa Fruit growers. This fruit company was incorporated in 1907 by L.C. Ellington, Andrew Linn, H.C. Busey, William J. Barrow, C.L. Greenwood, James Annand, and Jesse Reynolds. In 1908, James B. Lazear sold land to them, and Frank and Arthur Blide constructed the building. In 1912, an addition was added on that contained a large peach grader and an automatic box carrier. In 1918, heavy snow collapsed the roof, and apples were frozen. For Rogers Mesa farmers, this packinghouse was a closer place to take fruit. In 1926, the Lazear Fruit Company was incorporated. Robert White started another Lazear packinghouse in 1932 with Donald and John Patton. Later, Melvin and Raymond White took it over but saw it burn to the ground in 1972. (Both, HCHS.)

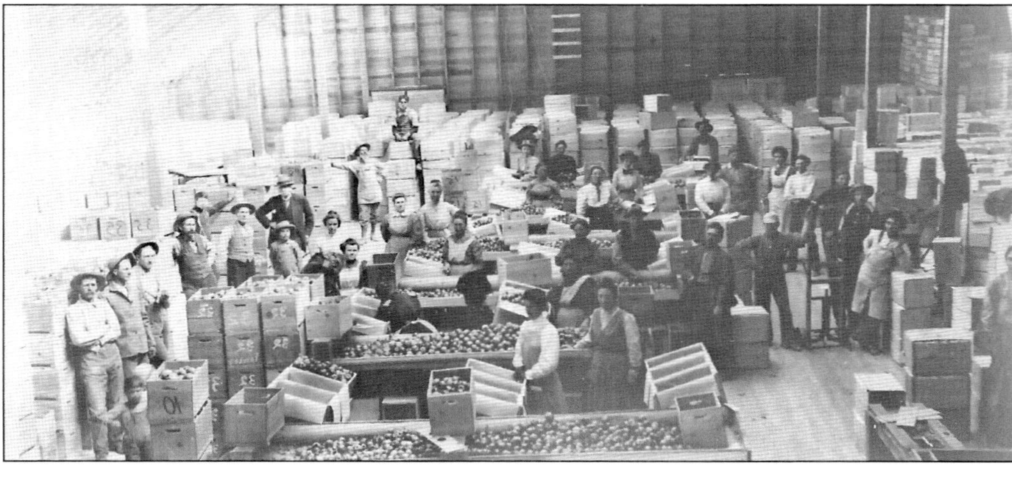

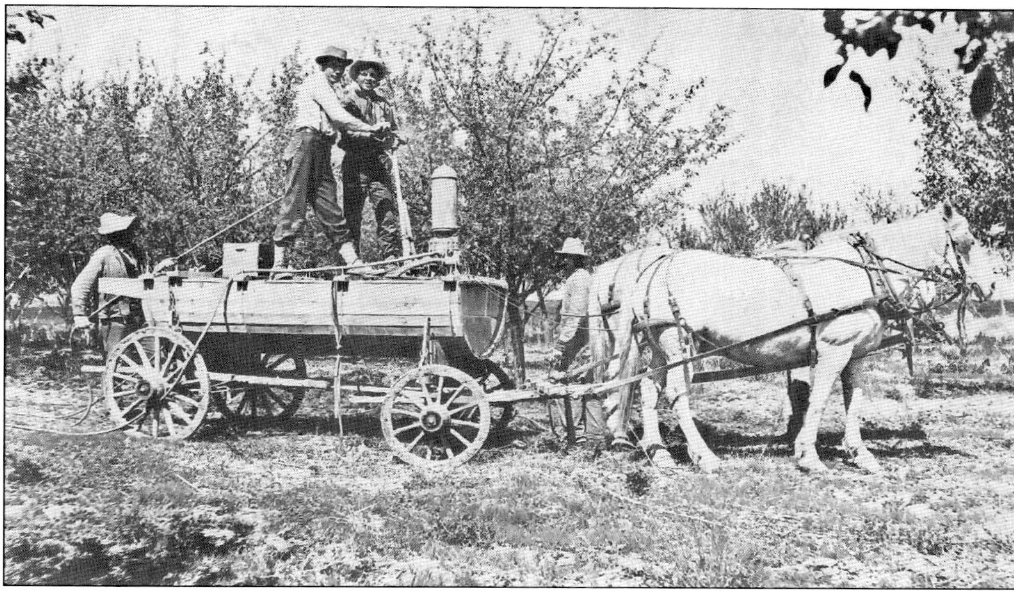

SPRAYING THE ORCHARDS. After fruit trees were brought into the valley, they began to mature and bear fruit. Although at first the trees were disease- and pest-free, as time went on and more people came, so did insects and diseases. In the April edition of the *North Fork Times*, an advertisement by North Fork Growers Association of Hotchkiss and Rogers Mesa was aimed at fruit growers. They had a complete line of supplies, including Swift's Arsenate of Lead, tobacco extract, Vreeland's Electro Dry Arsenic, lime, sulfur, whale oil soap, spray fixtures, repairs, and a full line of pumps. D.L. Blakley was the manager in Lazear, where Perry Slack purchased equipment to spray orchards. The fruit were prizewinners at many county, state, and national exhibits. (Both, HCHS.)

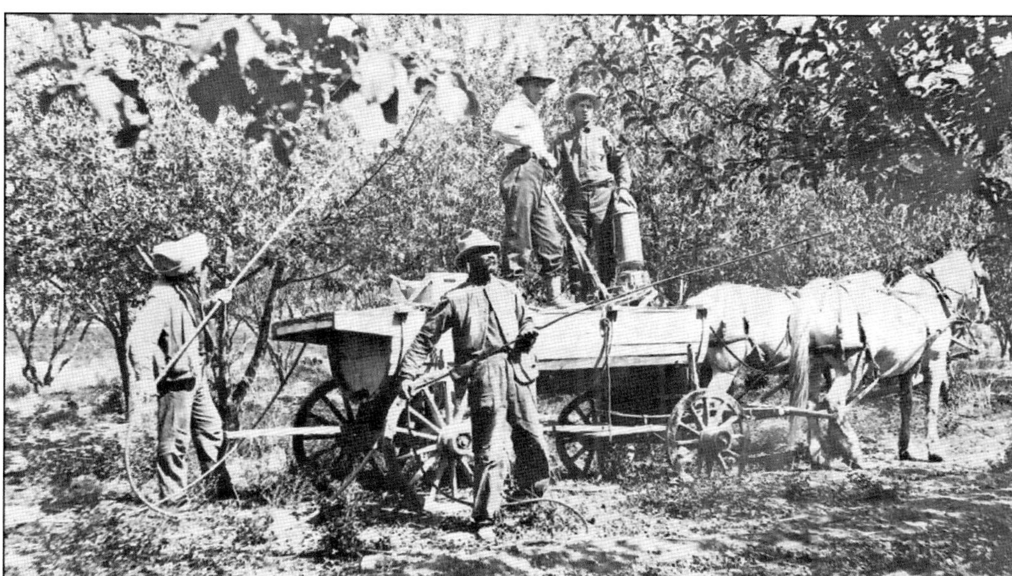

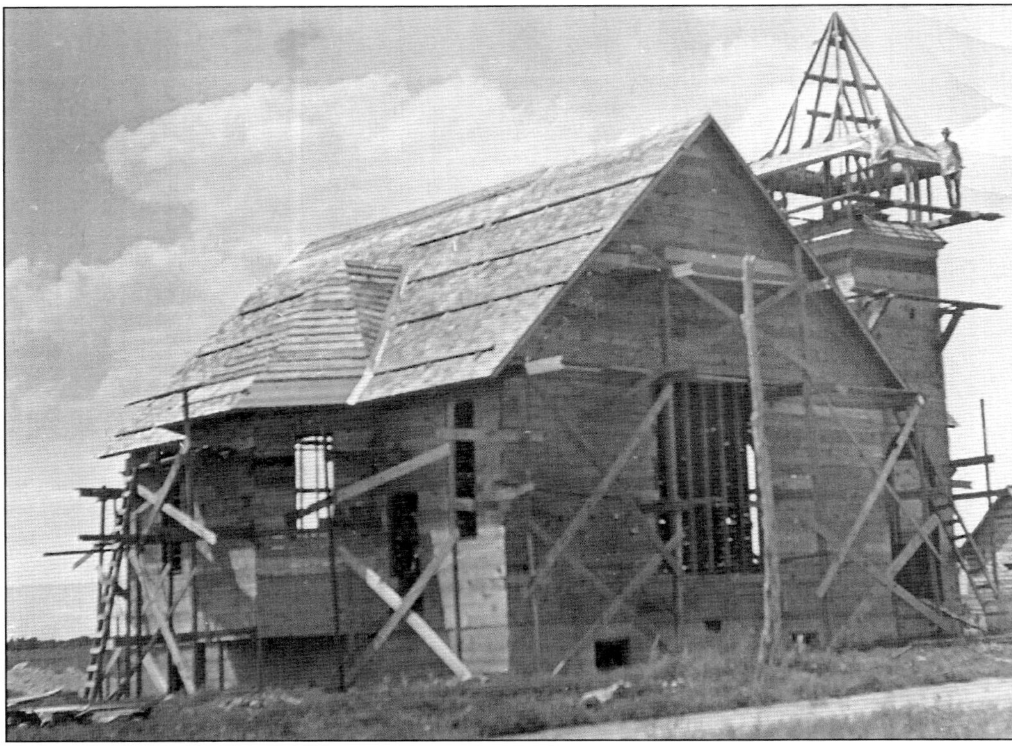

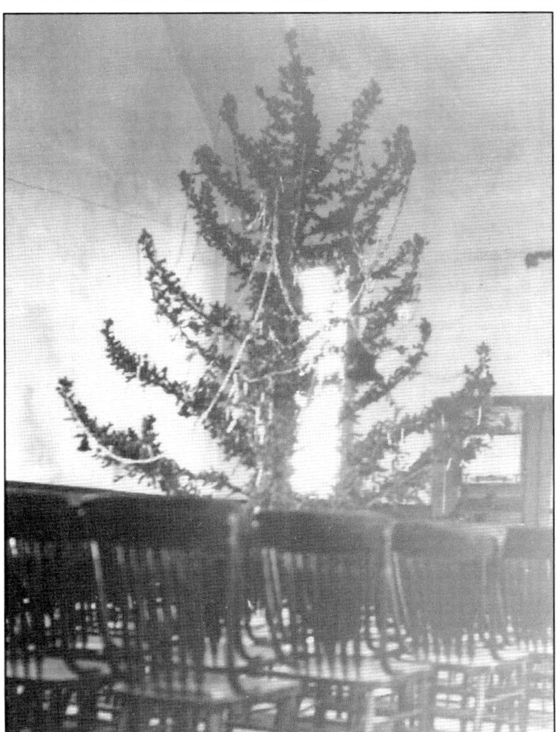

Lazear Methodist Church. In 1910, the ground for the new church was excavated. The Ladies Aid of the church had numerous dinners, socials, bazaars, and other events to raise money for building costs. Members subscribed amounts that they would donate as they could afford to do so. The church was dedicated in 1912, with James Dickey as the pastor. Wilford Allen was the first person to be baptized in the new church. To finish the inside of the church, each family purchased chairs for its own use. The young people's Sunday school class raised money for choir chairs. Another class bought pulpit chairs and collection plates. Friends of the Church donated the bell. James Lazear gave a Bible. There was a Catholic church in Lazear, but it was moved to Hotchkiss. (Both, HCHS.)

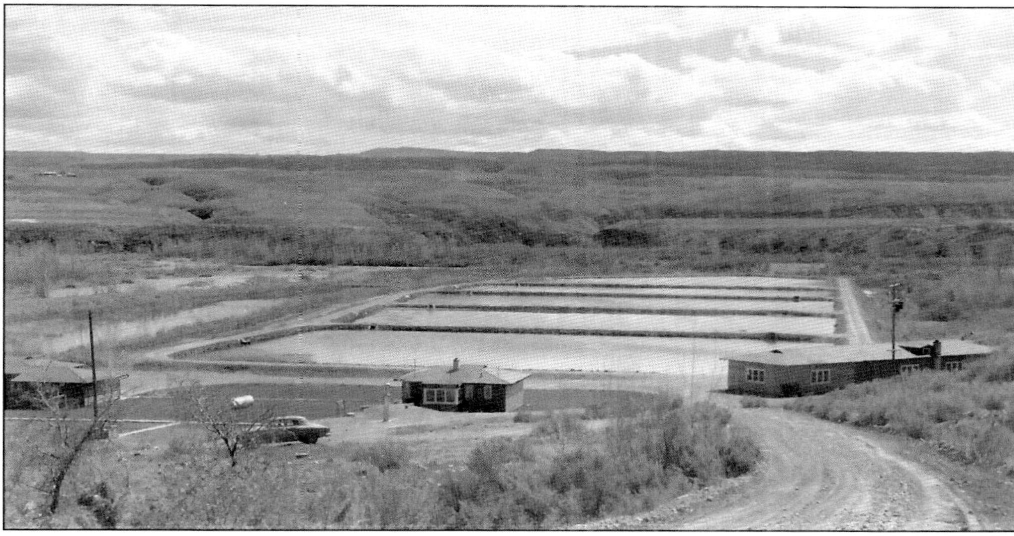

Fish Hatchery. On the south side of Rogers Mesa near Lazear is the Hotchkiss National Fish Hatchery. Charles Roberts and Jeremiah Clevenger obtained the land first in 1893. Through a process of selling and dividing the land, Paul Swisher and Chauncey Lee owned parts of the land. In 1937, Donald Bennett and Jess Norris leased springs on the land and built a small hatchery and rearing ponds. In 1948, Swisher sold the land to the State of Colorado, and this was the Chipeta Unit. An apiary owned by Ted Dowell soon became the site of North Fork Unit fish hatchery. In the 1960s, the two properties became a national fish hatchery. The springs that provide the water to them remain at a constant temperature of 56 degrees and flow 2,200 to 5,000 gallons per minute, which is ideal for trout production. (Both, HCHS.)

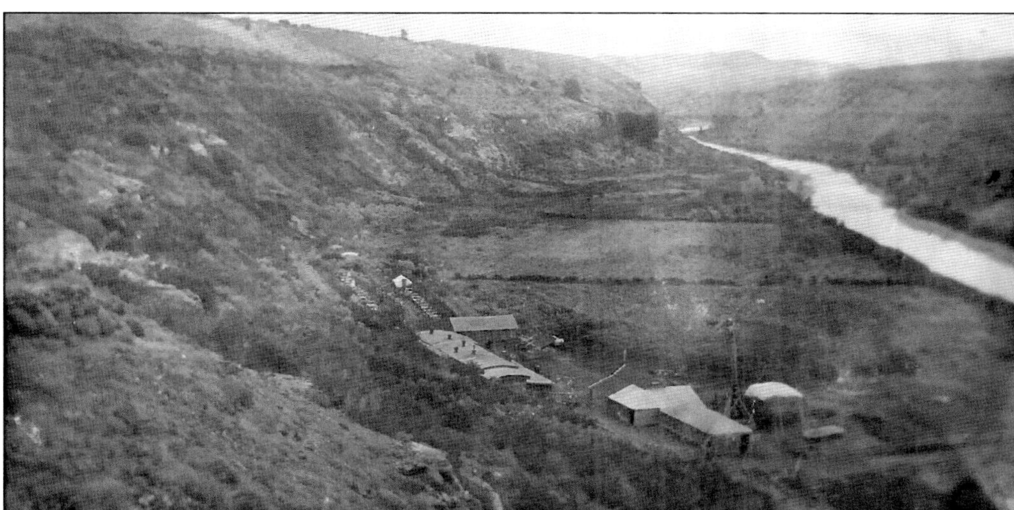

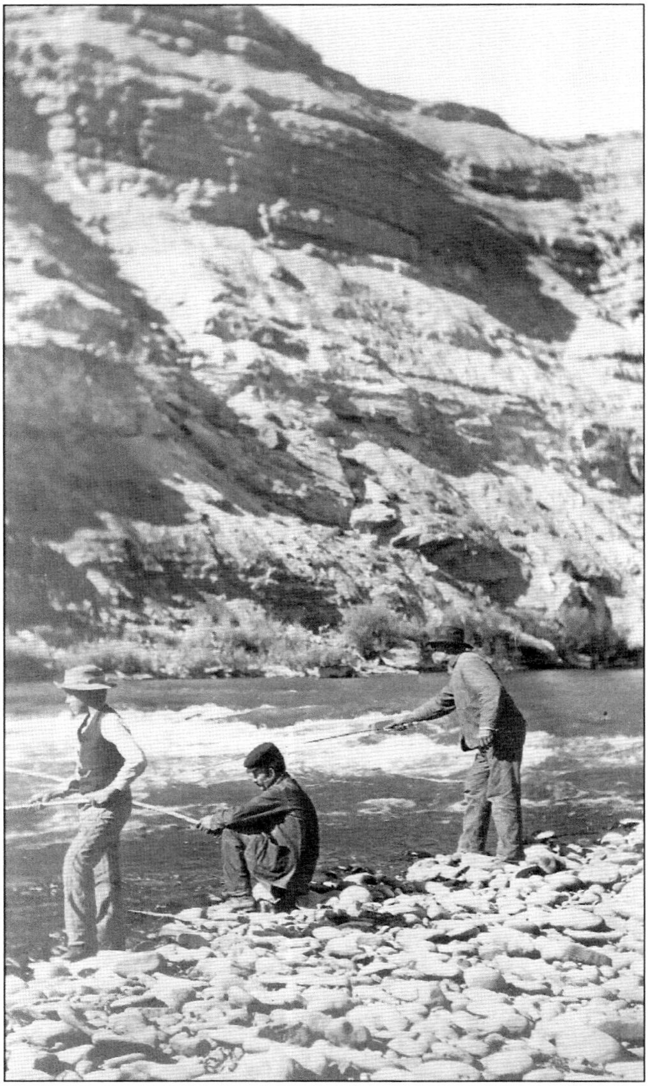

Time to Fish. The North Fork River is down a hill south of Lazear, where fishing was and still is a popular sport. Most of the fish were trout, and there was no number or size limit at that time, in 1910. Arthur Slack (left), ? Hall, and Perry Slack went on such a trip to the North Fork River to catch their supper (left). They cooked and ate their catch of trout while at the river (below). From left to right are Thomas Jamison, Perry Slack, and ? Hall. While Jamison lived with the Slack family, they took him on many fishing, camping, and hunting adventures, as told by the photographs he had. (Both, HCHS.)

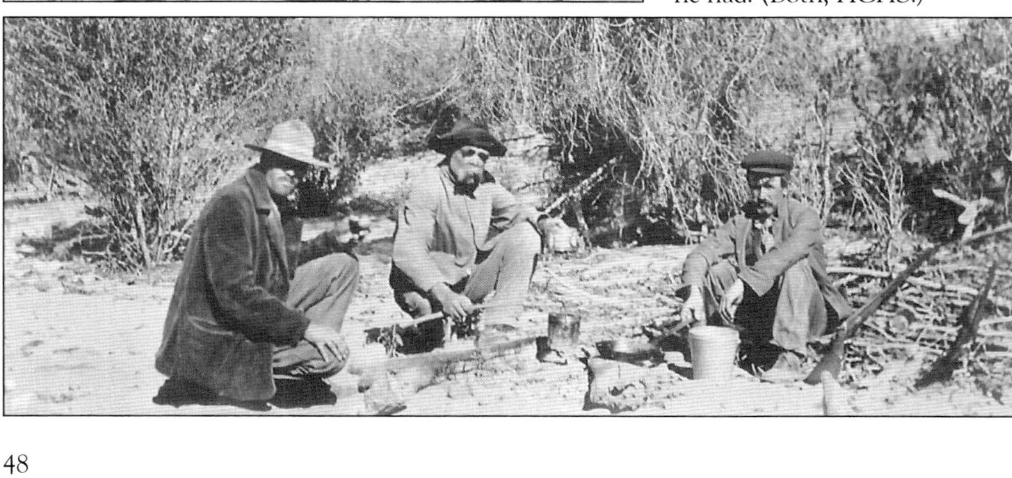

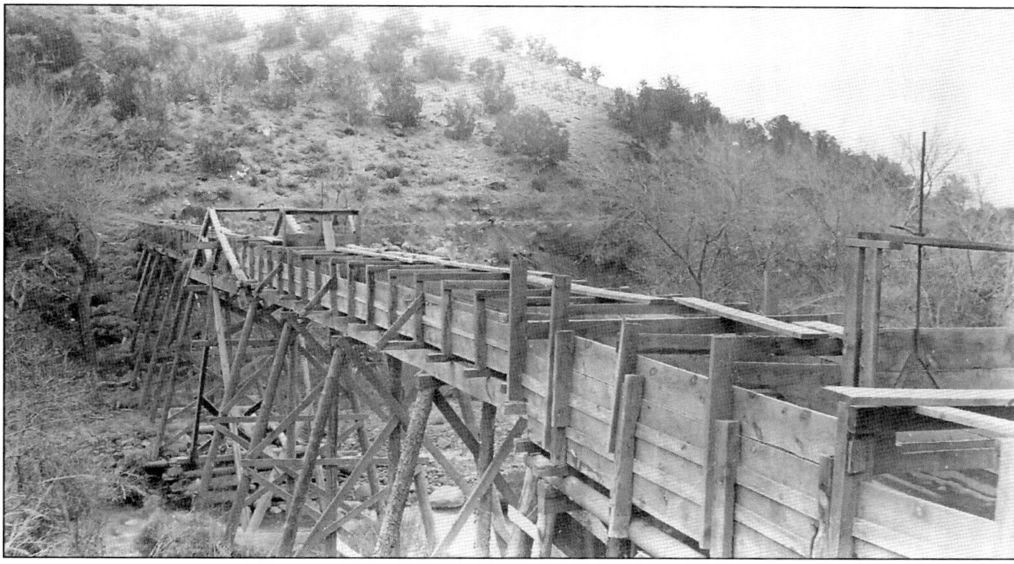

Irrigation Systems. Water used for this area came from the Fire Mountain Canal, which is still in use today. The head gate begins above Paonia by drawing water from the North Fork River. Above is a flume carrying the pipeline across a ravine. The canal was started in 1895. Other sources of water came from the Leroux Creek area with its reservoirs, which store water naturally. Claims were filed in that area, and man-made reservoirs were built later. Below is a divide box in a ditch. A farmer owned so many shares, and the box divided the water accordingly. At that time, the ditch carried 80 feet of water and was valued at $300,000. In order to get shares for some ditches, each shareholder had to work on the project. The number of days worked and whether he used a horse determined the share. (Both, HCHS.)

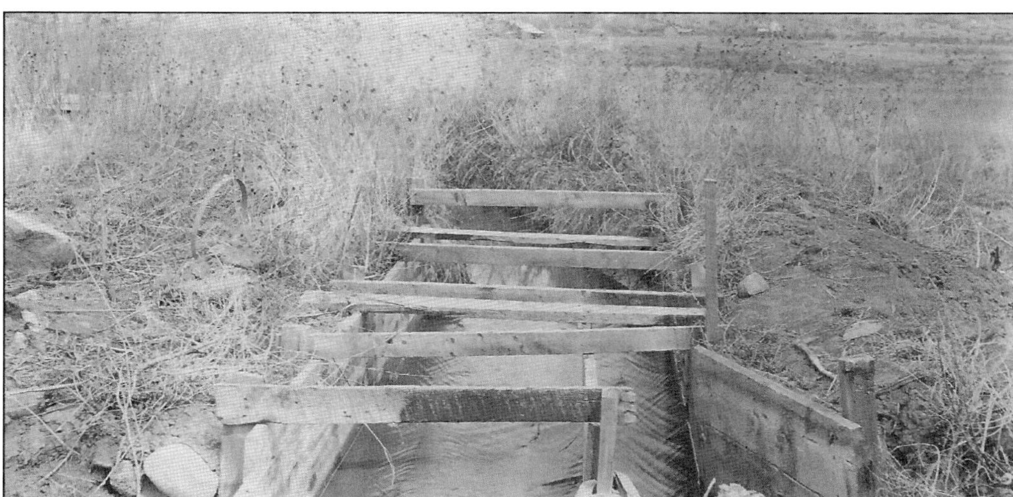

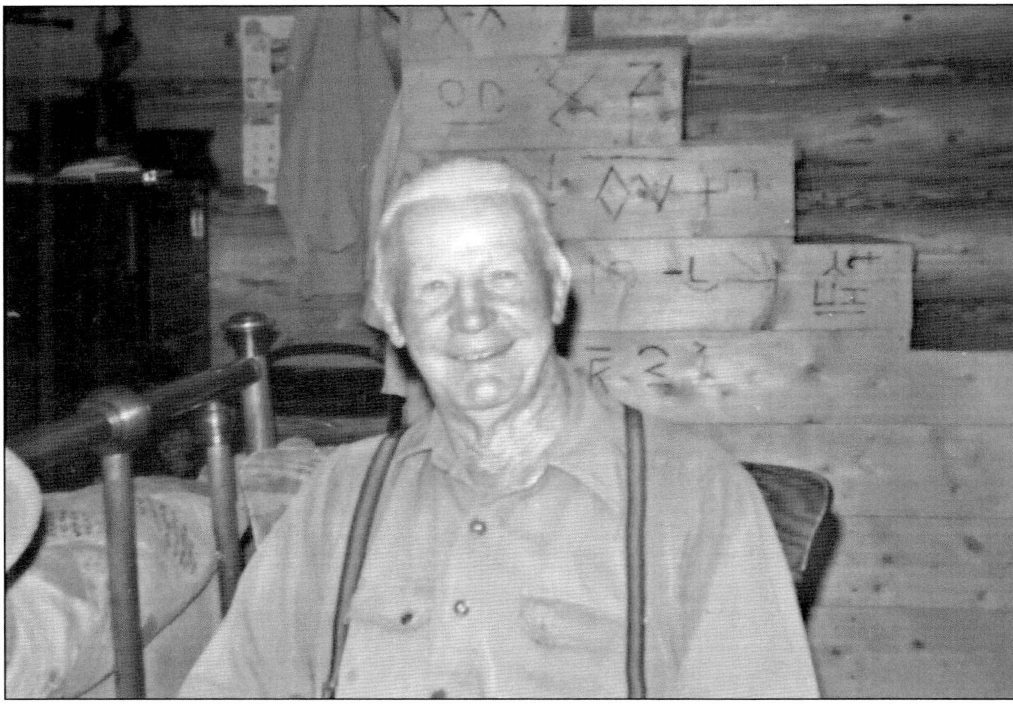

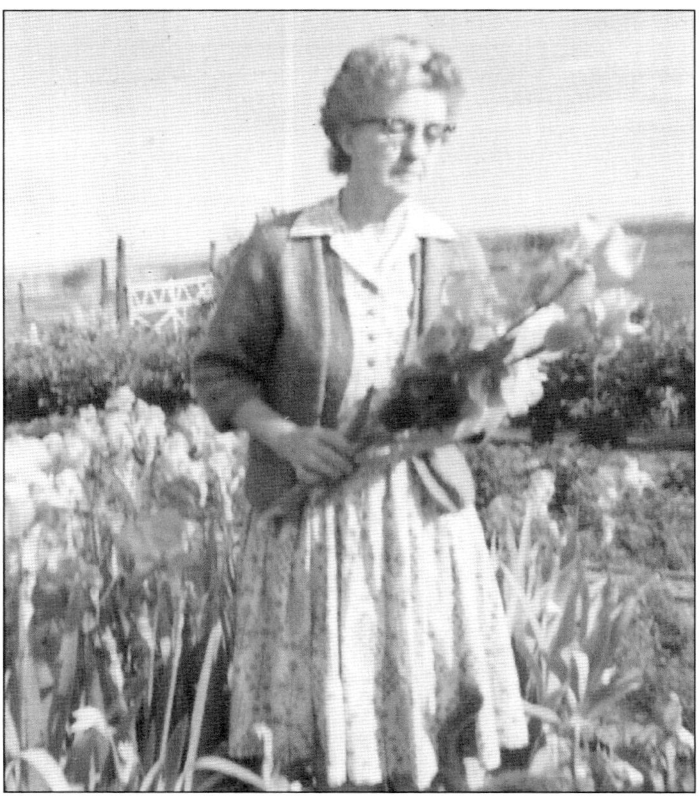

The Crouch Family. Katherine Wyatt Crouch came to Rogers Mesa in 1917. She and John were very well known people in Lazear. John was a deputy water commissioner for the Leroux Creek watershed for 37 years. He built a cabin in Doughty Park in 1937 and sold it to Jamie Carr when he retired. John's work would begin in early May at Duke Stomp, where he would walk or snowshoe in to oversee the use of reservoirs or ditches. There were no bridges and not much more than cow paths for roads. Katherine was well known for working for Royden and Ralph Girling as well as for Tom Coutts at the general store in Lazear for 53 years. Also important were the prized irises that she grew. (Both, HCHS.)

Three

Crawford and Surrounding Areas

Capt. George A. Crawford, who was scouting Indians before they were resettled, wandered through the area of Crawford in 1882. He met Harry Grant and told Harry that this place needed a post office. Harry listened and opened an unofficial post office. Joel Preston applied for an official post office, naming it Crawford. He was the first postmaster in 1883.

Duff Morrow owned the first store in Crawford and would travel to Gunnison for supplies before other businesses came. The Clipper Ditch was built, and the town was moved up the hill above the ditch instead of below it.

Crawford never got a railroad up to that area, though it was talked about greatly in 1910. George C. Harper and N.J. Oleson of Minneapolis were ready to build the road if $125,000 were raised. Some money was raised, and hopes were high, but the railroad never was constructed.

This area is mostly agricultural, and many ranches dot the countryside. The Crawford Dam was built in 1963 and provides storage for irrigation water and also recreation; and the area is popular for hunting, especially during the fall months. Sawmills once dotted the Black Mesa, providing lumber for the valley.

But what really makes this area pleasurable is the people. They are good, down-to-earth, hardworking, and proud citizens. Joe Cocker and his wife Pam have contributed greatly to the community by supporting the children of the valley. Wilson Rockwell represented the area well when he was in politics. Leslie Savage was instrumental in the development of the Black Mesa Road and the Crawford Dam, among many other endeavors.

The Black Canyon, that the first settlers struggled to travel by, is now a national monument, which draws many tourists to the north rim. The Gunnison River in the canyon is considered Gold Medal Water and Wild Trout Water. Former president Jimmy Carter has made the trip down it several times.

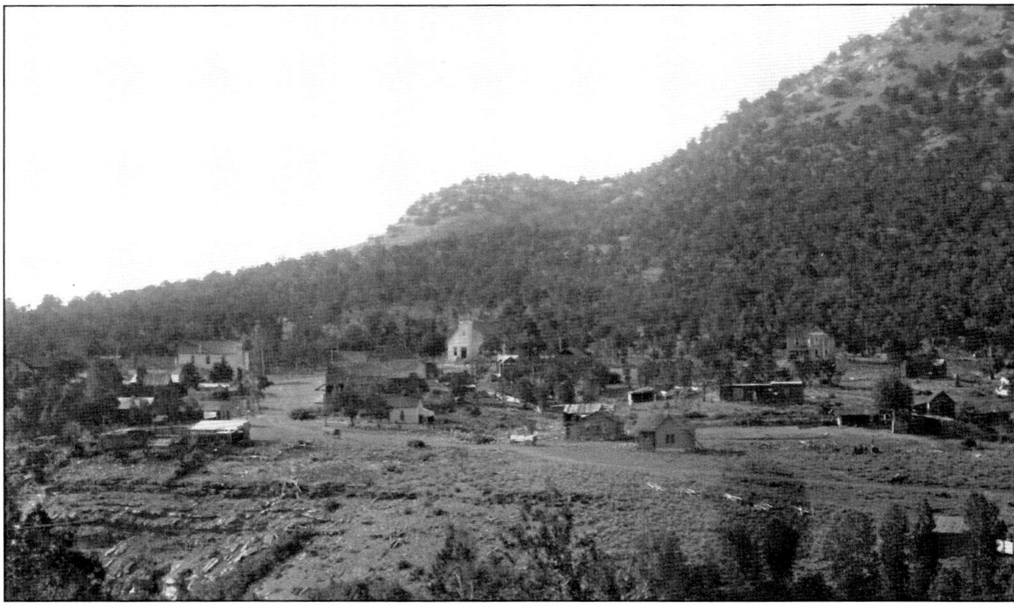

The Town. The first site of Crawford was down the hill from the present location, which is shown above. Harry Grant was the postmaster. Next came a co-op store and other small businesses soon followed. Because of the Clipper Ditch, the town was then moved up the hill to its present location in the 1890s. Eliza Ong owned most of the land above the first location of the town. After she turned her store over to Paul Kruemling and her son Floyd Zimmerman, things went better for the progression of the town. It was incorporated in 1910, and Charles Stoner was the first mayor. A church, blacksmith shop, creamery, school, and other businesses followed. The town was growing even though the railroad never came to Crawford. Below, Saddle Mountain is shown east of the town. (Both, HCHS.)

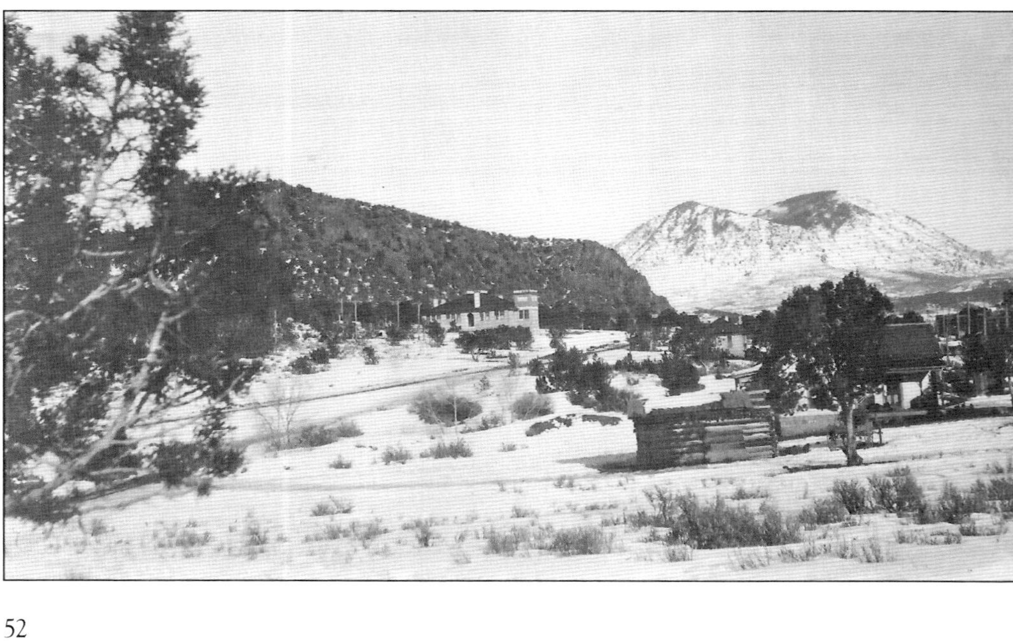

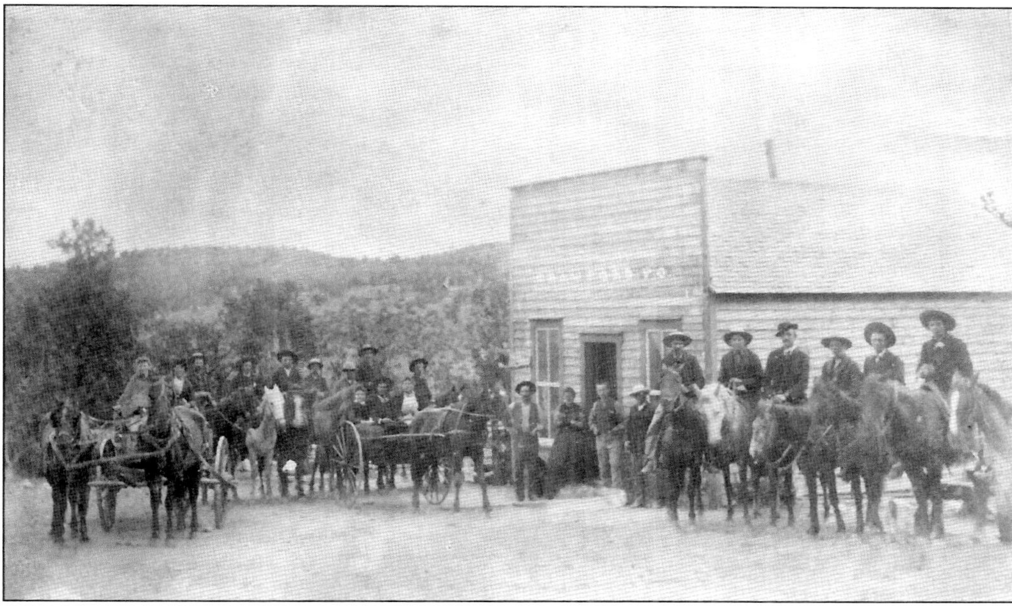

Eliza Ong. Pictured above in the center with a black dress, Eliza Ong was a tireless worker, often driving a wagon by herself clear to Delta for supplies for the store. If she needed lumber, she went to Black Mesa to a sawmill and loaded the lumber herself. It is said she carried two pistols under her skirt for protection. Her health began to fail, and she took Paul Kruemling in as a partner. He and her son Floyd Zimmerman began to run the store. Right before her death in 1899, she planned her own funeral. She also deeded the spot for the church and cemetery. After her death, more businesses began, such as Crawford State Bank, seen below in 1910. W.L. Savage, Willard Gould, Fred Foster, James Teeslink, and E.A. Browne were the directors. (Both, HCHS.)

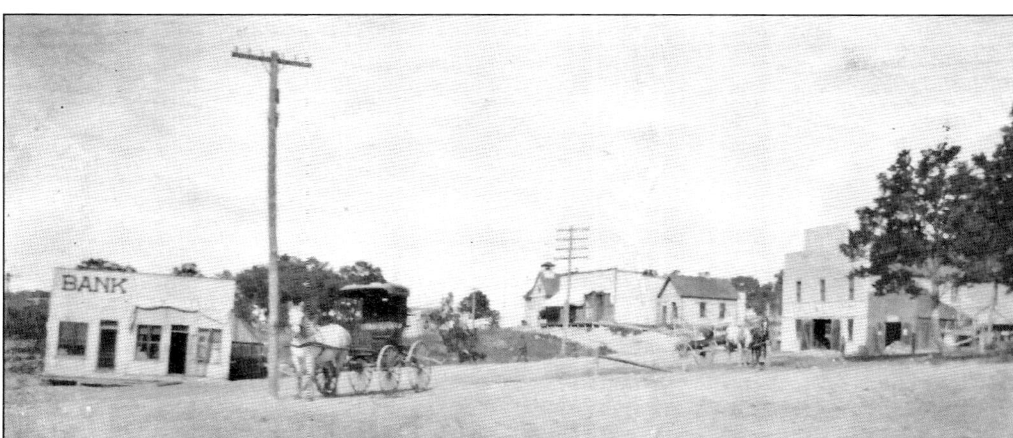

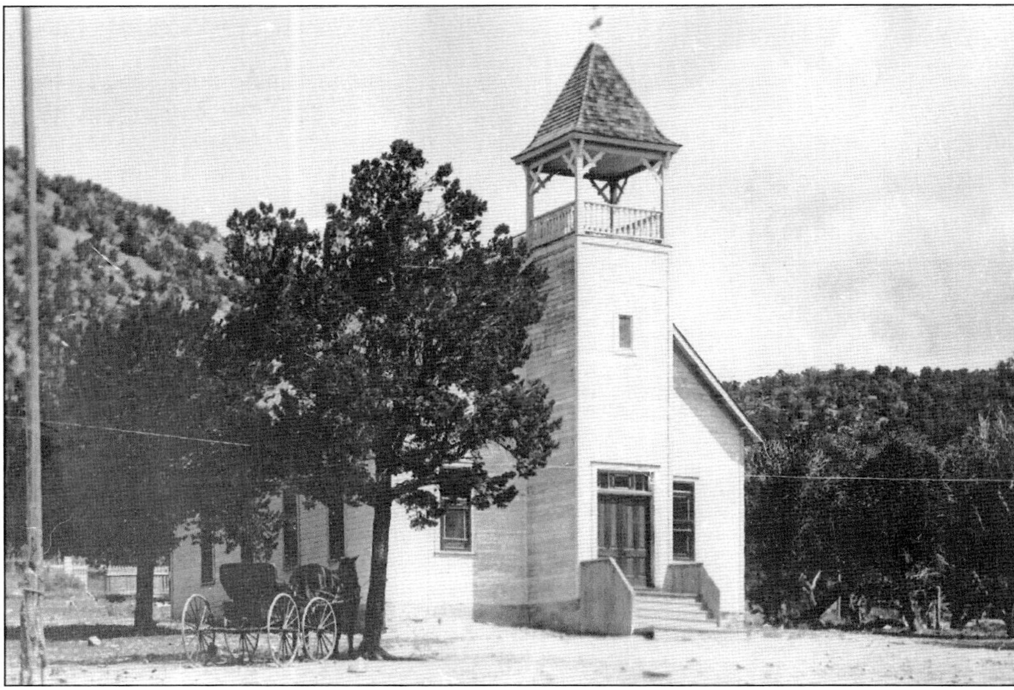

The Church. The Crawford Community Church was organized in 1899 and met above Eliza Ong's store. Needing a building of their own, the congregation sought donations. Lumber was free-of-charge at the Brock and Harpst sawmill. Zaum and Zaum built the church, which was dedicated in 1900. The cemetery is located directly behind the church. Memorial Day in Crawford is a big day when hundreds of people gather to decorate graves of loved ones, share dinner, renew acquaintances, and relive memories. In the 1930s, it was a day to decorate graves. Each year, it became a tradition to beautify the cemetery. On Memorial Day in 1914, the Crawford Cemetery Auxiliary served chicken and homemade noodles to 700 people. The tradition has carried on to this day, and various clubs participate. (Both, HCHS.)

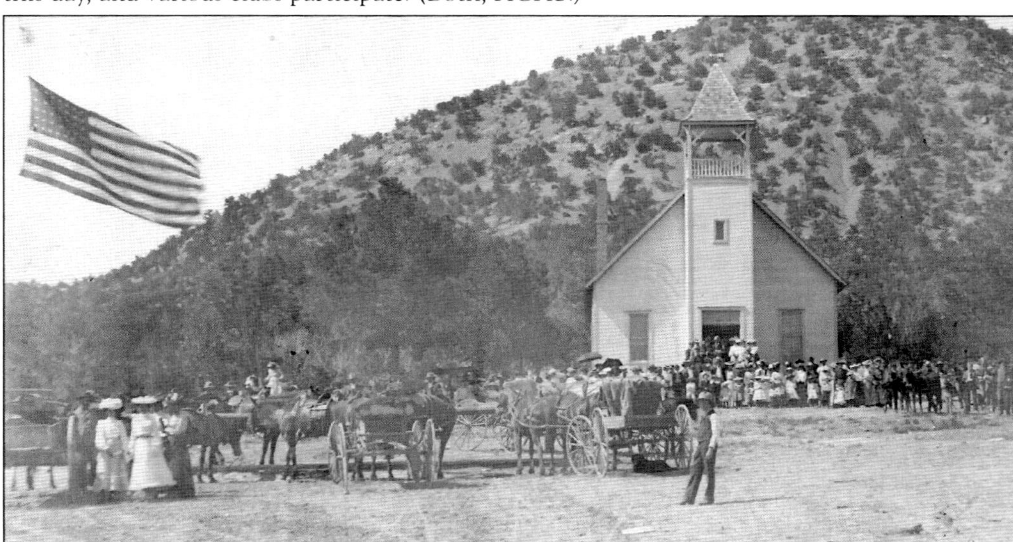

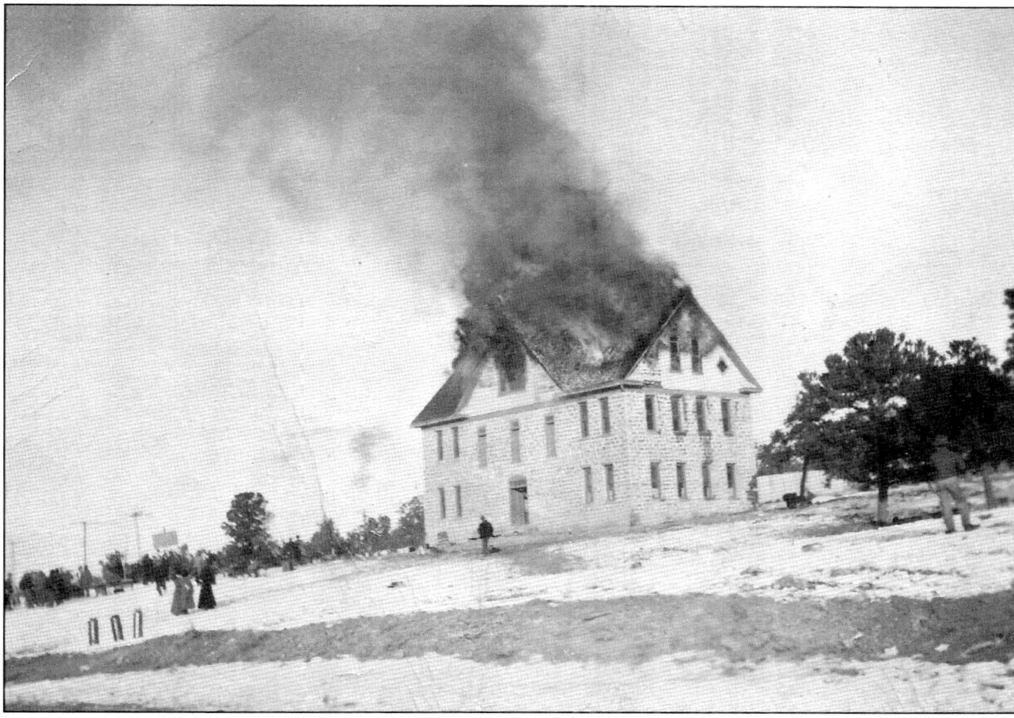

The Crawford School. Completed in 1906 for $16,000, this structure was made of native stone from the Smith Fork Canyon. In February 1907, there was to be no school one Friday as an earthquake was predicted. It never occurred, but some boys climbed a hill, rolled rocks down, and made as much noise as the anticipated earthquake. The first class to have high school graduation had two graduates in 1911. On December 12, 1912, a fire destroyed the building. One explanation of the fire was a faulty flue, and others say the sawdust used in insulation contributed to the blaze. A new school was soon built using much of the same stone from the bottom floor. Today, that building is a town hall. Crawford offers classes from kindergarten through eighth grade. (Both, HCHS.)

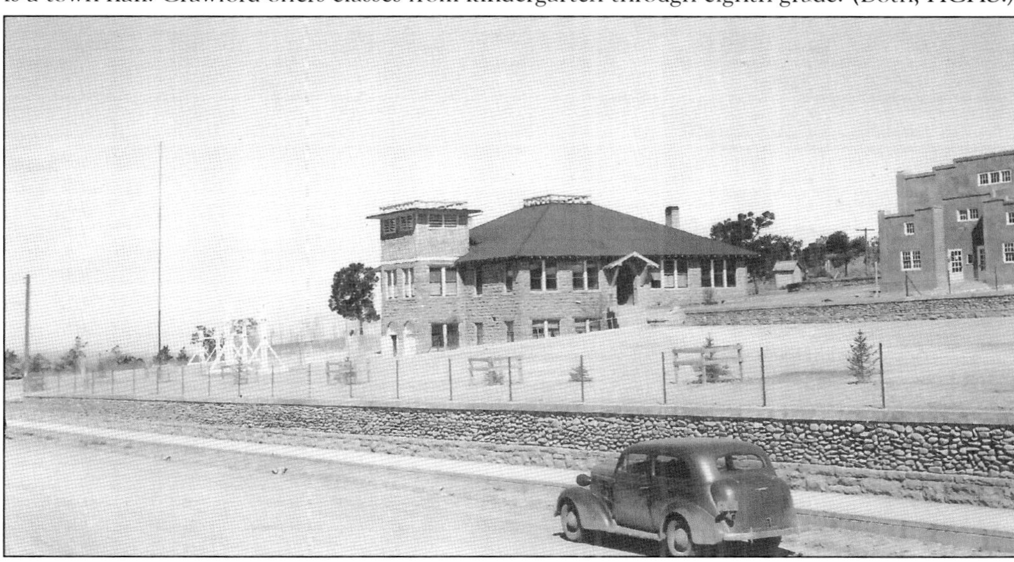

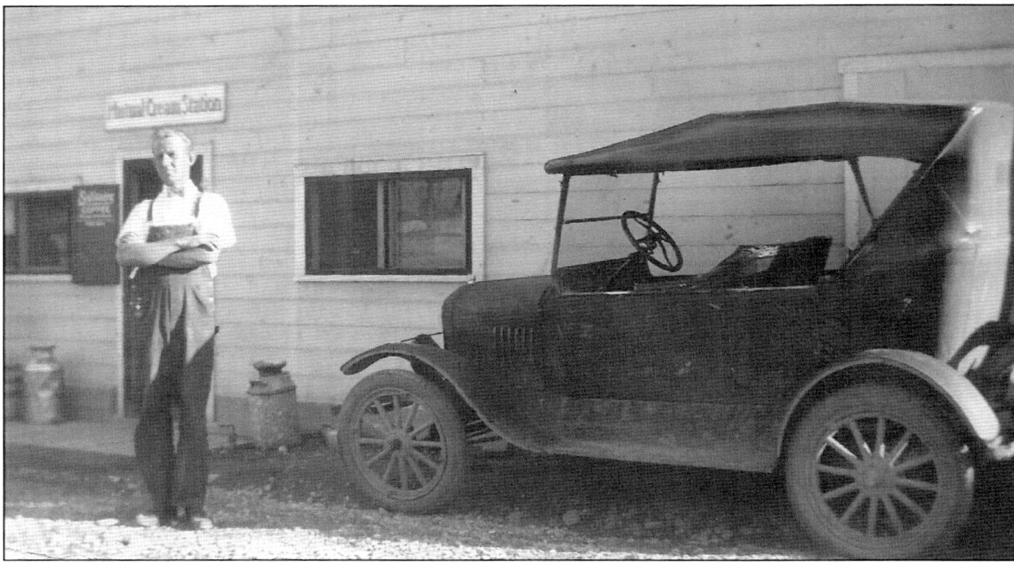

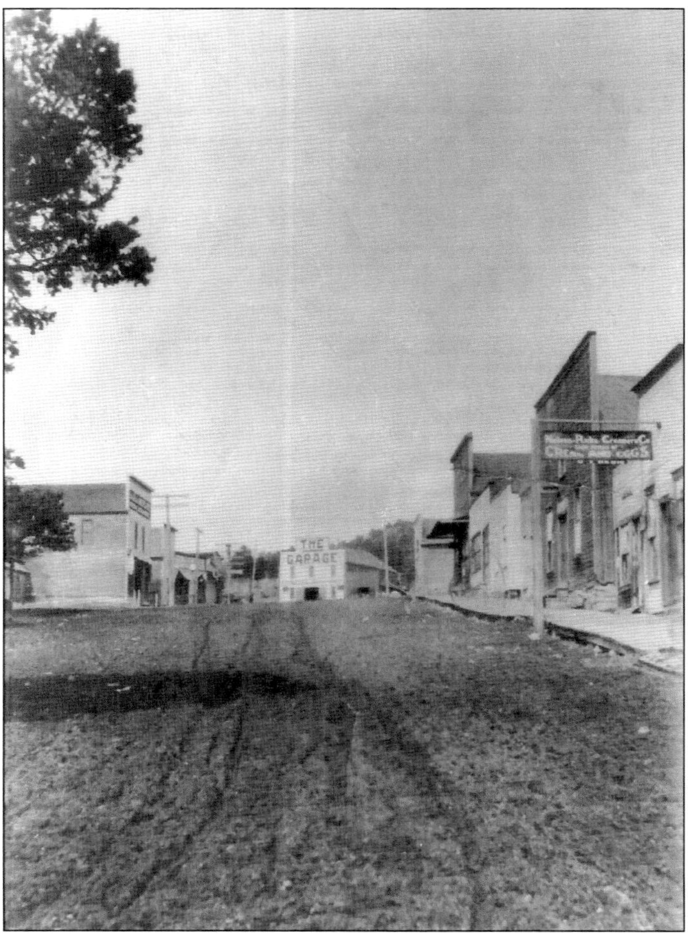

Cream Stations. These were important for farmers with cattle to make some money after World War I. The milk would be separated at home and the cream brought to the stations to be shipped to other places. The Mutual Cream Station was run by Leonard Busby. Solitaire Coffee, based in Denver, Colorado, is advertised on a sign on the outside of the creamery building. Solitaire advertised coffee or tea on many umbrellas also. Another station was known as Hollywood Cream. At left is a view of Main Street in 1929. Note a business called the Nelsea-Ricks Creamery Co., which sold fresh eggs as well as cream. Another way to utilize dairy products was cheese factories. Carl Karlen, who also had a cheese factory in Lazear, opened one in town. (Both, HCHS.)

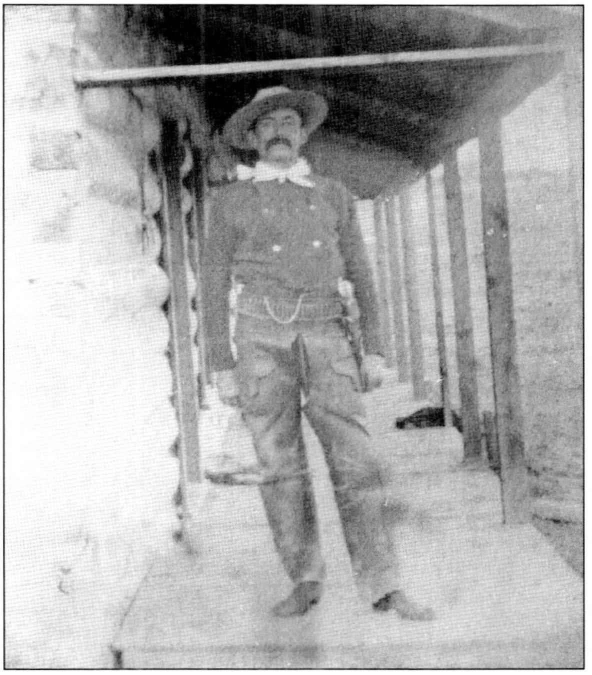

SAM HARTMAN. With partner Ed Kreighton, Hartman came to the Maher area in 1881, where he had one of the largest cattle ranches around. At one time, he averaged 1,500 head of cattle annually. He was a stockholder in banks and a major contributor to the Crawford church. One day, as he tried to step onto a moving wagon, his knee became caught in the spokes of a wheel, and his leg had to be amputated. Soon after, he was forced to sell the declining cattle operation to Robert Rockwell. Hartman moved to Hotchkiss and his daughter, Donna, was a teacher at Hotchkiss High School. (HCHS.)

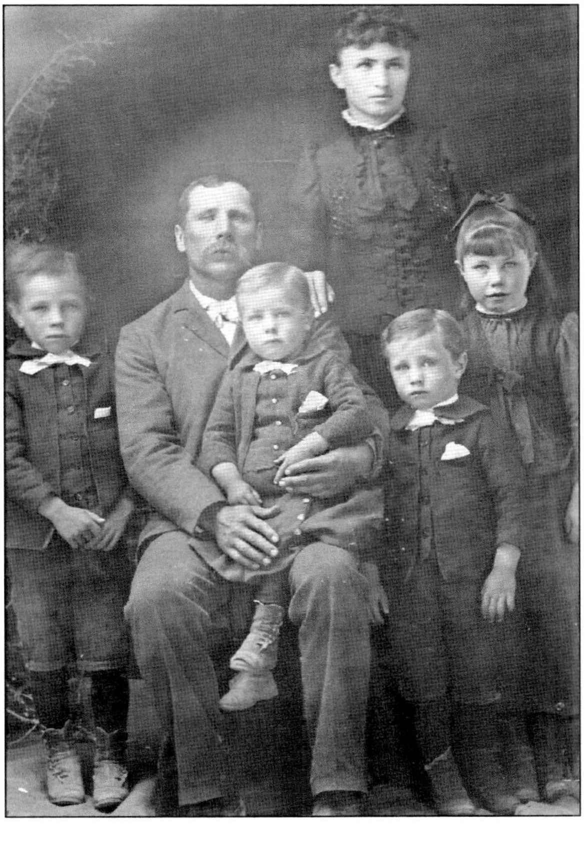

WILLIAM MCMILLAN. About 1882, McMillan came into the Maher area and homesteaded land. He sold his hay to Sam Hartman and other ranchers. Becoming a county supervisor, McMillan was able to buy more land and cattle. He then raised a substantial amount of hay and hired many to help with the hay season. In 1885, he married Katie McIntyre. Shown, from left to right, are Clyde, William holding Verdie, Katie Bell, Lester, and Hattie. (HCHS.)

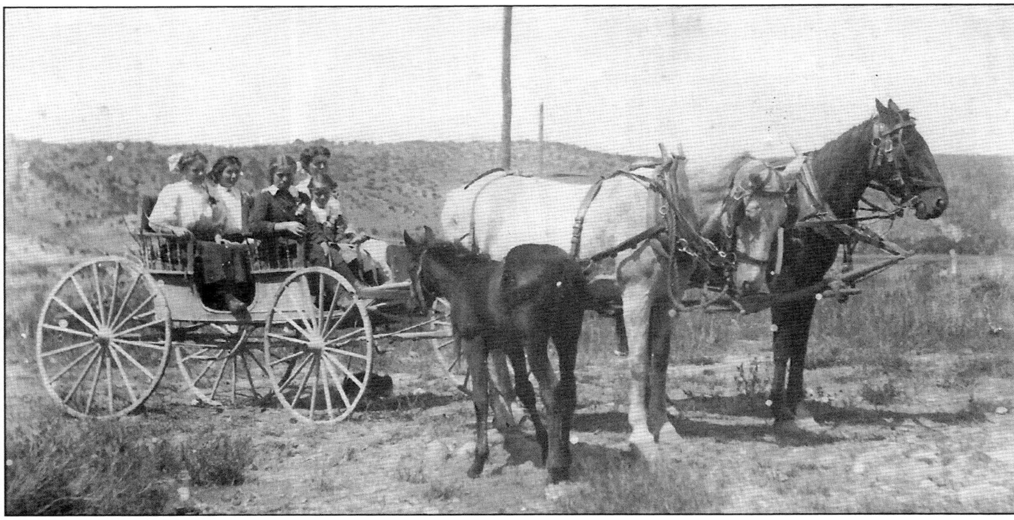

Transportation to School. The Tuttle and DeGraffenried girls of Maher are dressed to go to school. Rural schools were usually not close enough for children to walk to school. One way was to ride on horseback; or, like these girls, children could ride in a horse-pulled buggy. When one of the horses had a colt, the colt followed alongside its mother on the trip. (HCHS.)

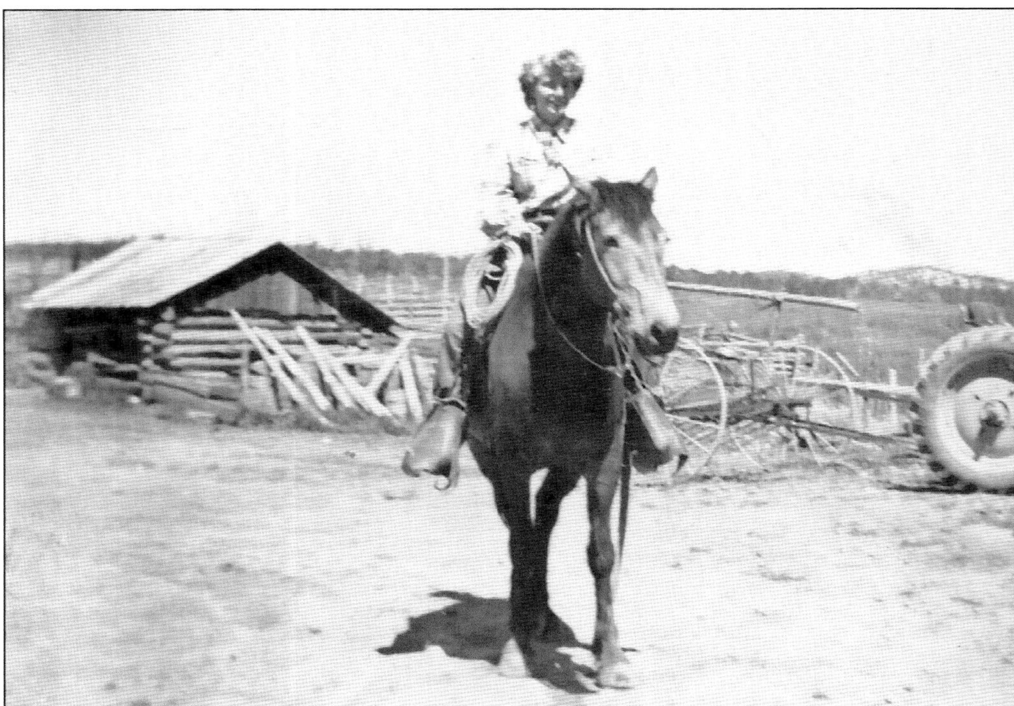

Margaret Ayer Deutsch. A genuine cowgirl, Margaret Ayer Deutsch (1933–2012) spent her life dedicated to the Crawford way of life. The Ayers had land in Maher, where Margaret rode horses, showed cows for 4-H, and helped with the ranch. After marrying, she was still a cowgirl at heart, but Margaret loved participating in Emblem Club, Needle Rock Club, Hotchkiss-Crawford Historical Society, the Methodist church, and other organizations. (HCHS.)

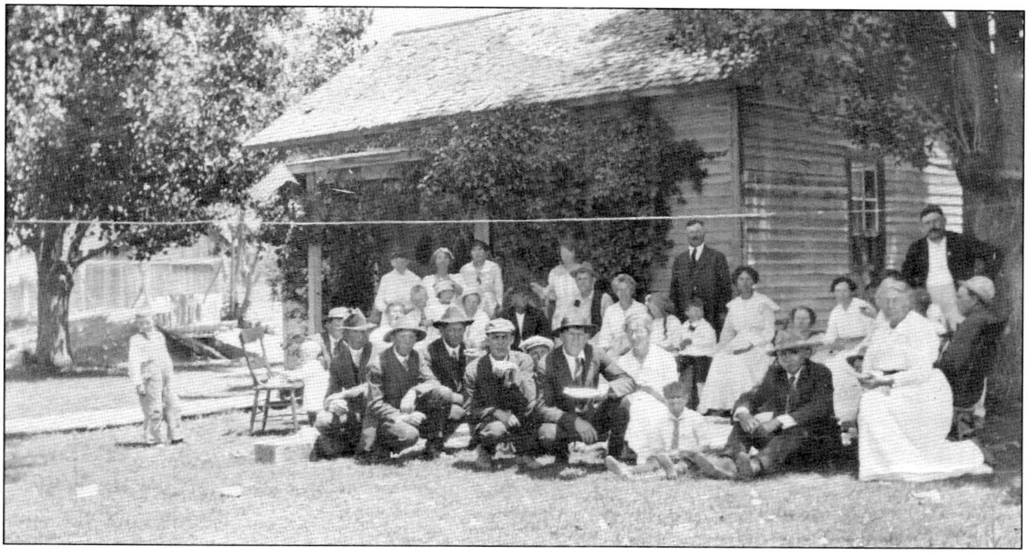

Picnic, 1920. The Turner ranch was on Missouri Flats, east of Crawford near Needle Rock. It was a great place to have a summer picnic after church. Ira and Emma Turner were married in 1909. They raised cattle, farmed with a team, cooked on a woodstove, and used a kerosene lantern for light. Ira's father, John, was on the first church board that built the church. (Dennis Turner.)

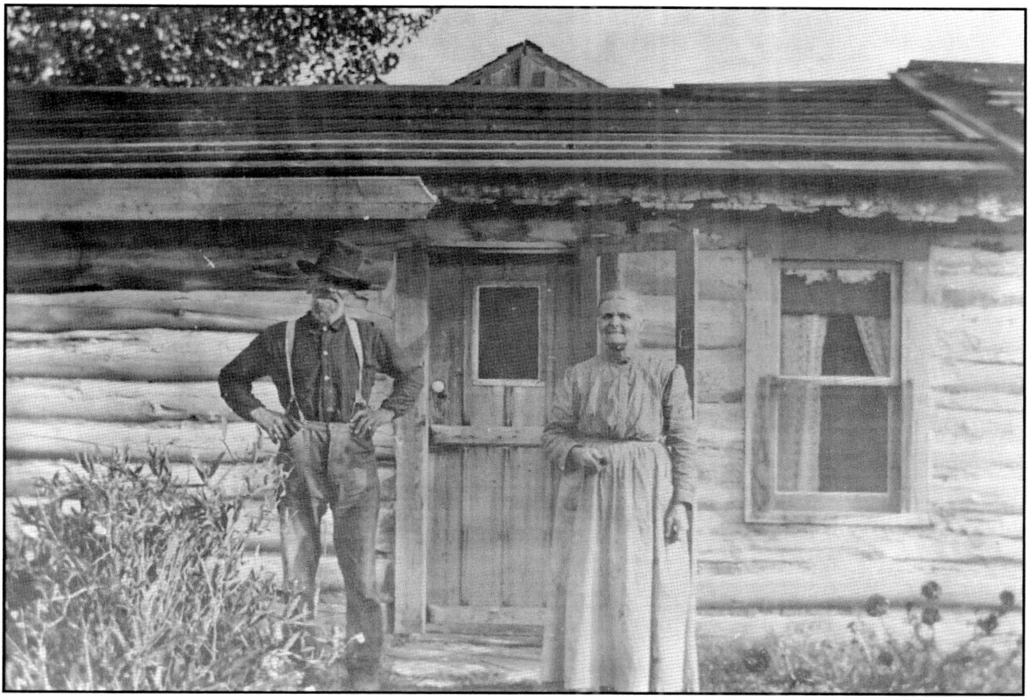

The Eiberts. In 1902, Valentine and Margaret Eibert came to Colorado from Oklahoma in covered wagons with Maggie and Frank Wooley and Flo and Will French. Maggie wrote a journal of the trip. In 1914, Valentine went to get a load of wood on Young's Peak. A gust of wind moved an umbrella on the road and spooked the horse. He was struck by the horse and killed. (HCHS.)

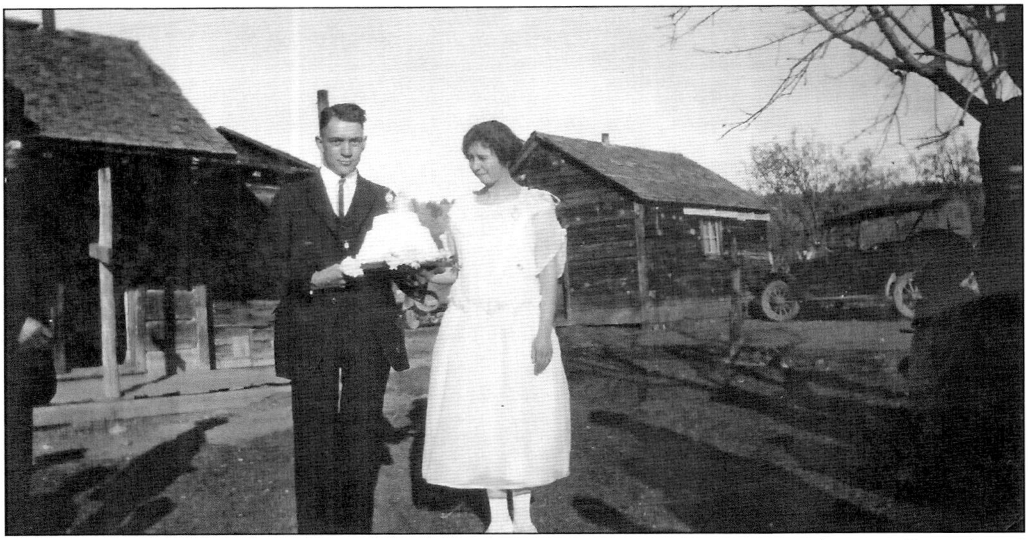

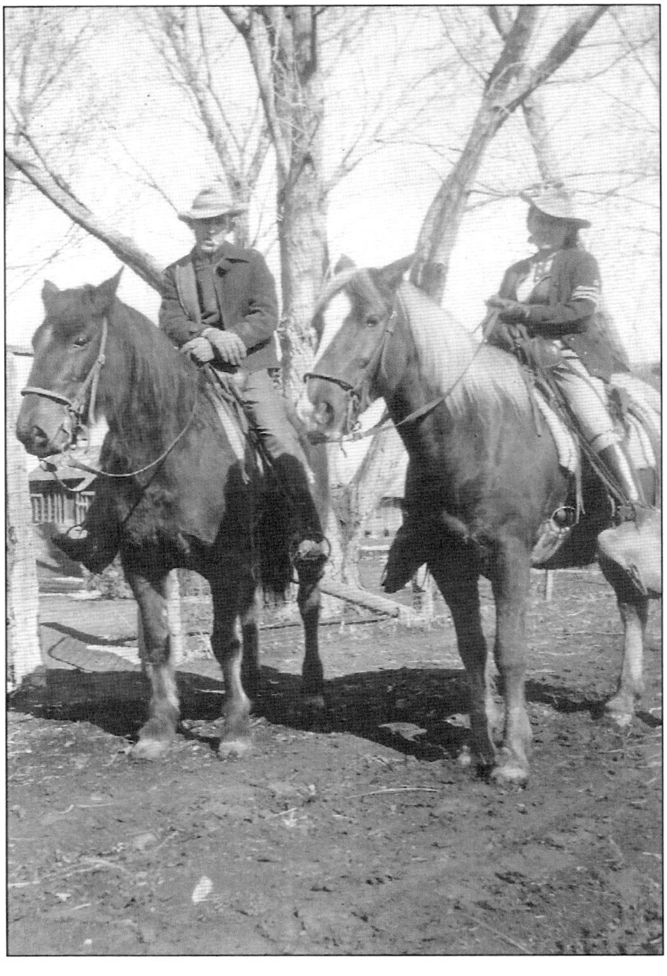

DREXELS. Clarence Drexel and Esther Den Beste attended college, but both returned to Crawford and were married in 1923. Clarence ran the family beekeeping business, did wiring for Rural Electric in Crawford, served as water commissioner, and was mayor of Crawford for 13 years. Esther, the eldest of 11 children, lived on Fruitland Mesa but attended Hotchkiss High School, living in town during the week. (HCHS.)

FRIENDS GO RIDING. Born in Crawford to Swan and Sarah Linman, Olaf Linman was a good friend of Janie Savage. Linman rode for many ranchers in the area and loved horses. Janie was the daughter of Leslie Savage and sister to Martha. Janie married Fred Hagie, and they had a grocery store in Crawford from 1939 to 1946. They returned to Crawford in 1962 and ran the store until Fred passed away. Janie liquidated it in 1985. (Dennis Turner.)

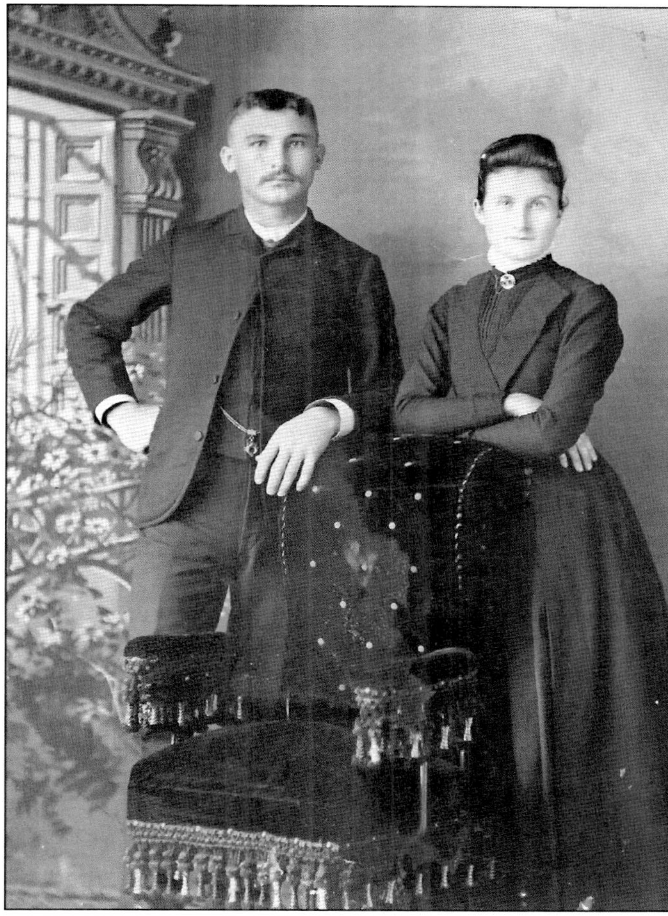

The TeSelle Family. A Dutch Reformed congregation moved to Colorado in the early 1900s after John Simpa crossed paths with Willard Gould. This was a bilingual community with strict beliefs. The majority of the social activities were church, school, and family, with John Teselle as the Dutch Reformed preacher. Church was held at his house. The most interesting farm belonged to the TeSelle family. The ruins still stand today and barely show the ingenuity of it. The circular barn had a silo in the middle and a ramp to the top. A milk house made of concrete had airholes for circulation. Outside was a trough to keep the cream cool until it was brought to market. (Both, HCHS.)

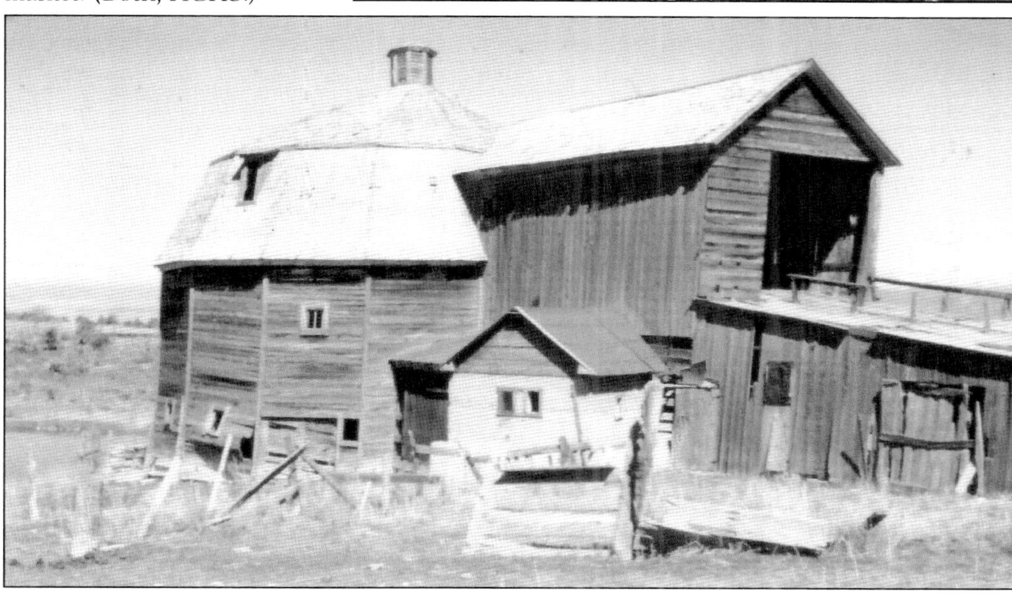

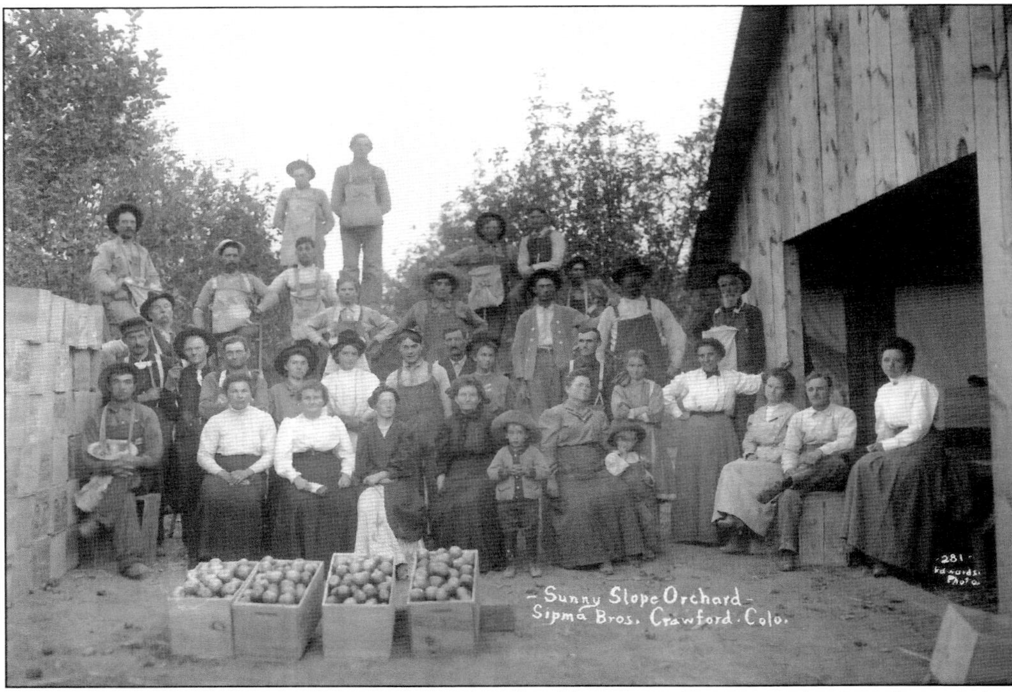

Simpa Fruit Farm. The dream of orchards full of fruit was the reason the Dutch settled on Fruitland Mesa. They had plans to plant orchards but soon realized that water was insufficient, the seasons were too short to produce a profitable crop, and wildlife ruined the trees in the winter. They then grew crops and raised cattle for meat, milk, and cream. (HCHS.)

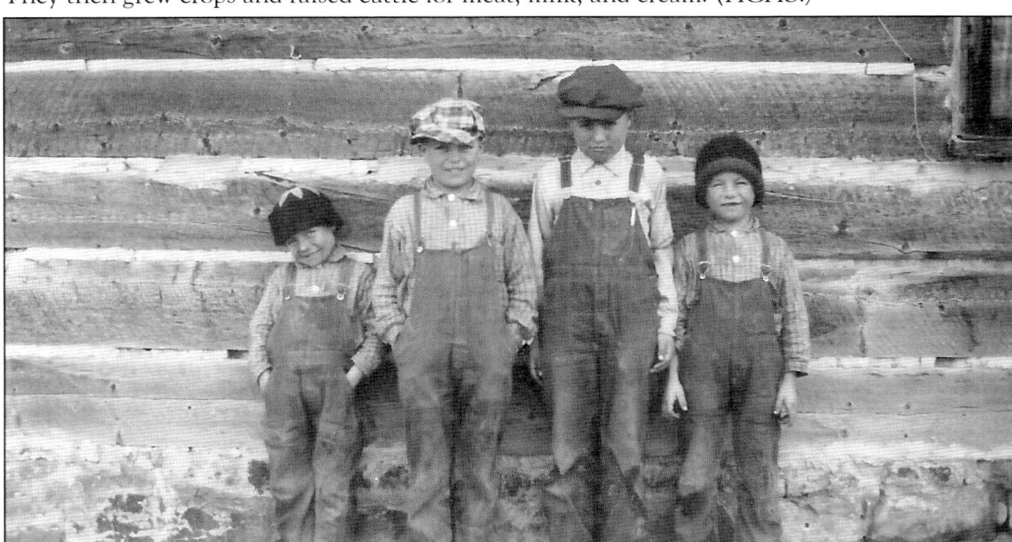

DenBeste Boys. From left to right are Ray, who did not have much to say before age five but later was a band director and taught math; Howard, who never lost a drop when he slipped while climbing a fence with a full bucket of fresh milk; Jim, who was the eldest and later a frontline officer in World War II with the 41st Division; and Walter, who was musically inclined, called square dances, and made root beer that exploded all night. (HCHS.)

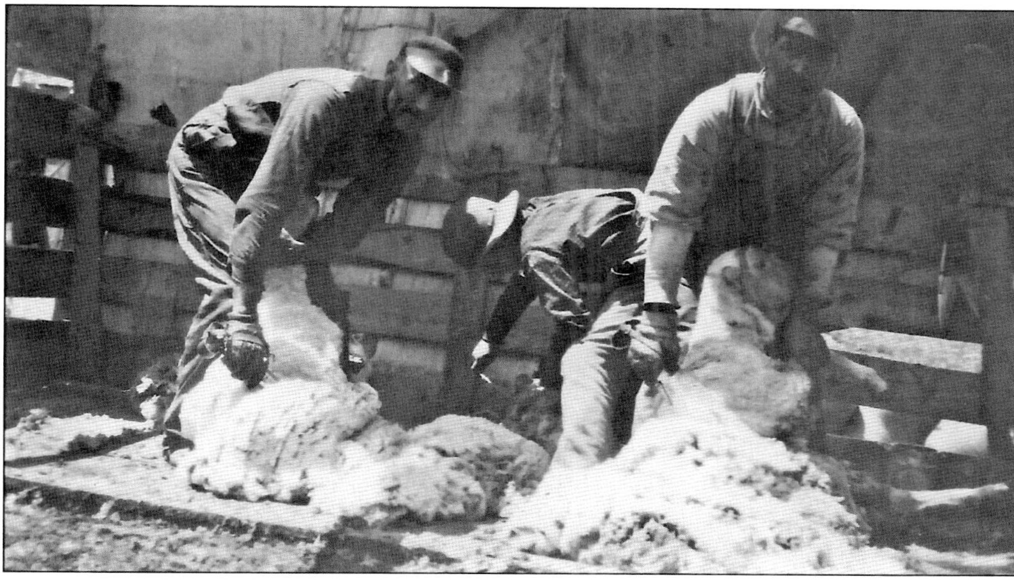

SHEEP, 1920S. Though cattle are still the main livestock in the area, sheep were also raised. This area never had the range battles that other locales had before the Taylor Grazing Act went into effect in 1934. Then, the Department of the Interior controlled how long the sheep would graze in areas. Shearing was done by with hand-clippers in the beginning; now, traveling units of professionals use state-of-the-art equipment. In early times, the sheep were sheared in the spring before lambing season, and the wool was packed into large burlap sacks. The wool was transported by wagons to be shipped out by train or sold to buyers. It is still a family affair, with some of the finest wool grown in this valley. (Both, Hetty Todd.)

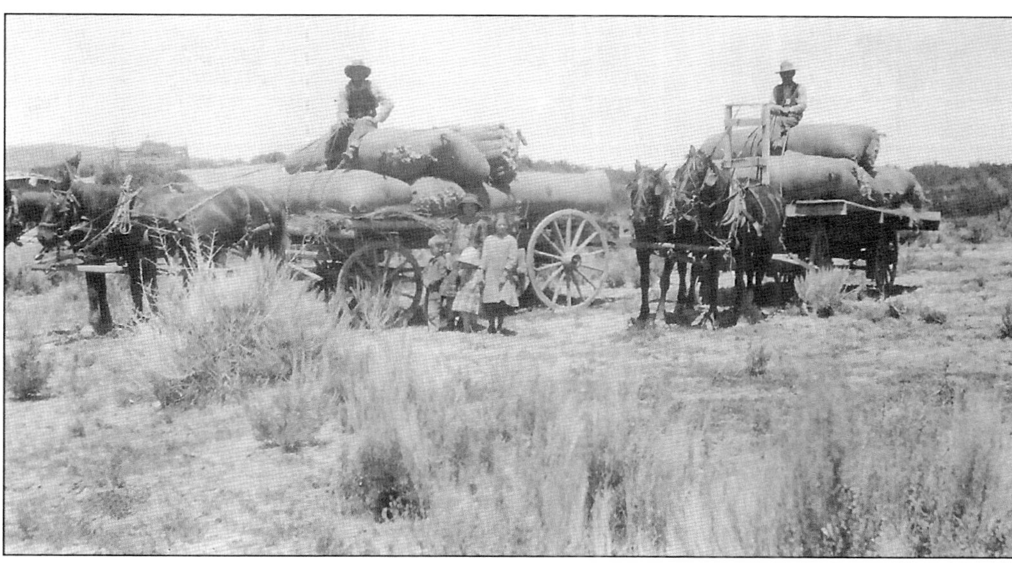

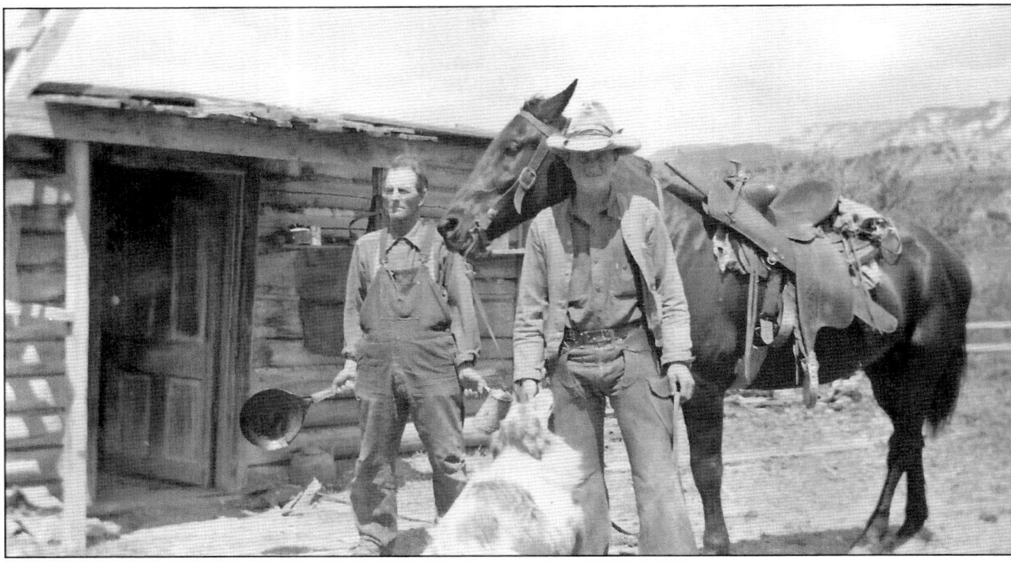

The Life of a Cowboy. The Crawford area is known for cowboys. Above, this young man may be ready to hunt, look for stray cattle, or drive a herd to summer pasture. He has a dog by his side, chaps on to protect his legs, and a rifle on his horse in case of encounters with unwanted predators. While spending time at the cabin, the other man fixed him food in a cast iron skillet and a pot of coffee. Below, Ira Turner is fixing a meal on a stove outside and Grant Ferrier and Everett Deutsch are playing with a colt at the Little Robinson cow camp on the way to Navaho. (Above, Hetty Todd; below, Dennis Turner.)

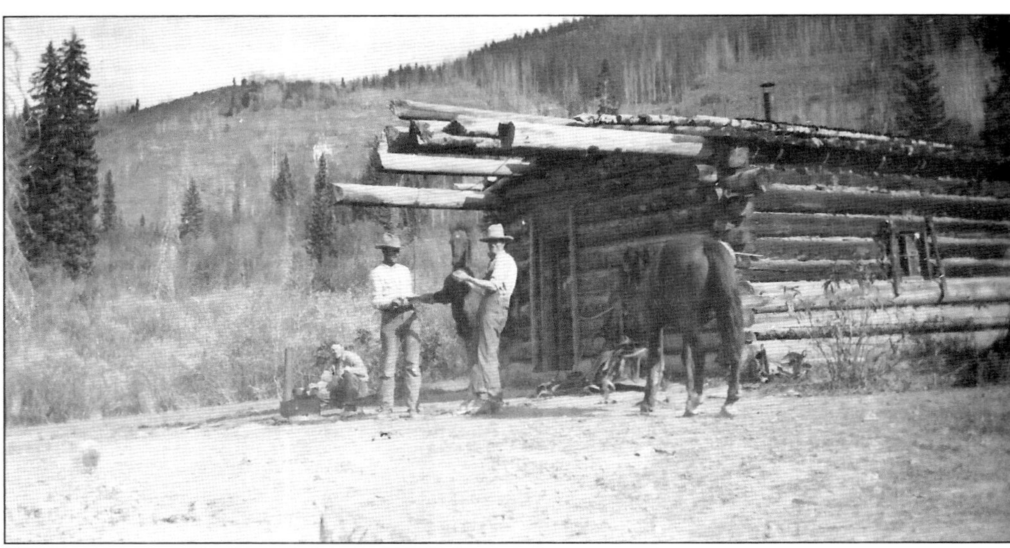

BRANDING. After the calves were born in the spring, an important day arrived before the cattle went to summer pasture. It was branding day, and the cattle were counted, sorted, roped, and wrestled. Other tasks were performed, which include vaccinating, castrating, ear-marking, and dehorning. At right, George Tracy has roped over 90 calves in an hour, keeping the mothers away for this period. He brought a roped calf to the wrestlers, who held the calf down, and then the brand was burned into the hide with a specially made hot iron. Below, from left to right, Franklin Ferrier, Harvey Barsh, Clell Turner, and Everett Deutsch take part in a day of branding near Needle Rock. Branding is a form of identification that determines to whom the cow belongs. All brands are registered. (Right, HCHS; below, Dennis Turner.)

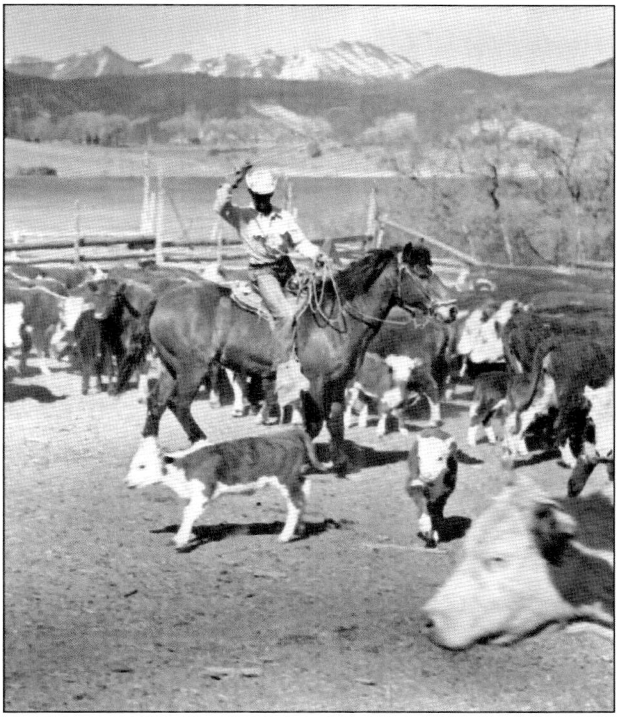

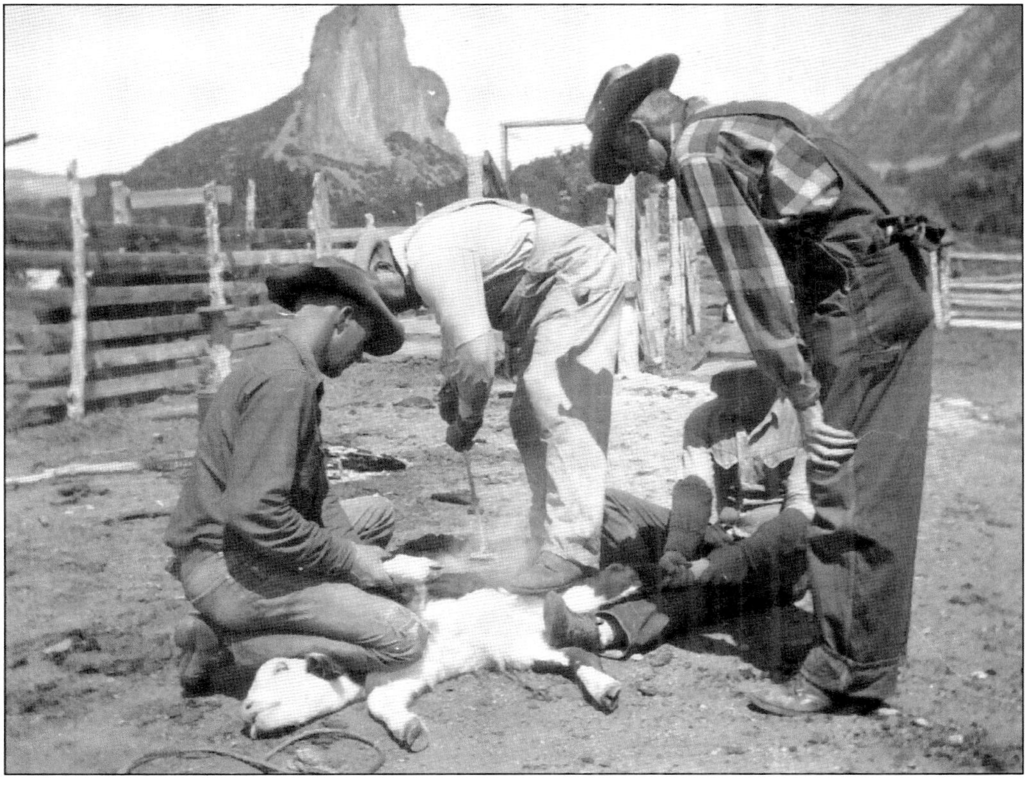

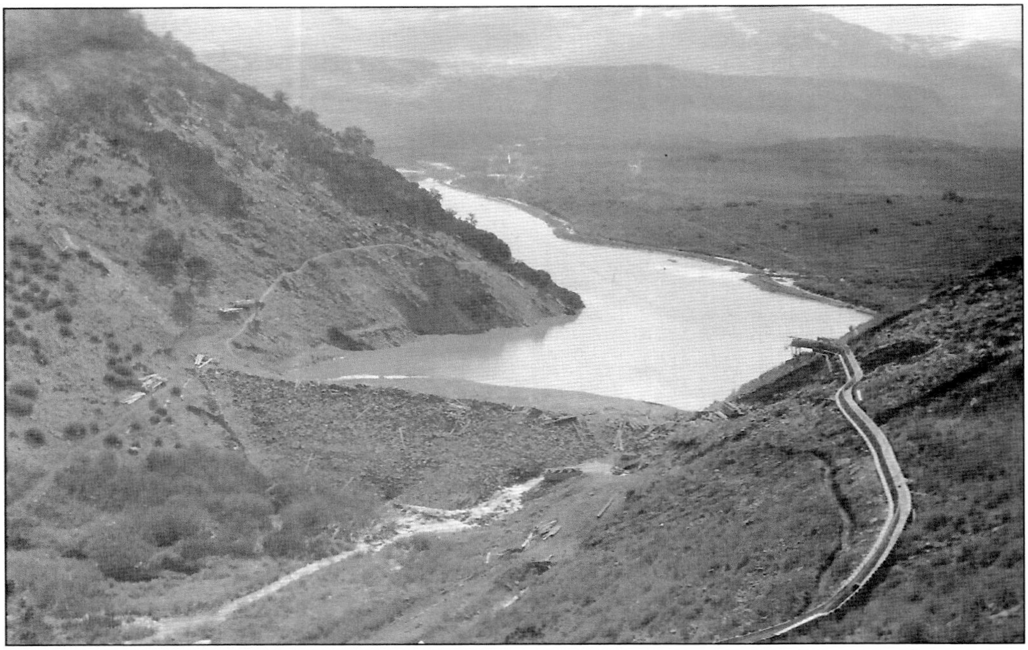

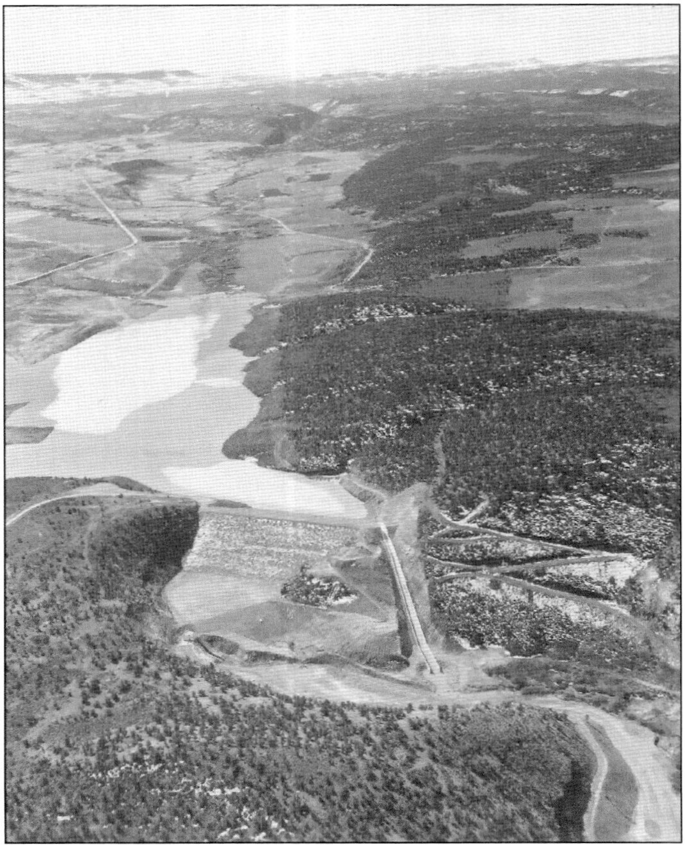

Water Projects. It was the idea of the Gould family to be able to hold the spring runoff and provide irrigation water to Fruitland Mesa for their dream orchards. In 1901, four Gould brothers organized a company. In 1907, the company became known as the Fruitland Irrigation Company. A ditch about 20 miles long would supposedly irrigate 20,000 acres of land. The reservoir was a complex system, taking years to build. It proved satisfactory, but through the years has needed endless repairs and updating. The Smith Fork Project (Crawford Reservoir) was part of the Colorado River Storage project and was finished in 1963. The reservoir uses a siphon to carry water to ditches. Currently, the lake attracts many visitors year-round for fishing, boating, and camping. (Both, HCHS.)

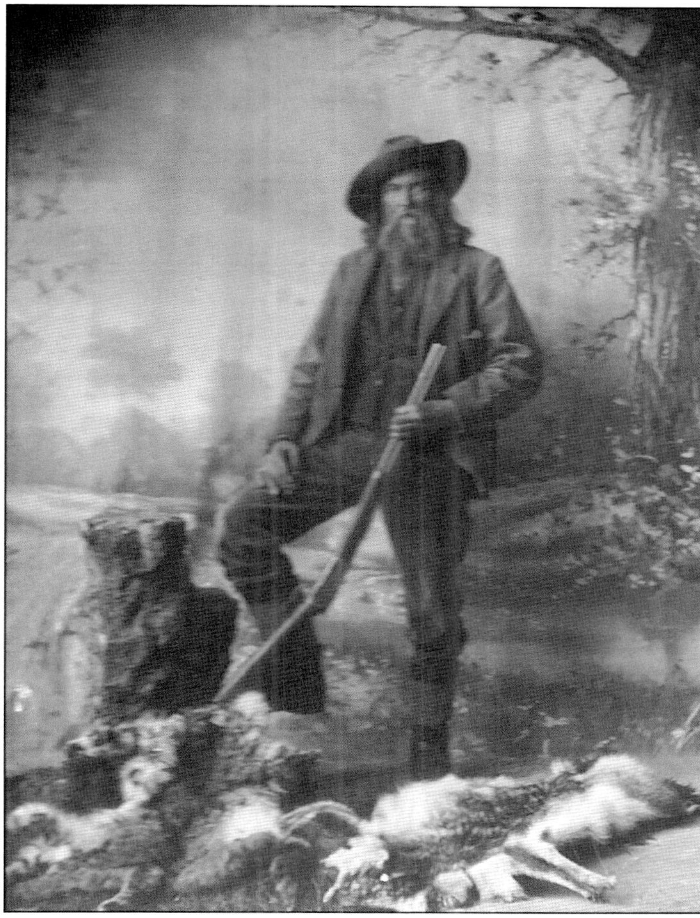

Moccasin Bill. His real name was Bill Perkins, and the story goes that he got caught in the mountains during a storm and had nothing on his feet except for moccasins, which froze to his feet. So, he glued more moccasins over them to keep them dry. His feet were then enormous and so was his legend. He came to Colorado as a government scout in 1860 to watch the movement of the Indians. One winter, while trapping in the Gunnison country, he came upon an Indian who was almost frozen to death. Perkins saved his life and was befriended by the Indians afterwards. Known as a legendary bear hunter, he died in Colorado in 1904. Below, he is pictured with his daughter and grandchildren in later years. (Right, Hetty Todd; below, HCHS.)

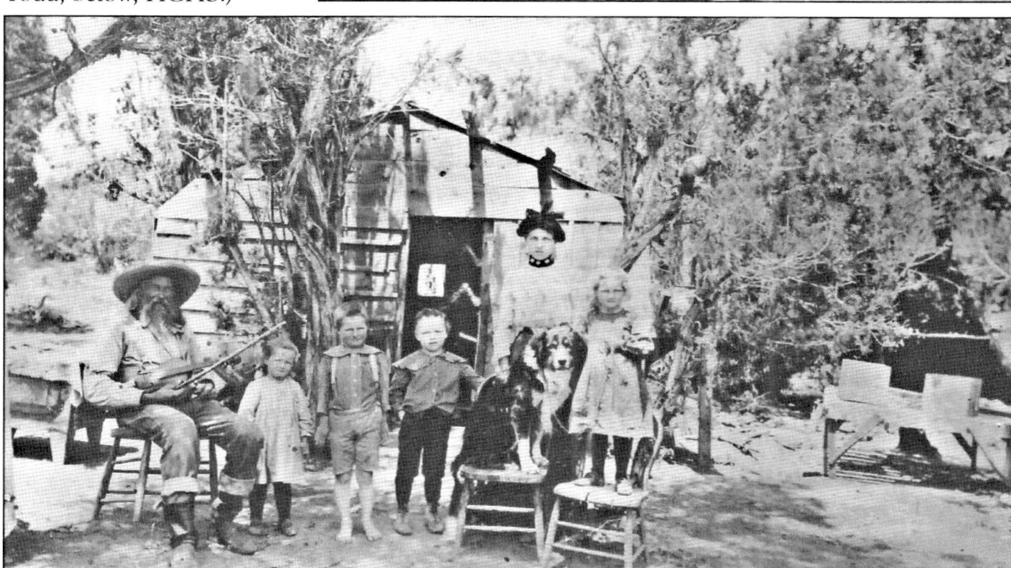

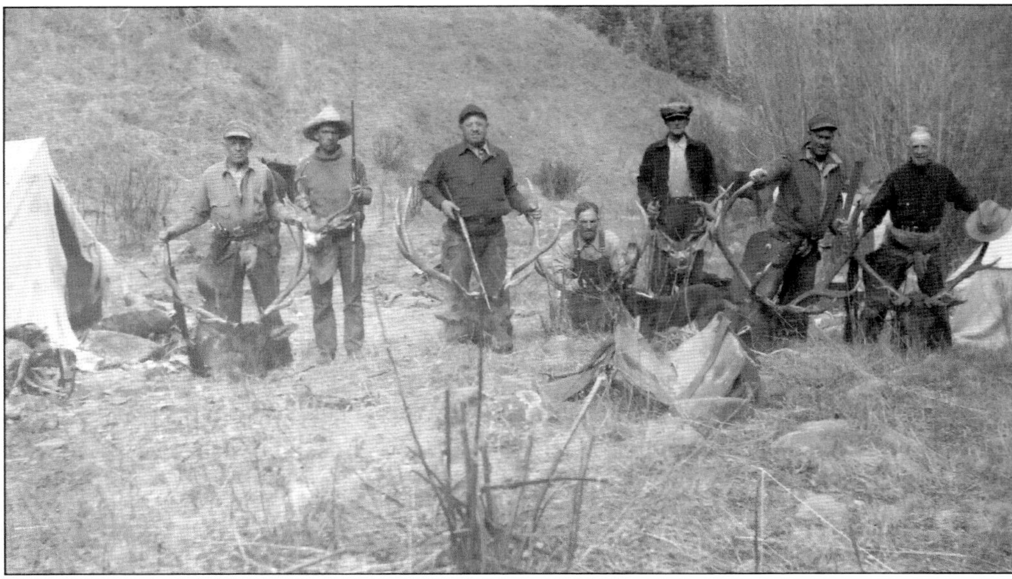

The Great Outdoors. The first settlers reported abundant wildlife, especially on Fruitland Mesa. Populations of wildlife diminished so much that it was illegal to hunt for game until a certain season, and a license was required. Keeping the proper ratio of wildlife was frustrating. Many used the meat, unlike those who just wanted a rack as a trophy. Hunting seasons now are highly regulated and a lucrative business in the fall. Fishing in waterways is well known in this area. The Gunnison River in the Black Canyon boasts a Gold Medal Stream and continues down to its confluence with the North Fork of the Gunnison River. Below, these pioneers caught any amount and size of trout they wanted. Mother Tuttle has the skillet ready for a fish fry with Fred Bender (left) and George Tuttle. (Above, Hetty Todd; below, HCHS.)

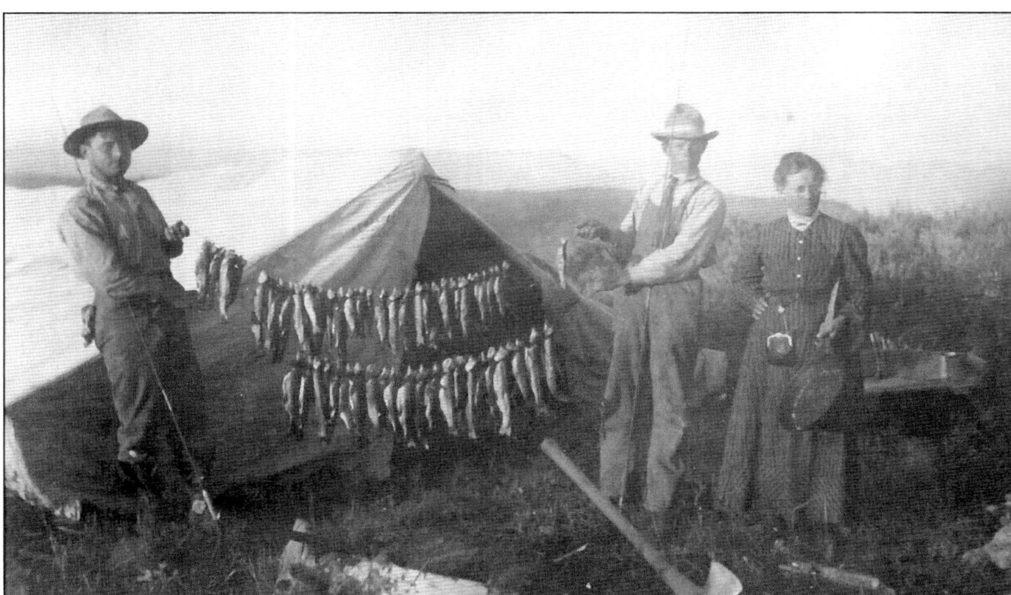

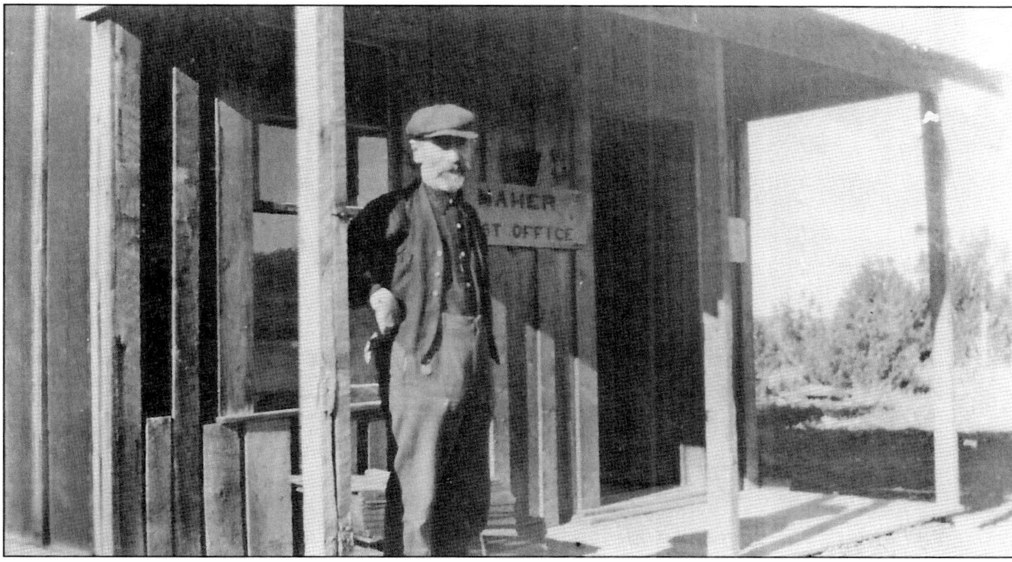

Maher Post Office. In 1884, Caleb Maher applied for a post office, which was run from his house. Thereafter, each postmaster hosted the post office until Paul Kruemling took over in 1918. He opened a larger store in conjunction with the post office. This became the official post office until it closed in the 1960s. (HCHS.)

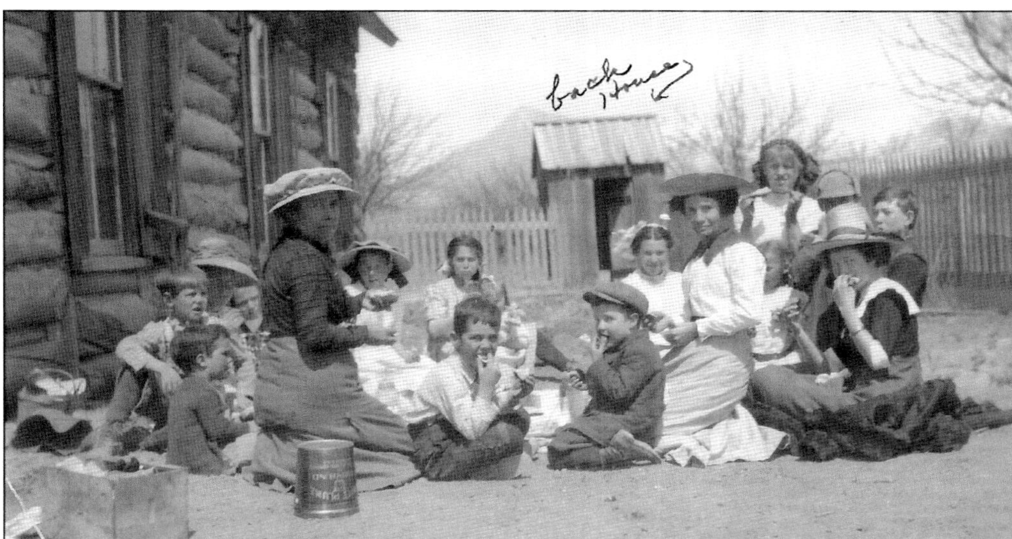

School at Maher, 1912. The end of the school year was signified by a picnic. Here, a group of students enjoys a picnic with teacher Edna McCully. In 1884, a meeting was held in Maher (Montrose County) to establish a school district. All 25 voted for the organization. Later on, if a student graduated from eighth grade, he or she had to pay tuition to go to school in Crawford, which was in Delta County. (HCHS.)

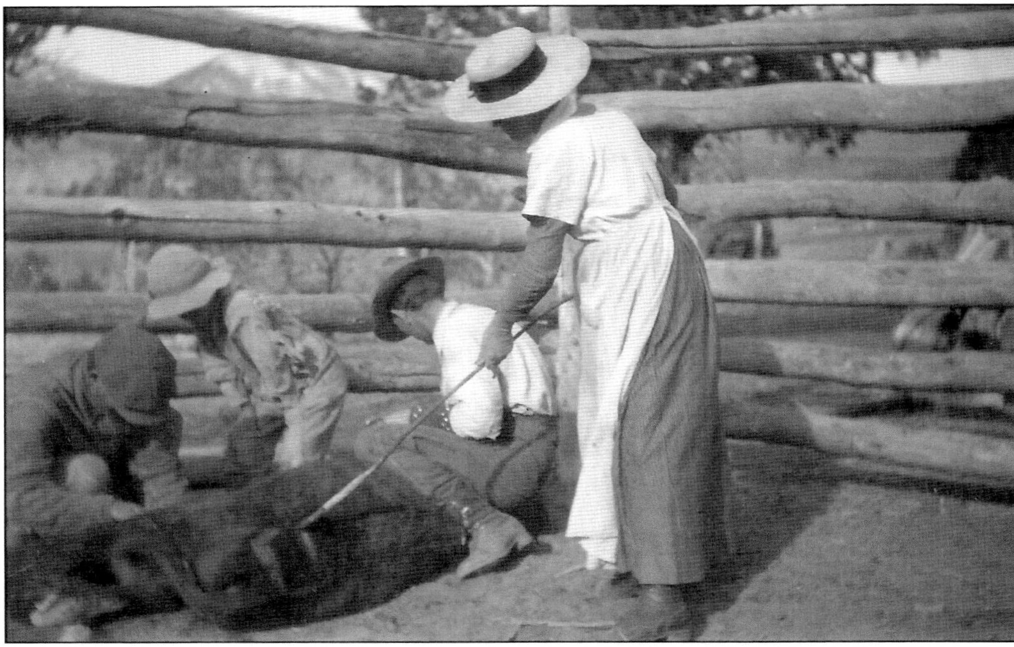

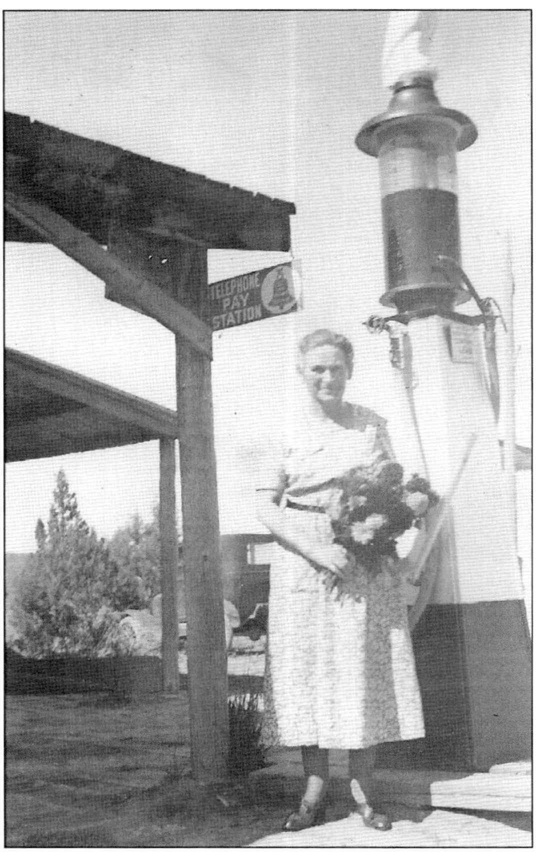

CARRIE COLLINS. Born in Grayson County, Virginia, Carrie Brewer married Luther Collins after teaching in the Blue Ridge Mountains. They honeymooned in Washington, DC. In 1902, they headed home to Colorado a couple of months after the first train arrived in the North Fork area. Carrie became the postmistress of Maher in 1925 and retired in 1945. She was a community-minded person and loved being around people. In this image of the Maher Post Office, a gas pump is visible. The post office also had a long-distance telephone. Homes had local service only. (Both, Hetty Todd.)

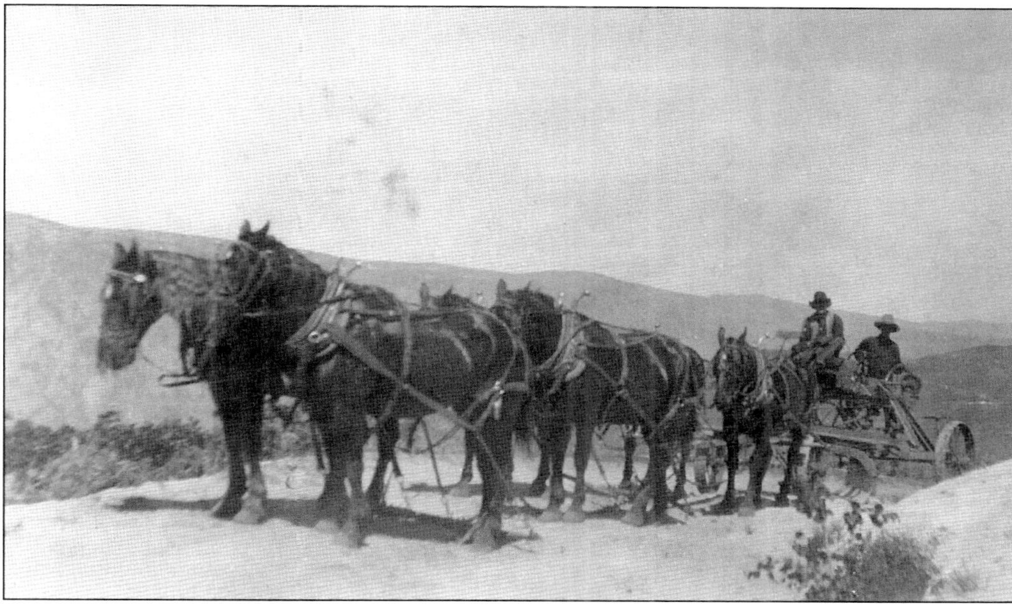

Black Mesa Road. On a route traveled by the first settlers, the Black Mesa Road was started in 1912. In 1913, the commissioners drove over it and said the road was as good as it could be, and a celebration should be held soon. In the 1920s, Roy Cotten grades the road at White Point with a team of horses. Ed Bates is the "blade man." This road is now called "the old road." A paved road to follow the rim of the breathtaking Black Canyon of the Gunnison River was next. Today, that road is part of the West Elk Loop, a state scenic highway. Many turnouts from the road provide views of the gorgeous scenery. (Both, HCHS.)

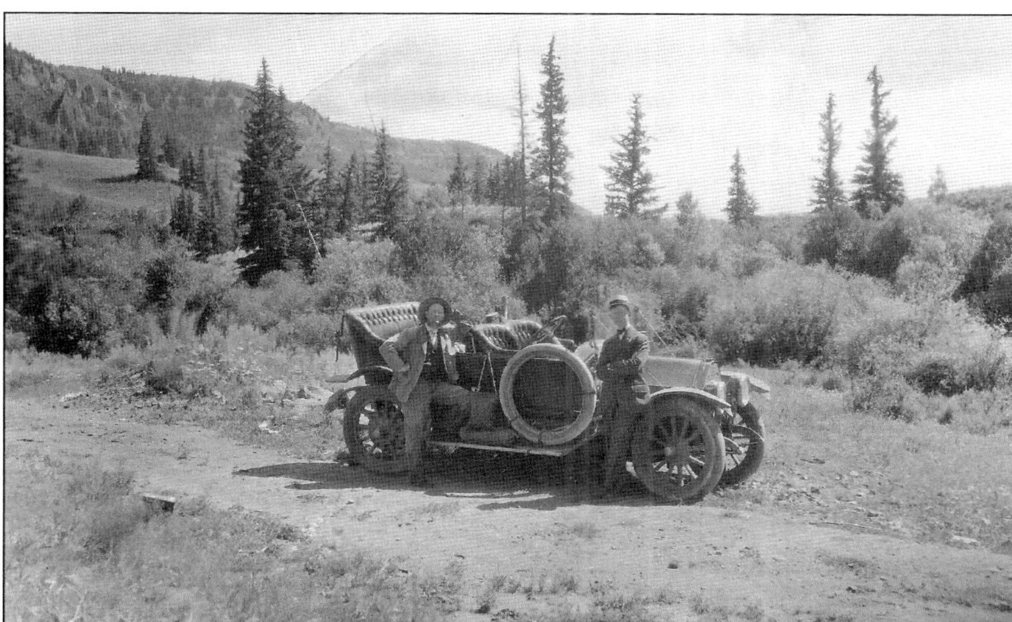

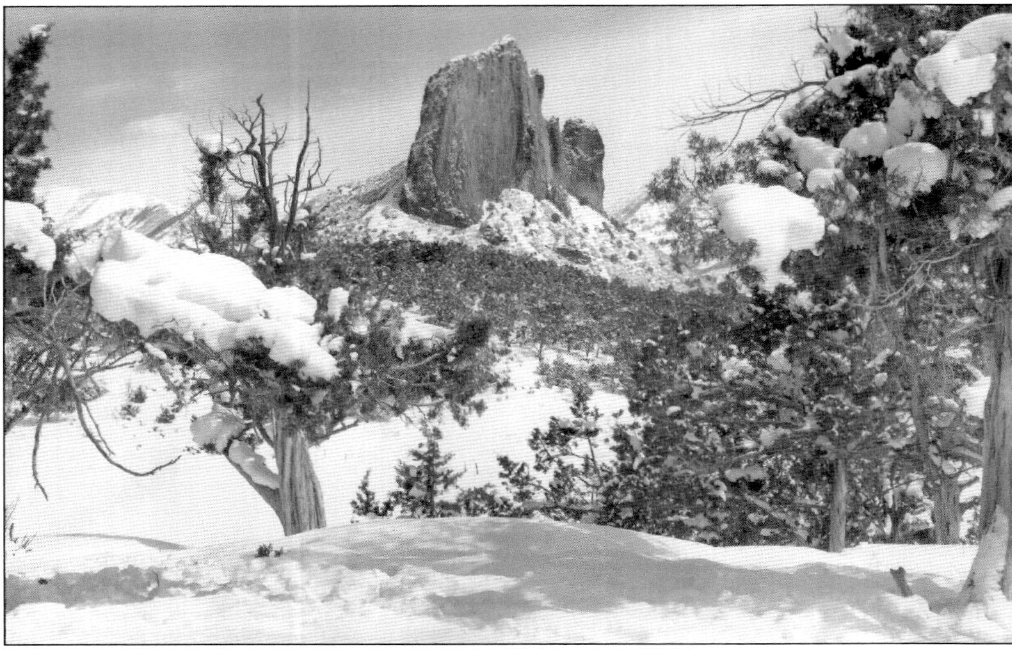

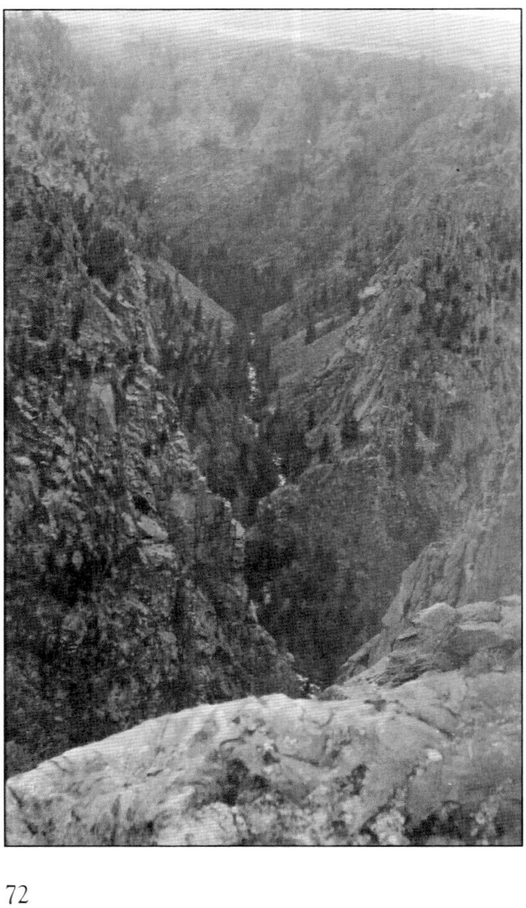

Landmarks. East of Crawford is Needle Rock (above), a large volcanic rock jutting 700 feet out of a hillside. It is north of the Smith Fork, with the Missouri Flats between it and the town. Needle Rock Club was organized in 1933 and met at Helen McKissen's home. A civic-minded club, it has always benefited the area. Income from farm sale lunches, quilt raffles, and white elephant sales still helps the organization today. South of Crawford is the Black Canyon (left). The depth of the canyon is immense, and the walls are steep. The greatest depth is 2,722 feet, at Warner Point. The first explorers to see it were the Spanish in the 1700s. In 1882, the railroad came through but was abandoned in 1955. In 1933, the canyon became a national monument, and in 1999 it was declared Black Canyon of the Gunnison National Park. (Above, Dennis Turner; left, HCHS.)

Four

PAONIA

Legend has it that founder Samuel Wade wanted Peony to be the town's name when he sent the Latin spelling of *peony* (*paeonia*) to the Post Office Department. Unfortunately, the *e* was left off, and Paeonia became Paonia. In 1891, Wade located the post office on his 1881 homestead west of Paonia's current Grand Avenue. William Clarke claimed the property to the east beyond Grand Avenue. It was hoped the town would be on the Wade property, but the river began to wash out so much land that Paonia was moved to its present location.

Before Paonia became a town (1891–1902), settlers had been extremely busy digging irrigation canals and planting fruit trees. In 1882, fruit trees were brought in by wagon from the nearest railhead at Gunnison. At night, campfires kept trees warm as they traveled over Black Mesa to Crawford to Paonia. Fruit attracted the attention of buyers when it won six awards at the 1893 Chicago World's Fair.

Paonia, cradled in the valley dominated by the beautiful Mount Lamborn, was incorporated in 1902. The first mayor was W.T. Baetjer (1902–1903). Some 200-plus residents would increase to 1,000 by 1909. Paonia was booming because of the arrival of the narrow-gauge Denver & Rio Grande Railroad in 1902 (widened to broad gauge in 1906). Hotels, boardinghouses, and places to get supplies and food were needed. Land was selling at the outrageous prices. Hopes were high.

Telephones, electricity, and domestic water were concerns. In 1904, the town boasted three churches, 22 mercantile stores, two banks, and an electric light plant. New emphasis was placed on education in 1903, when Paonia completed a large school. For over 25 years, fruit was king. But then the September freeze of 1912 occurred. The peach crop was damaged, and pests began to make an appearance. The good times were coming into question. Perhaps one of the answers would be "black gold" (coal) discovered in the surrounding area.

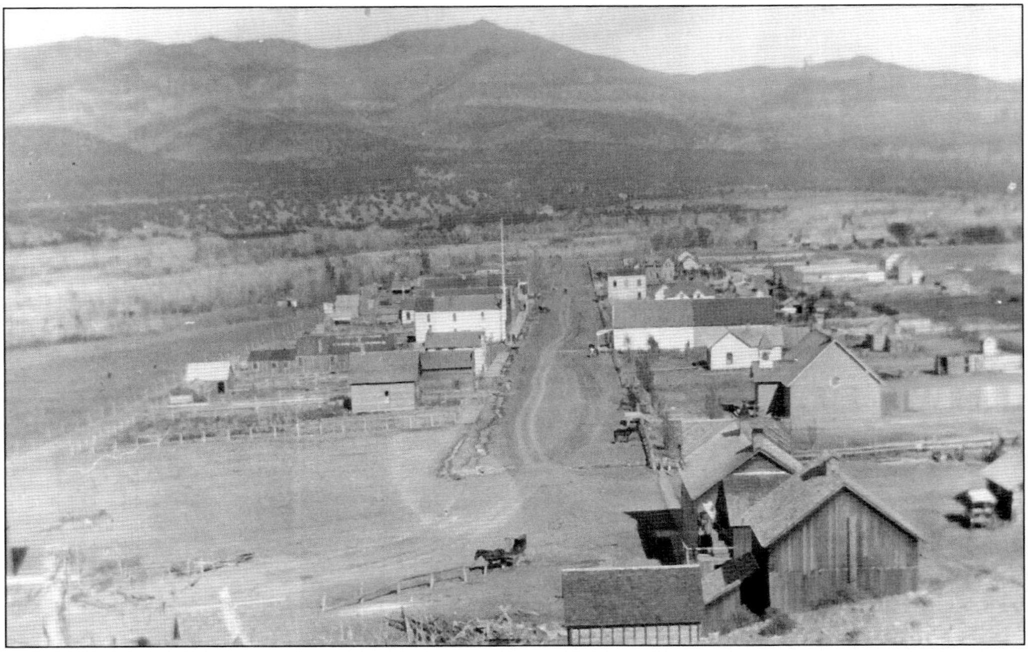

Paonia in Spring, 1898. By 1882, Samuel Wade had established a store in his log cabin and the first schoolhouse was built. Thomas Wand's mercantile store in 1889 provided settlers with all their needs, and Paonia was incorporated in 1902. In early years, the North Fork Fruit Growers Association and Nelson Brothers Fruit Company handled fruit. In 1920, one thousand railcars of fruit were marketed. (NFHS.)

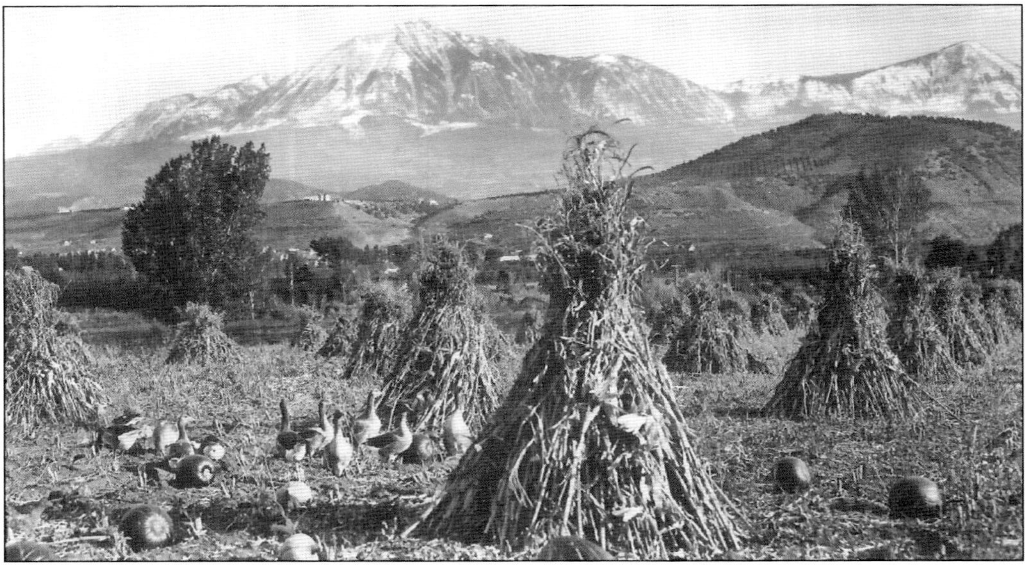

Autumn Splendor, c. 1930. The 1905 *Souvenir of the North Fork Valley, Colorado* promotional book extolling Paonia introduces the area with a poem by Dr. Edward Fayette Eldridge: "Like a nest in a royal garden, Where the birds are soothed by song / Through the day, aflame with glory, and cradled the fair night long; / Like a rose in a sheltered arbor, Smiling the livelong day / Lies the beautiful town—Paonia—where the North Fork wends its way." (NFHS.)

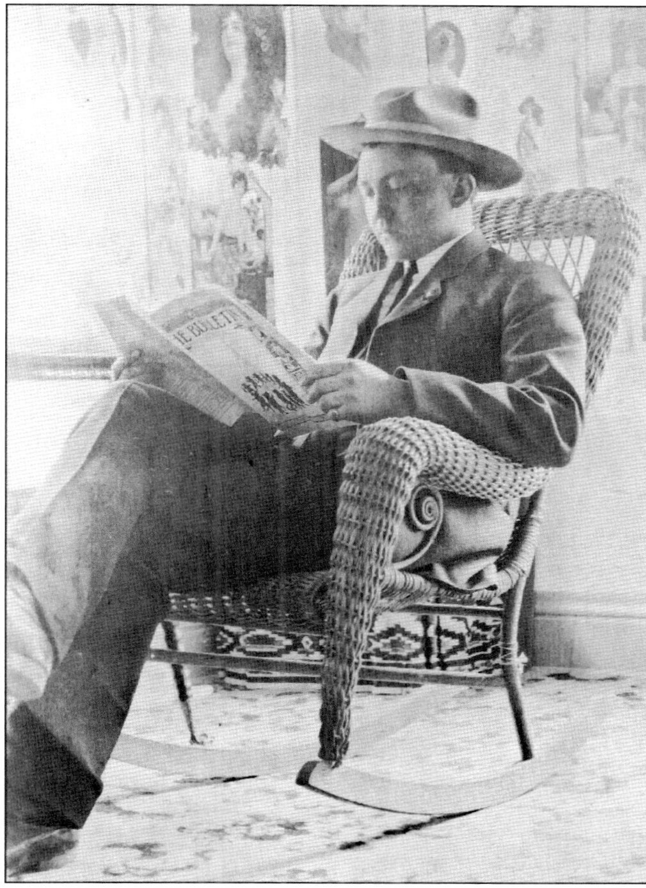

WALTER EUBANKS. Walter Eubanks's son Wallace "Wally" was curator of the Paonia Museum (1974–1993). Excavated after the Paonia Library was completed, the basement museum's location was Grand Avenue. Wally excerpted articles from the (1904–1960) Paonia newspapers—*Gazette*, *Newspaper*, *Progressive*, *Paonia Newspaper*, *Booster*, and *Paonian*. The three-volume *Resumes of Items in the Paonia Newspapers* is an invaluable resource for research. Wally's mother was Helen Dorrance Eubanks. Pictured below is the 1911 Dorrance ranch team. As a child, Wally often visited the German Mesa Dorrance ranch. From this experience, and his family heritage, he developed his great love for Paonia. (Both, NFHS.)

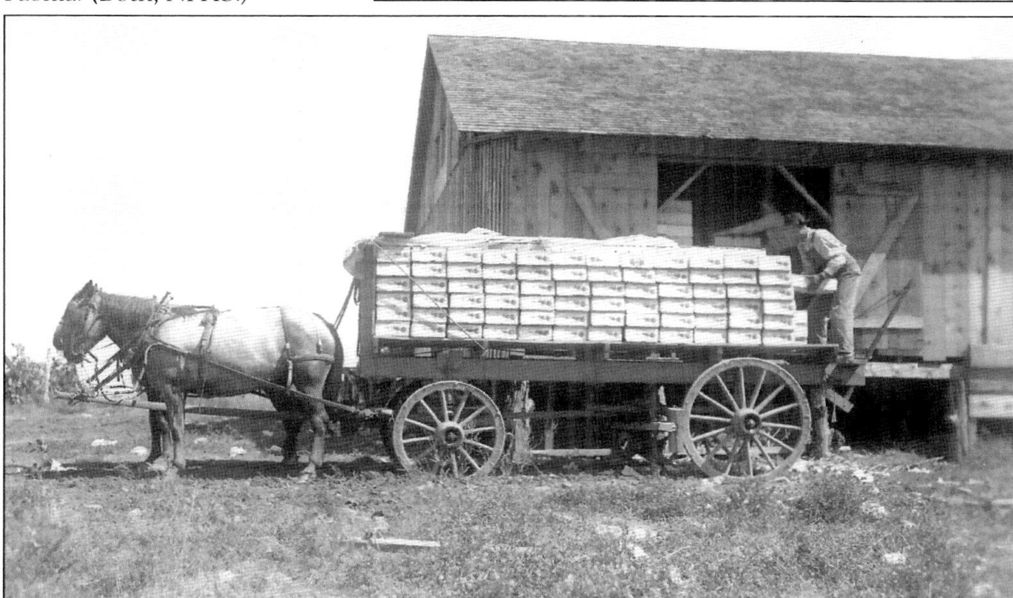

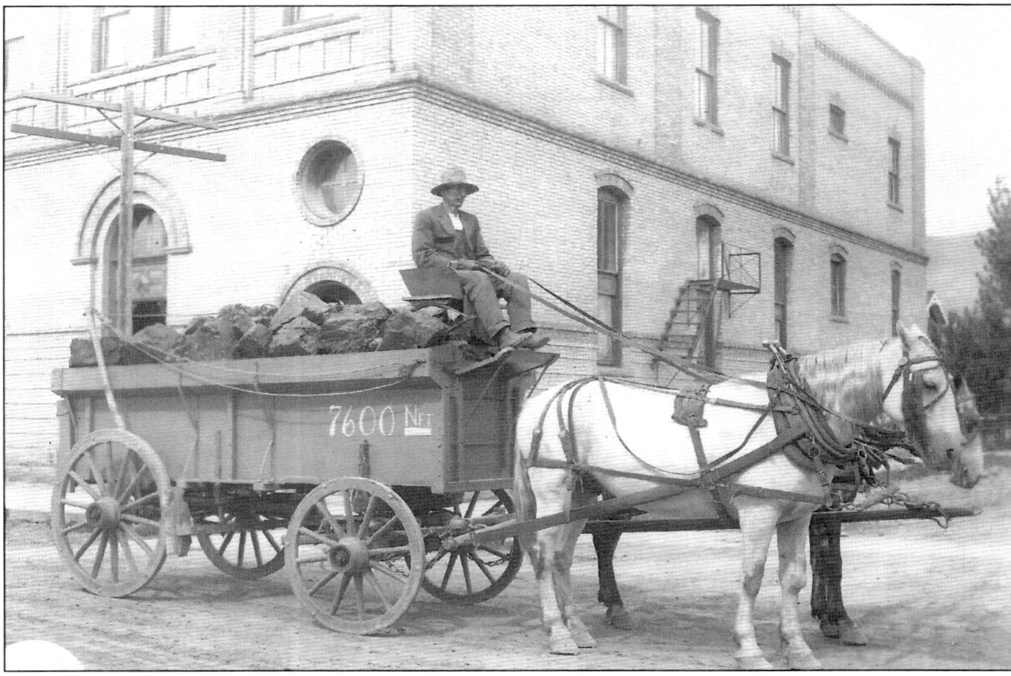

COAL WAGON. Pictured in 1915 at the opera house are Sylvester Hall, a white horse called Old Ned, and a second team horse. They are taking coal to the Fruit Exchange Evaporator in a newly finished wagon from the V.W. Kemp shop. Constructed by the Independent Order of Odd Fellows (IOOF) in 1907 as a meeting place, the opera house was a gathering place for plays, Chautauqua, fruit house dinners, dances, minstrel shows, silent films, evangelistic crusades, class plays, graduations, and election-day balloting for 70 years. A train with 200 passengers arrived in Paonia to join 300 others in the dedication of the IOOF Hall. Shortly before daybreak, the train returned revelers to Delta. This remarkable building was destroyed by a fire caused by an electrical short. (Both, NFHS.)

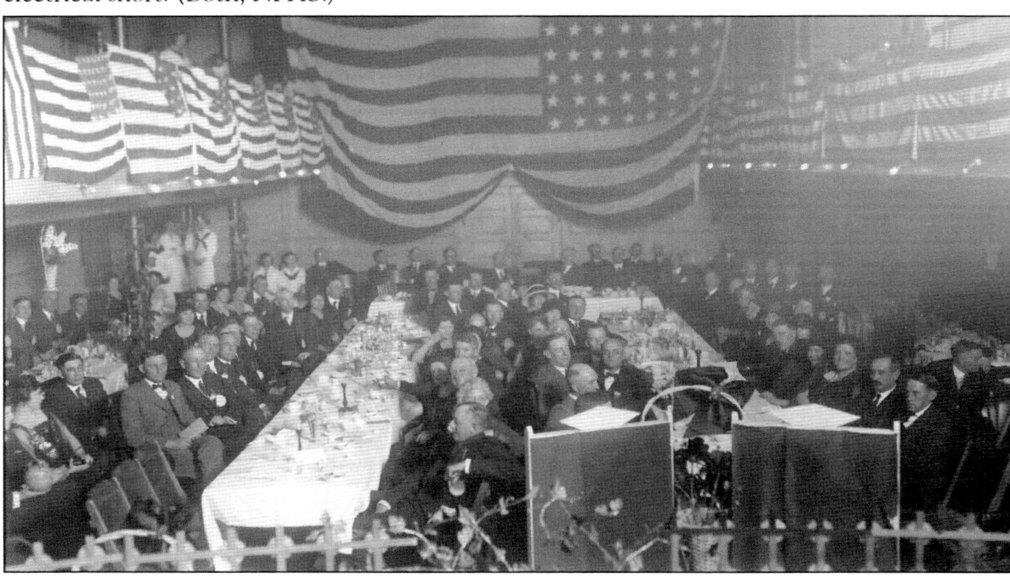

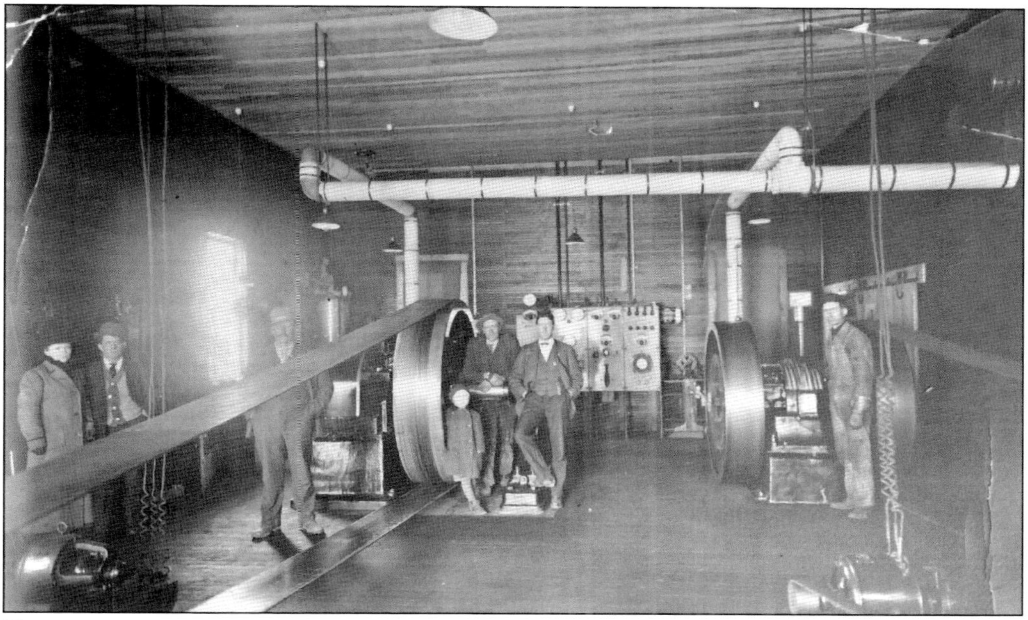

TELEPHONES AND ELECTRICITY. At right, a crew is stringing telephone lines. Dr. Follansbee wanted his patients to have telephones in their homes, so he donated $1,500 and asked others to donate $50 apiece to form a cooperative. By August 1904, ninety people had telephones. Electricity was provided to Paonia with light generators and engines. Jimmy Beasley operated the electricity plant, shown above, which shut down at 11:00 p.m. Many dances had to continue in candlelight. In 1906, amid controversy, the town purchased the plant for $4,836. Pictured above in 1911 are, from left to right, Harry "Shorty" and Pearl Edwards, Charles Carlson, Ed Nutting (Paonia town official), Vern Rawalt (water and power commissioner) and Grant Heter (power plant mechanic). (Above, NFHS; right, Evelyn Edwards Audin Brown.)

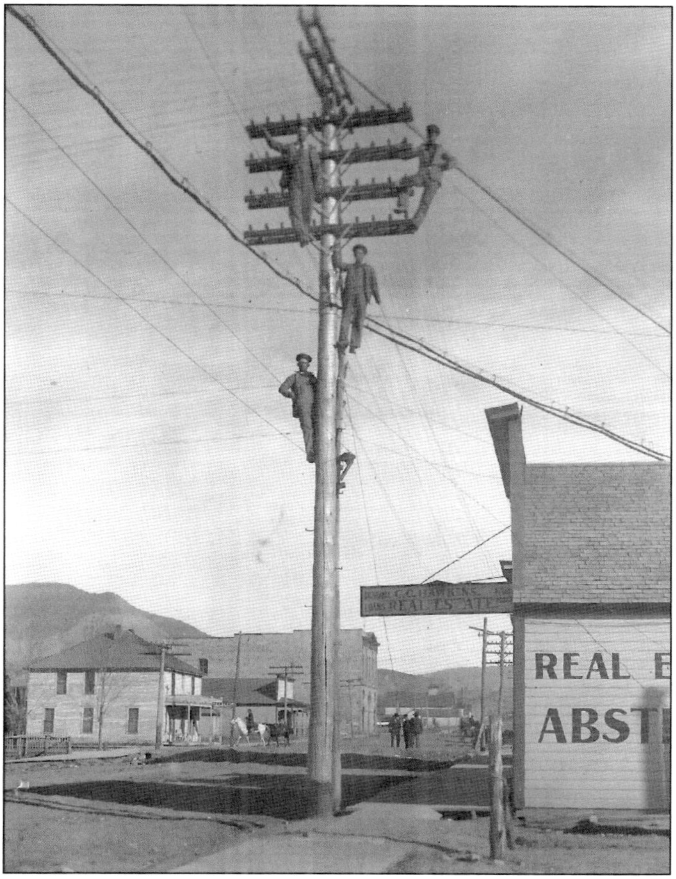

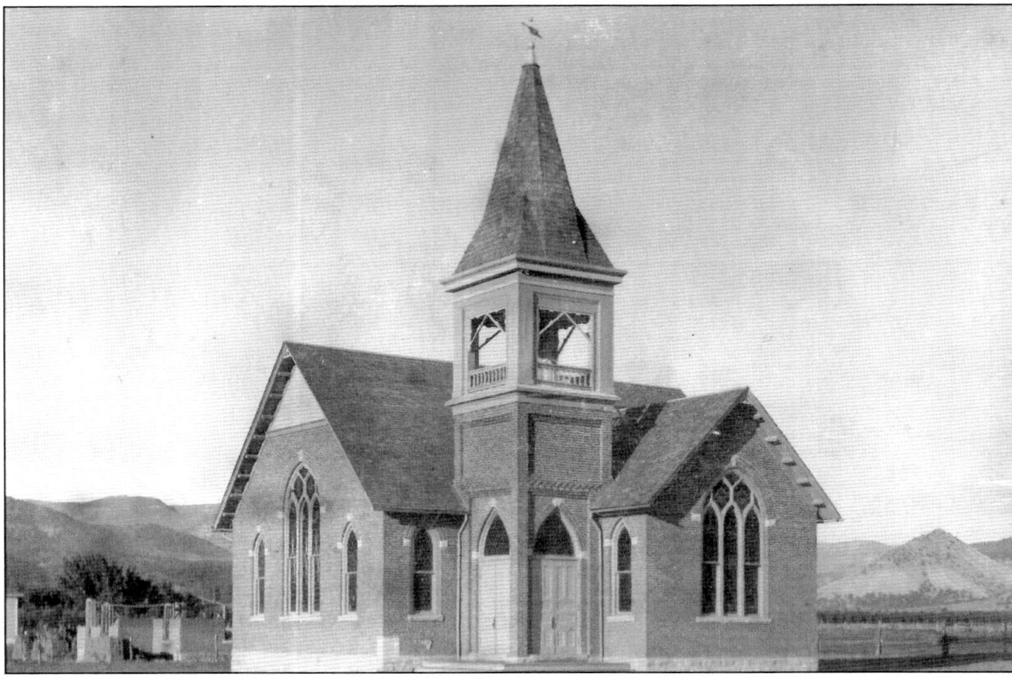

METHODIST CHURCH, 1899. This is the oldest church in Paonia. Circuit rider Rev. Henry Harpst organized Paonia, Hotchkiss, and Smith Fork in 1894. Twelve members met to start the church, hiring J.W. Martin as pastor in 1893. By 1906, there were 190 members. The interior is not elaborate or ornate, in keeping with early Methodist teachings. The church bell warned Paonians of fire. (NFHS.)

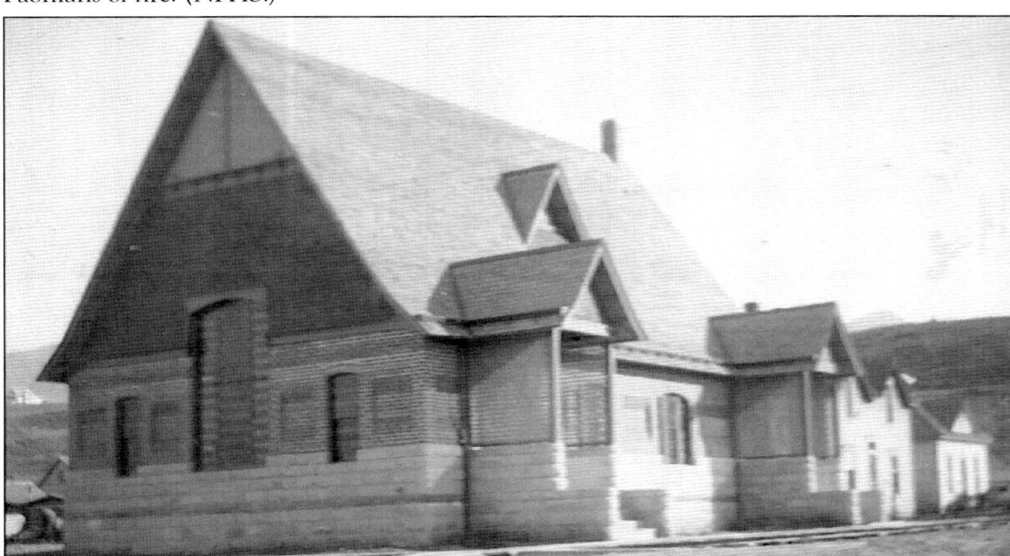

FRIENDS' CHURCH, 1904. In 1903, the Religious Society of Friends bought four lots along Third Street for $700 and hired pastor Maria Dean at a salary of $55 per month. The Early American–style church has a striking ceiling made of sections of wood strips in diamond patterns. The sections were glued in C.P. Allen's garage. Many Quakers came from Earlham, Iowa. (NFHS.)

Christian Church. This 1906 church remains to this day. A Kimball organ arrived in 10 boxes weighing three tons in May 1908. The pipe organ, the first in Delta County, was played by Mrs. K.M. McMillan. It was returned in March 1915 because the church could not pay for it. Limestone was quarried by Sege Stratton north of Paonia. Contractor J.A. Hurst was known for his beautiful stonework on the Friends Church, the Fruit Exchange Bank, and the First National Bank. Designed by Rev. J.K. Hester, the church included a Gothic turret, Romanesque windows (curved at the top), Gothic ceiling beams, and a Victorian steeple. Pictured at the Christian Church are members of the Grand Army of the Republic from Paonia and nearby towns remembering veterans from the Civil War at a Memorial Day service. (Both, NFHS.)

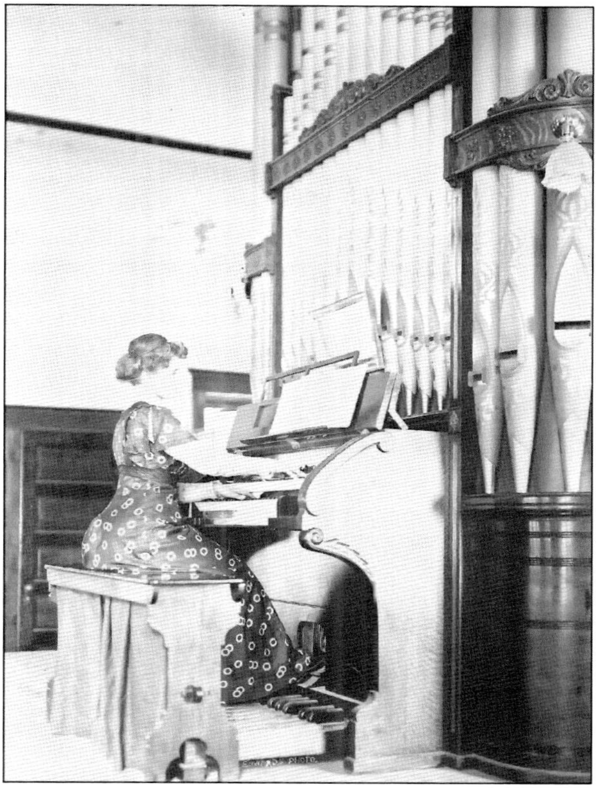

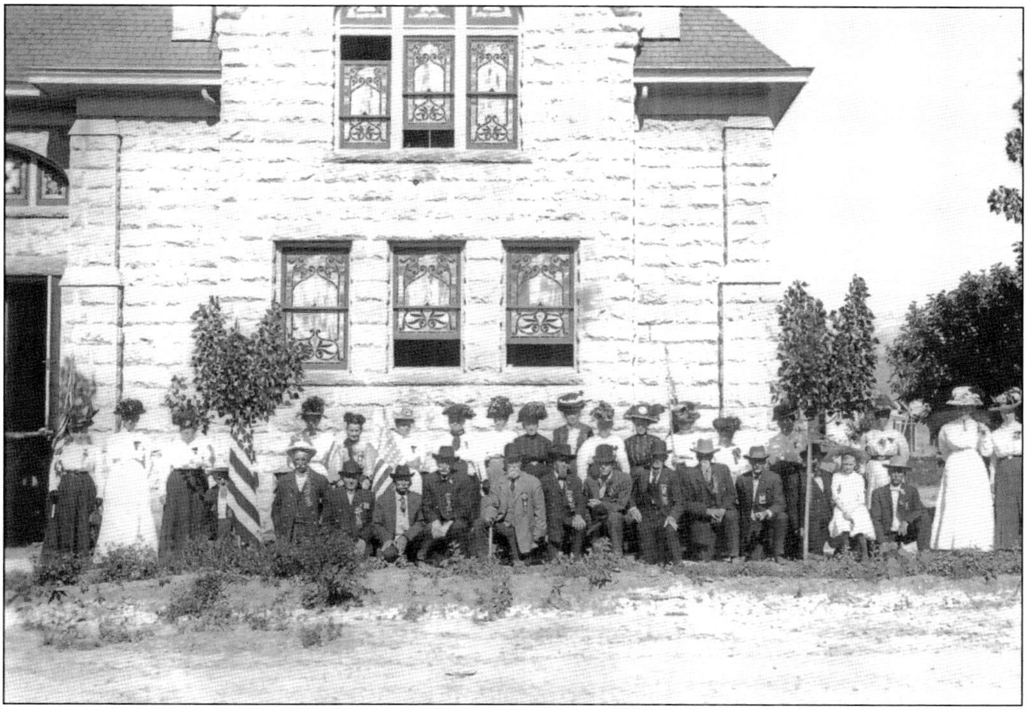

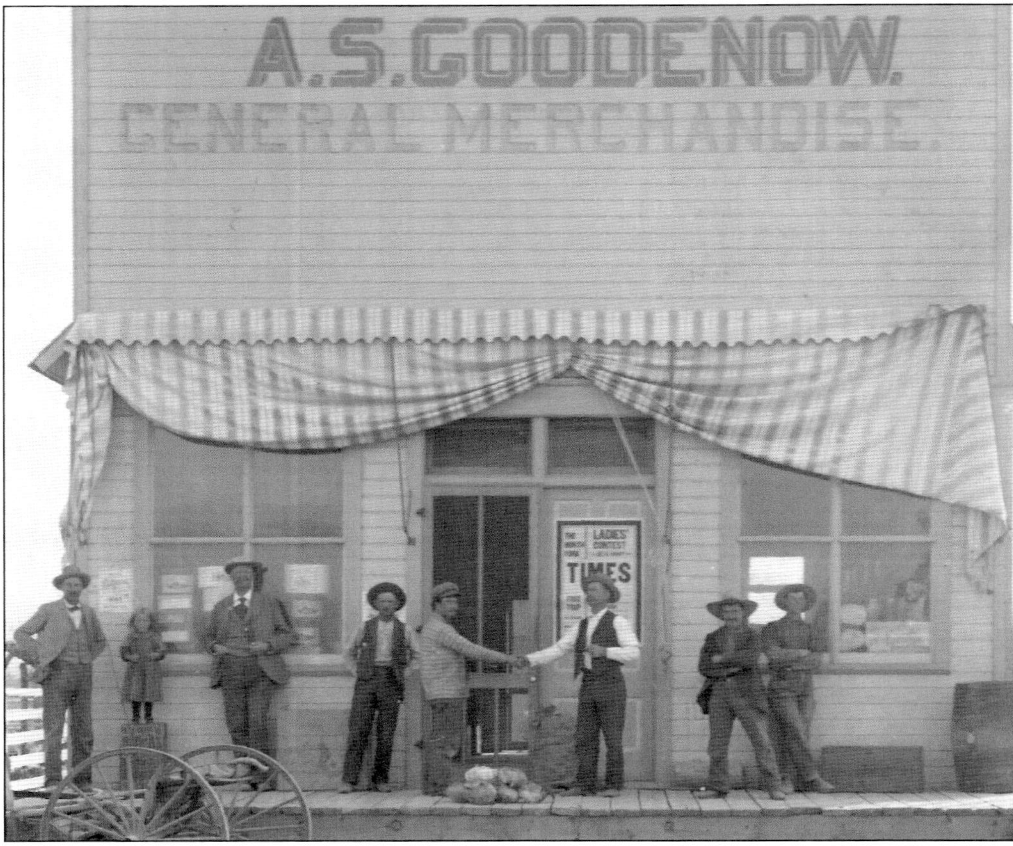

A.S. GOODENOW GENERAL STORE. This mercantile store provided a potpourri of products, such as tin and ironware, crockery, gentlemen's furnishings, groceries, dry goods, boots, and shoes. The beautiful brick house built for the Goodenows, later surrounded by M.P. Gonner's rose gardens, became American Legion Post No. 97. It was named for Ralph Wilson, who died in World War I, and Frank Head, who lost his life at Pearl Harbor on the battleship *Iowa*. Two hundred area men served in World War I. Besides Wilson, 2 were seriously injured, 10 died of the flu, and 3 died of other illness. (Both, NFHS.)

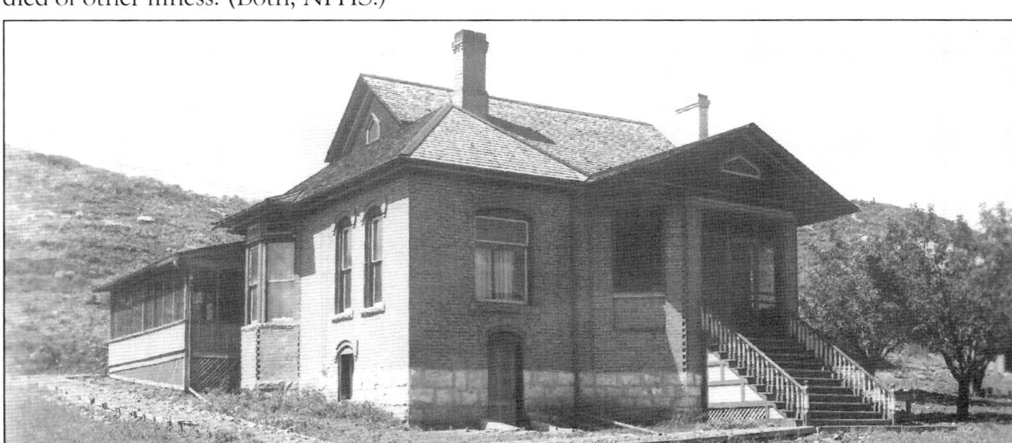

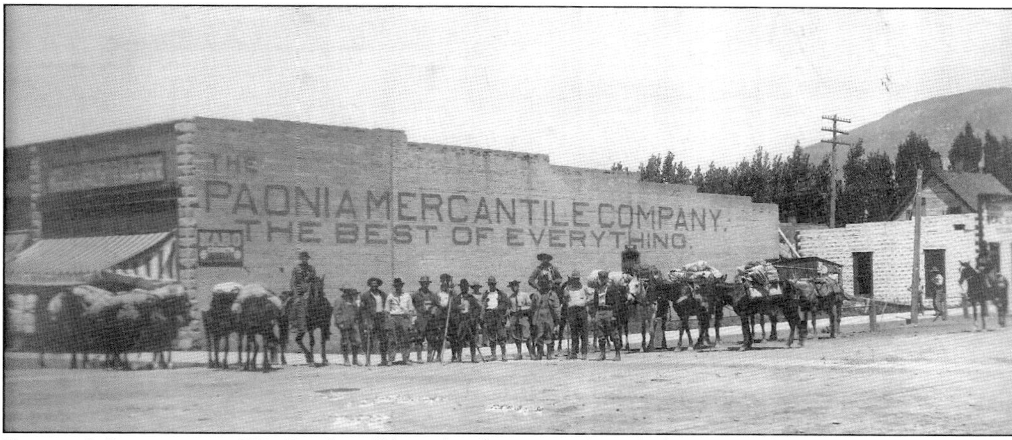

Paonia Mercantile. F.R. Rockwell bought this store, founded in 1898, from A.S. Goodenow in 1902. (Rockwell was the superintendent of the Denver & Rio Grande Railroad.) Pictured is the advertisement for the large 1904 building. In June 1912, the store ordered a carload of salt for ice cream. Another early mercantile store was owned by Milton Spencer. He also served as banker, locking cash in a strong box for safekeeping. (NFHS.)

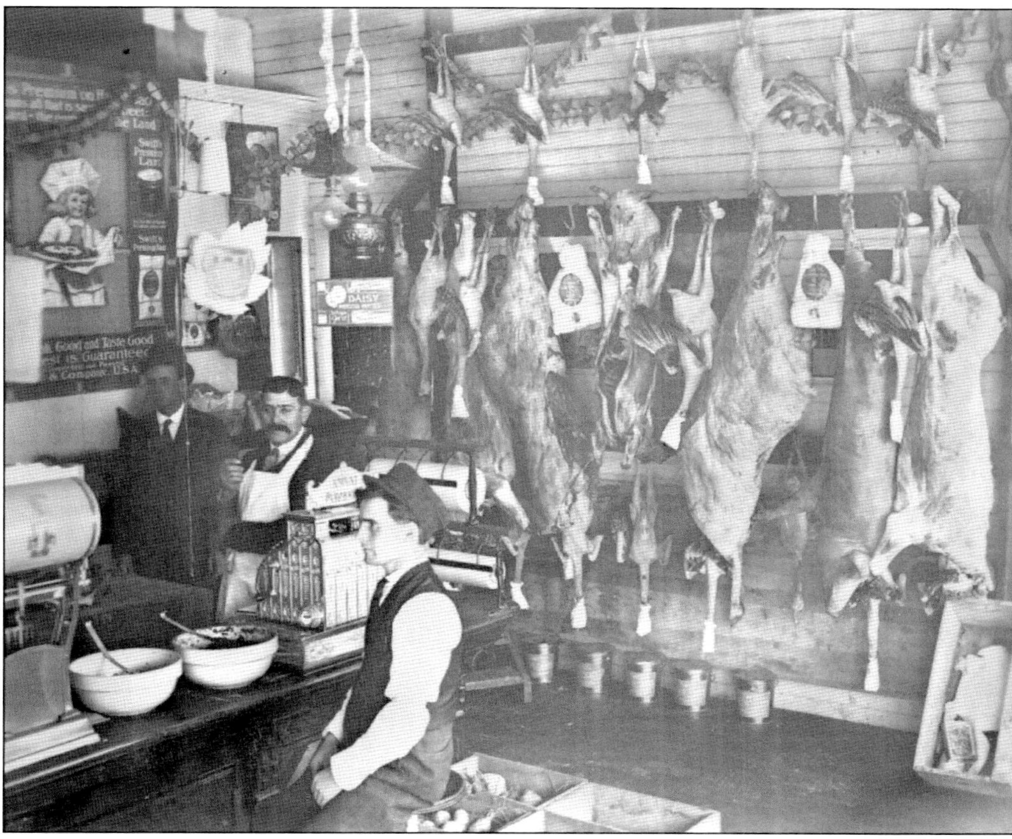

Peoples Meat Market. Owned by Phil Eisenkramer, who came to Paonia from Lake City, the store had a phone connection to Delta by 1904. Advertised in December 1911 were beef hindquarters at 11¢, front quarters at 9.5¢, and bacon at 30¢. The beef came from Crawford. (NFHS.)

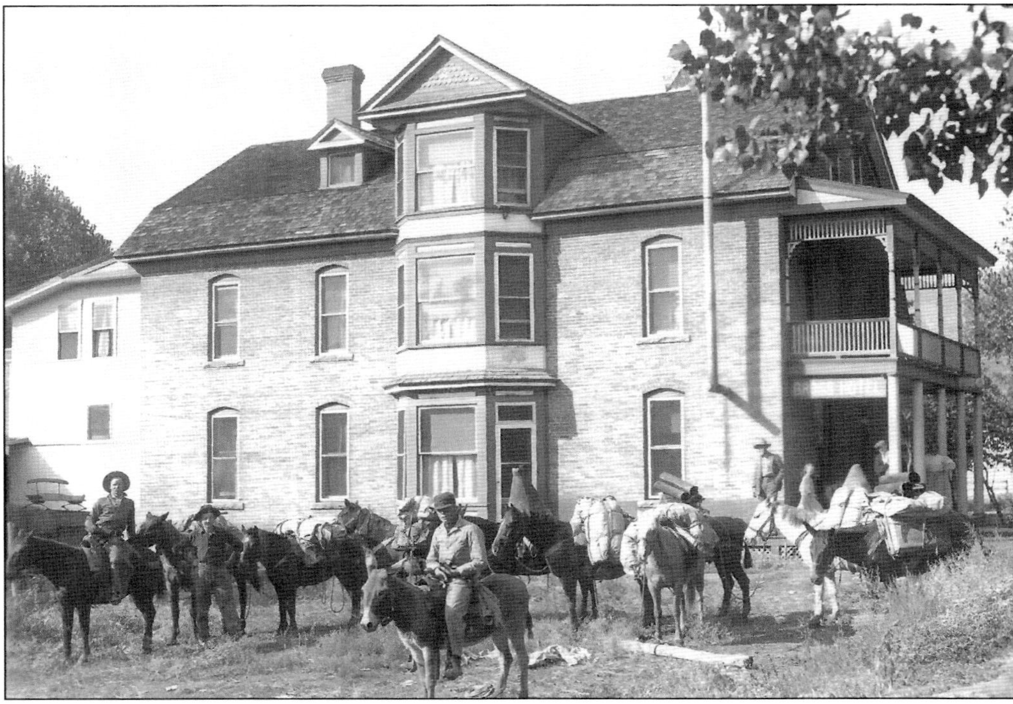

Bross Hotel, 1906. Built from bricks fired from soil taken from the basement, the present hotel is a beautifully restored bed-and-breakfast. Owning the establishment from 1906 to 1925, William T. "Daddy" Bross drove his team to the depot to pick up fruit brokers from Denver. Fruit workers were less fortunate; they were crowded into bunkhouses. (NFHS.)

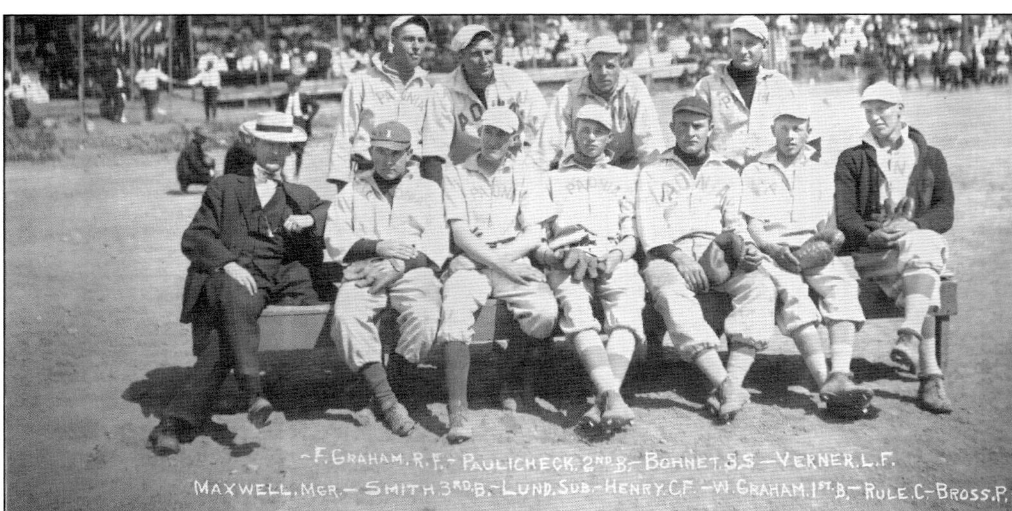

Baseball Team, 1912. Pictured to the far right, Otto Bross was a well-known Paonia pitcher. He had an offer to pitch for Walla Walla, Washington. The Paonia team won the Western Slope championship on August 22, 1914, by defeating Cameo 10-1 and 5-3 in a doubleheader. A crowd of 450 witnessed the Paonia victory. (DCHS.)

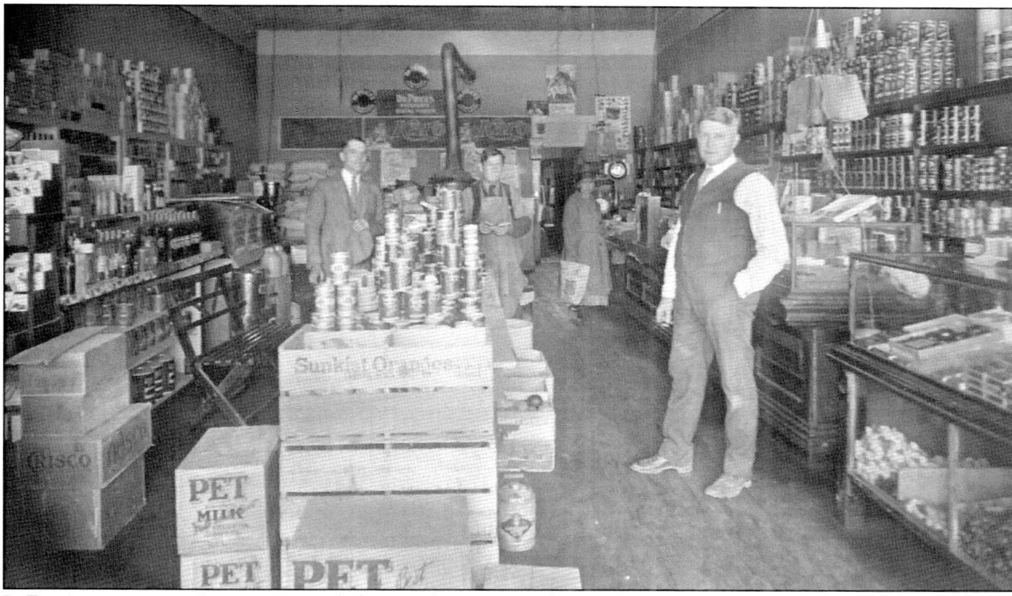

L.R. ARMSTRONG STORE. From left to right are traveling salesman Port Lyons, Charlie Van Deren, L.R. Armstrong, and an unidentified shopper. Armstrong worked for the Paonia Mercantile from 1912 to 1919. Louise Armstrong married Robert Rockwell, Colorado's representative to Congress from 1941 to 1950. (NFHS.)

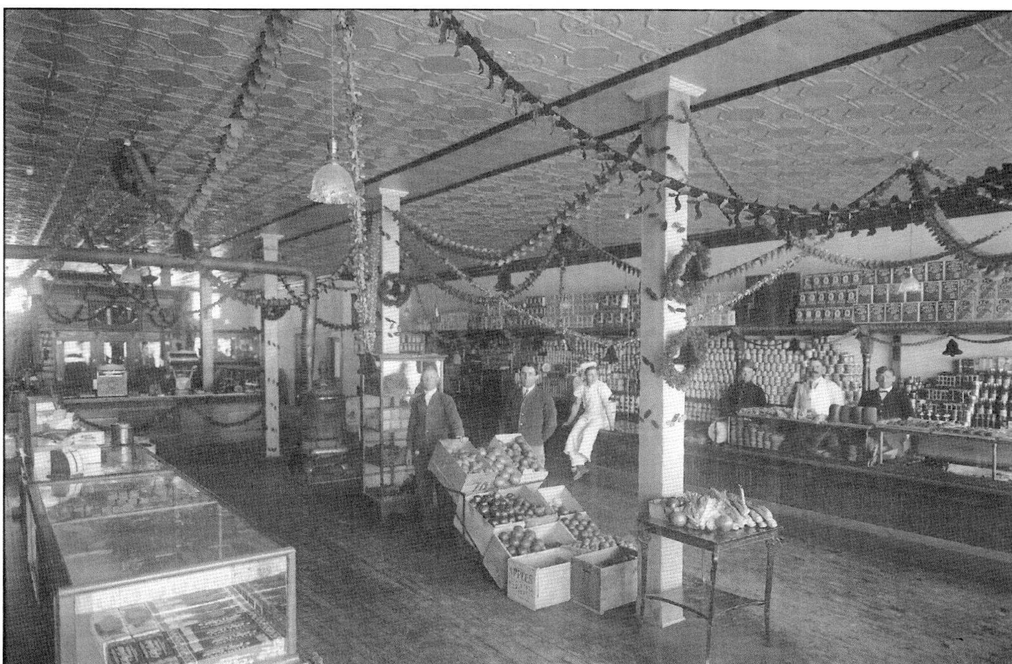

DEWOODY, ELDER GROCERY. To market bread, a gold piece was once baked into a batch of bread sold to customers. A 1912 advertisement reads: "We will roast your Christmas fowls and meats and deliver hot to your door at 11 a.m. Christmas Day for low figures." Employee Melvin Wade, Ezra Wade's son, married Nina DeWoody. (NFHS.)

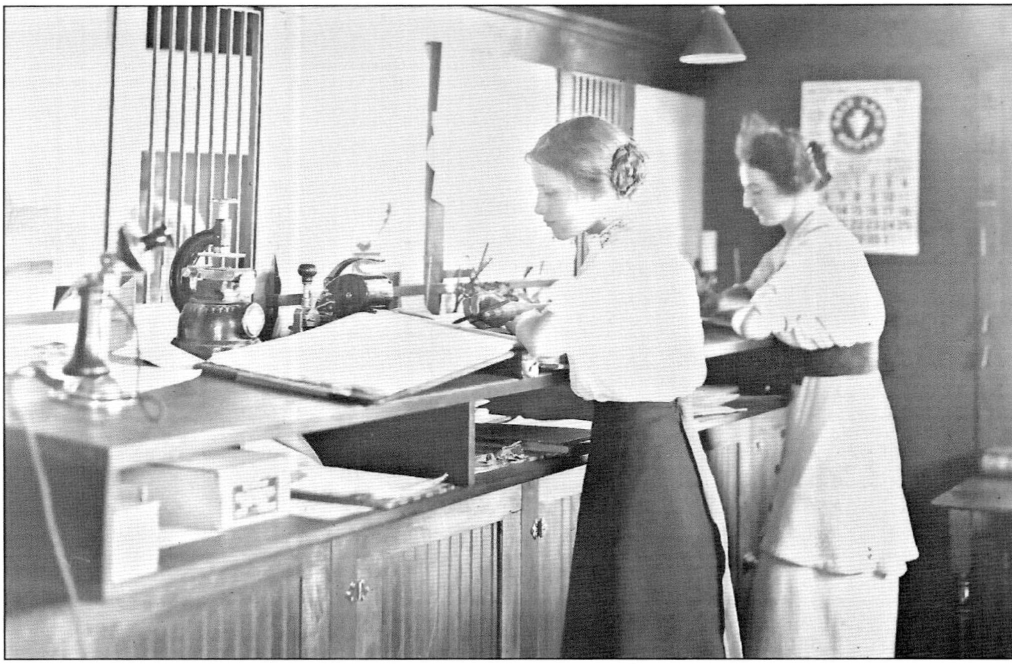

First National Bank, 1903. The First National Bank cost $6,500 to build. The first president was Ed Curtis. Except for the striped canopy, the exterior of the building remains unchanged. Today, it is the Blue Sage Center for the Arts. In 1904, bank resources were $26,000; in 1919, assets were $267,625.33. A prominent banker was M.H. Crissman, active in Republican politics. President Franklin Roosevelt closed the banks in 1933. This bank reopened, but the Fruit Exchange Bank did not. The 2012 bank is located at 133 Grand Avenue and has been renamed First Colorado National Bank. (Both, NFHS.)

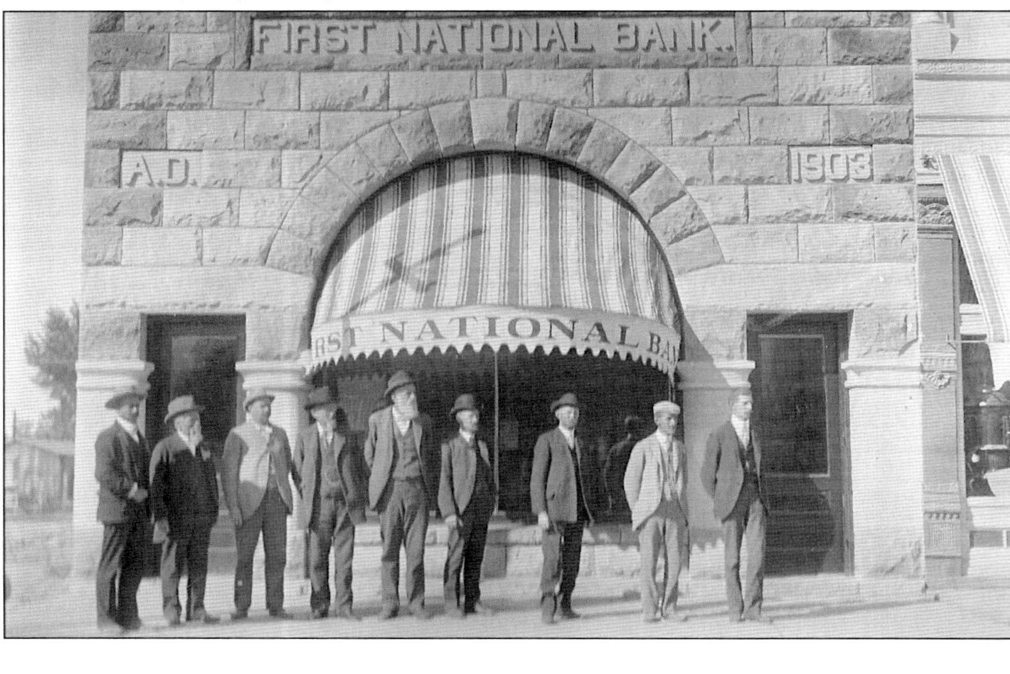

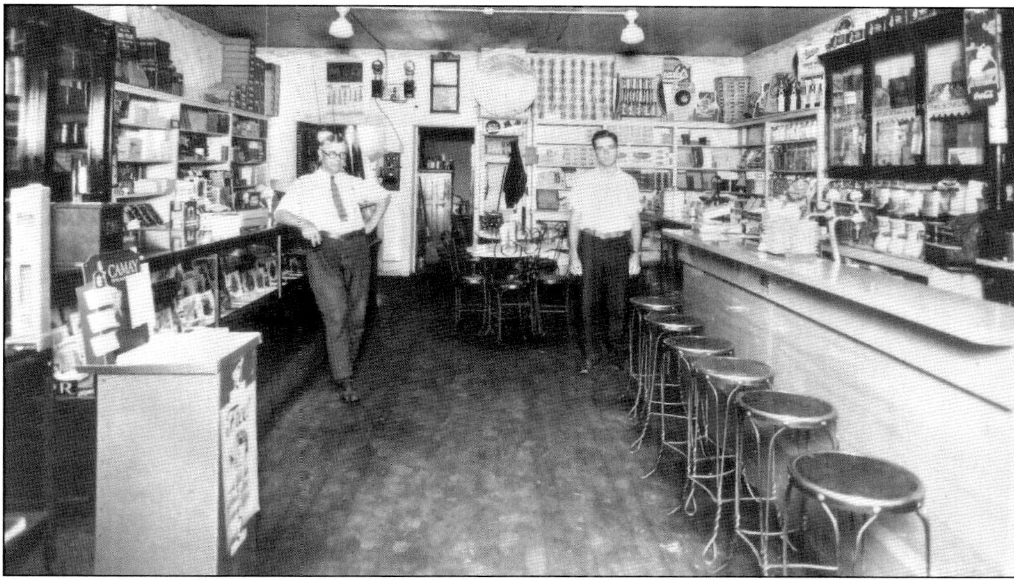

W.R. Bradshaw Confectionery, 1927. From 1912 to 1950, the confectionery provided malted milks prepared from fresh cow's milk. The cow was milked at Bradshaw's home on the block just behind the store. At Christmas, a large amount of hard candy displayed in bins was sold. Penny candy was very popular with Paonia youngsters. (NFHS.)

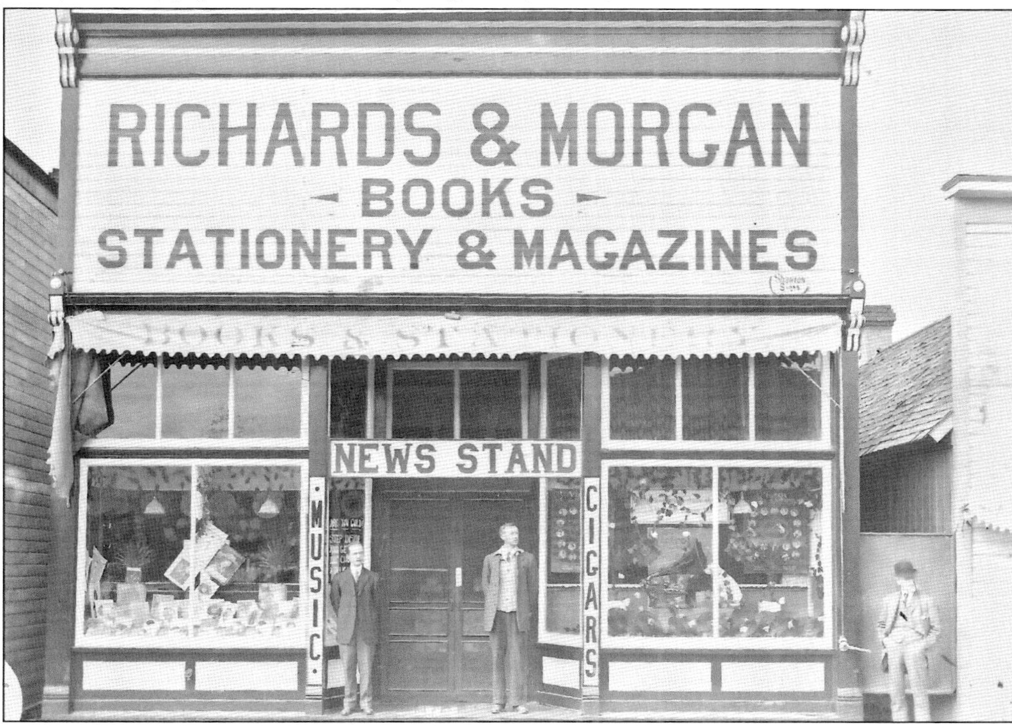

Richards and Morgan Books. Try a tango sundae. This building has housed many interesting stores during its history. In 1915, the bookstore became Richards Drug and Stationery Company, which moved to the larger Paonia Mercantile building in 1917. (NFHS.)

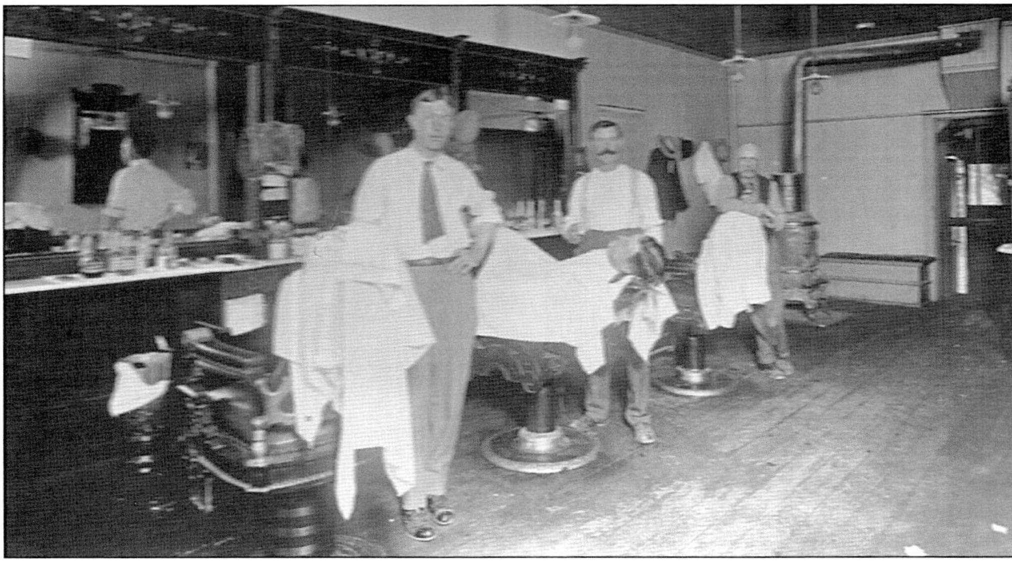

Barbershop, 1910. Guy Patterson (left), Frank Shields (center), and Guy's father, Alvin Patterson, exercise their barbering skills at the Patterson Barbershop on Grand Avenue. In June 1905, town council ordered all barbershops to close on Sundays. (NFHS.)

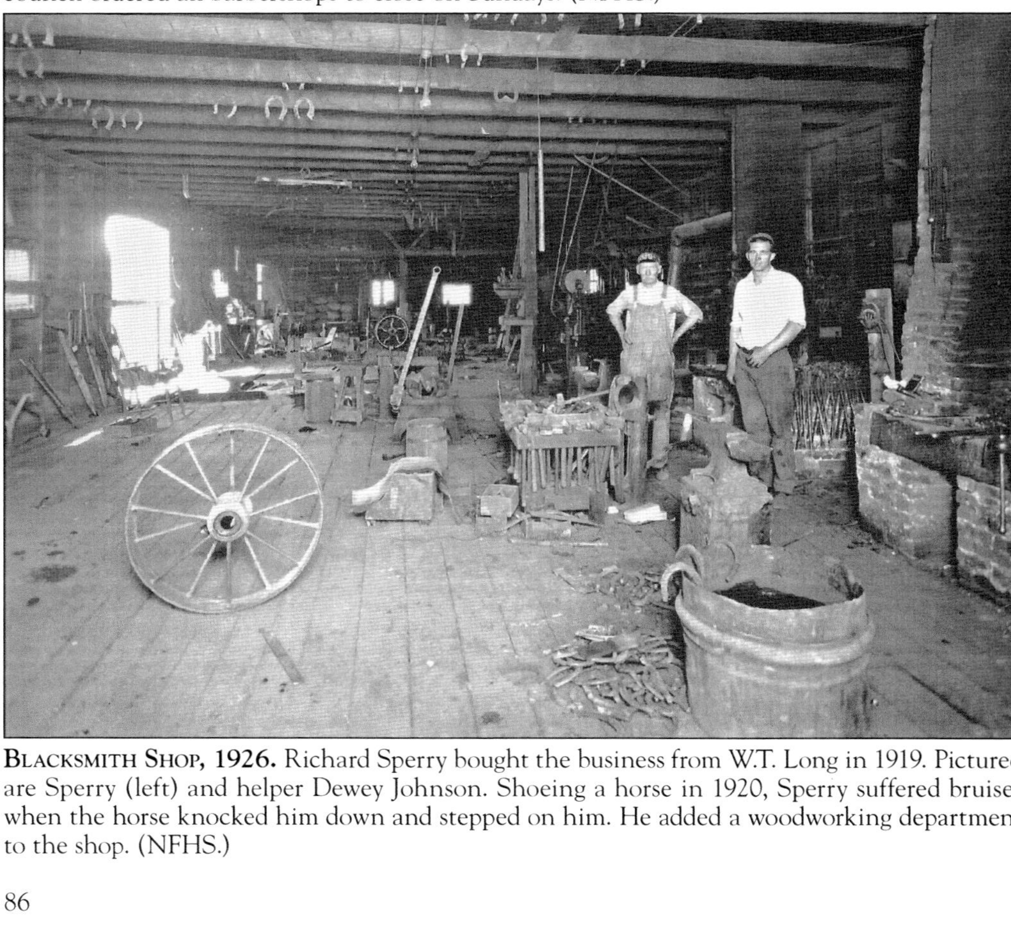

Blacksmith Shop, 1926. Richard Sperry bought the business from W.T. Long in 1919. Pictured are Sperry (left) and helper Dewey Johnson. Shoeing a horse in 1920, Sperry suffered bruises when the horse knocked him down and stepped on him. He added a woodworking department to the shop. (NFHS.)

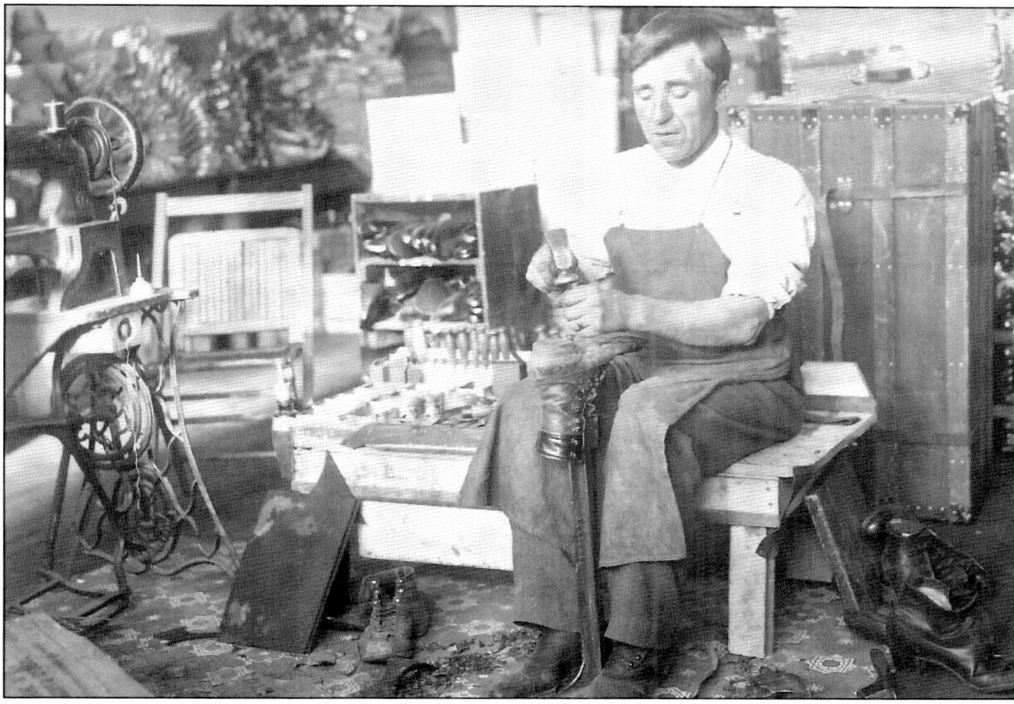

SHOEMAKER. Theodore Beckman (not the unidentified shoemaker in the photograph) collected dimes as payment for his shoemaking services. He tossed them in a corner behind his equipment. Hearing about a break-in at another store, he decided that he should take the dimes to the bank to be counted. There were 8,400 dimes weighing 80 pounds. Beckman was able to buy a large car. Another business that made shoes was the Paonia Harness, Boot, and Shoe Shop. E.B. Grable, proprietor of the 1905 shop, also repaired bicycles. In 1916, J.W. Shrader owned the shop. He displayed a saddle with a silver saddle horn. He sold Studebaker wagons and buggies as well. (Both, NFHS.)

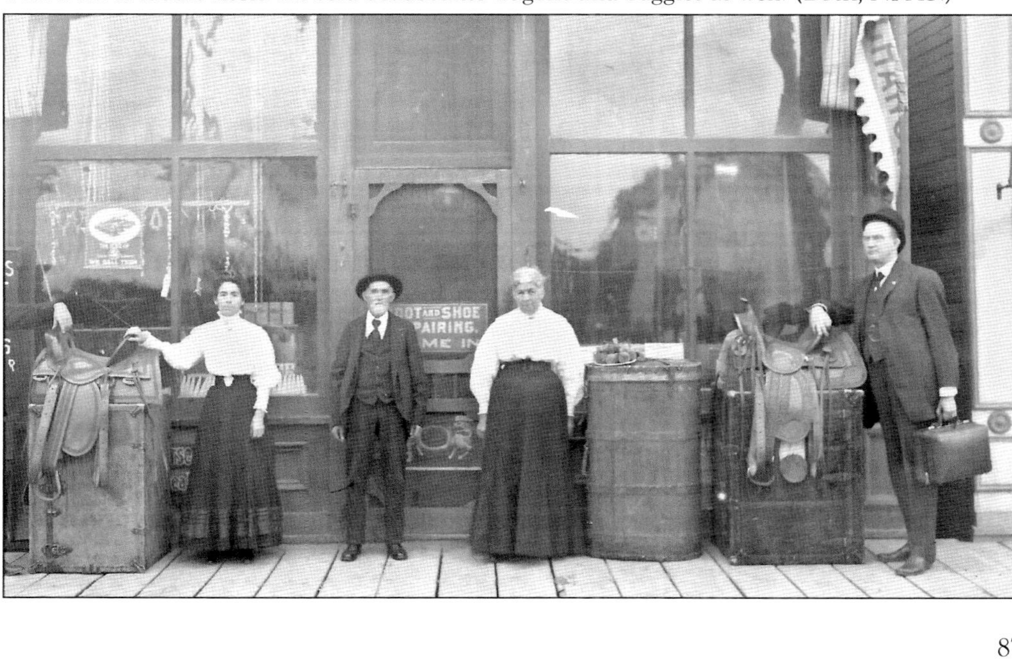

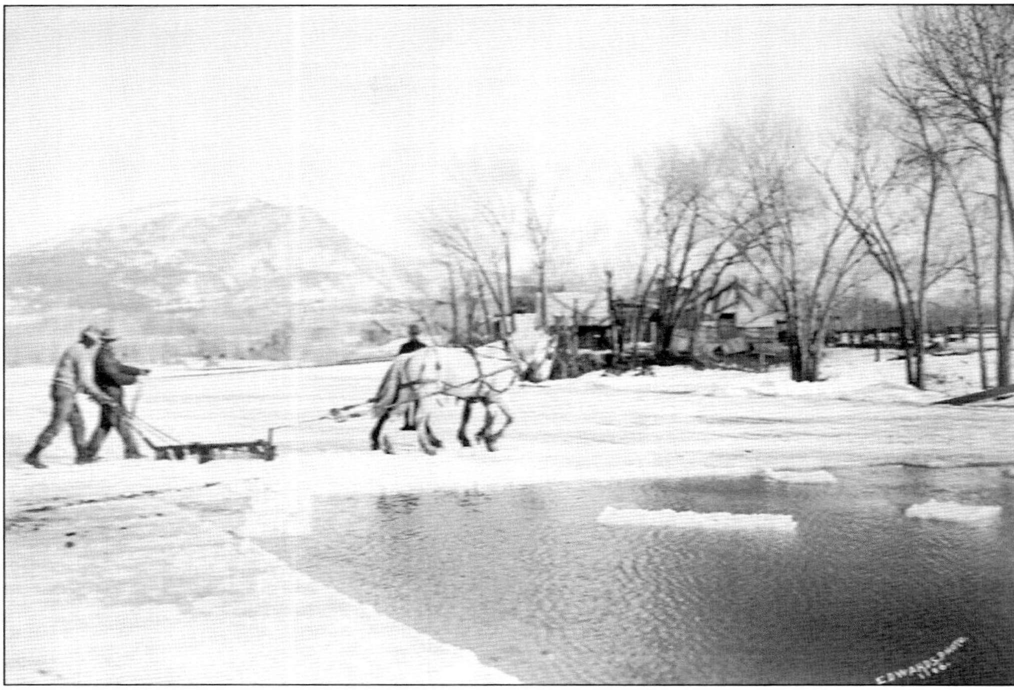

ICE CUTTING. In November 1905, flamboyant Parker Balch filled an ice pond for winter cutting. Ice was stored in sawdust in an icehouse. Bert Norris and J.W. Taylor cut ice at Somerset. In 1913, The Denver & Rio Grande Railroad stored 20,000 tons of ice at Grand Junction for use in refrigerator cars. (NFHS.)

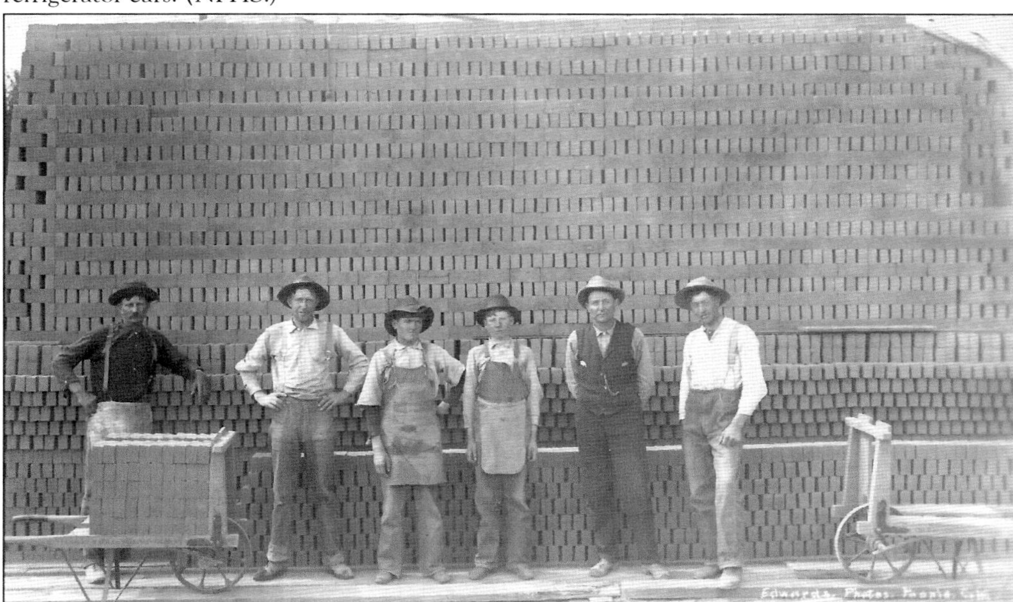

BRICKYARD. Delta Brick Yard, in 1906, was trying to put Paonia brickyards out of business by selling and delivering brick to Paonia for $8 per thousand. Locco and Noe (Paonia Brick and Paving Company) was threatened. (NFHS.)

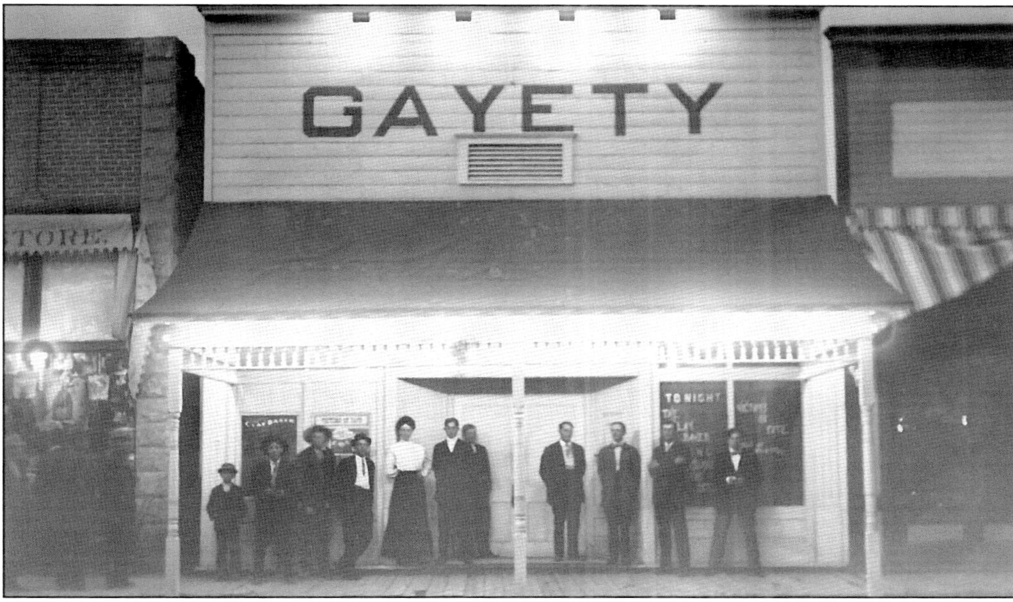

Gayety Theater. With a pianist banging out music, silent movies were *Seth's Temptation* and *Ten Nights in a Baroom* in 1911 and *Pranks at School for Young Ladies* in 1910. The *Little Red Riding Hood* matinee on December 27, 1911, cost 5¢ for children and 10¢ for adults. (NFHS.)

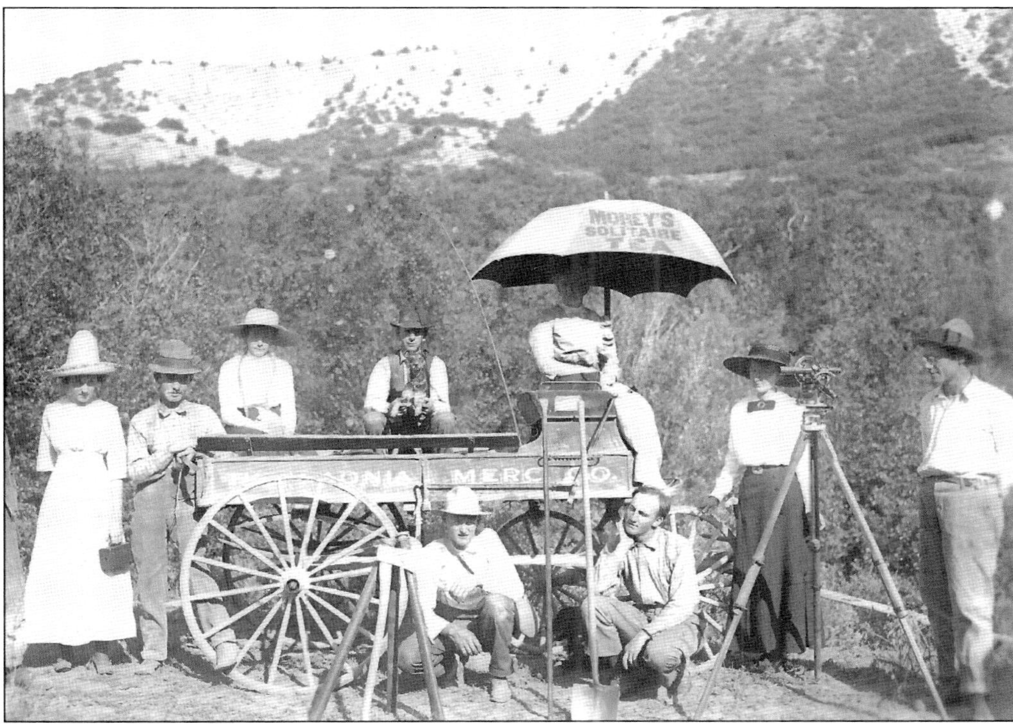

Survey Crew Picnic. This nicely dressed group is enjoying mountain views through the surveyor's tools, and one is escaping sunburn by staying under a large umbrella atop a wagon from Paonia Mercantile. No woman appears without a hat, even in this bucolic setting. (NFHS.)

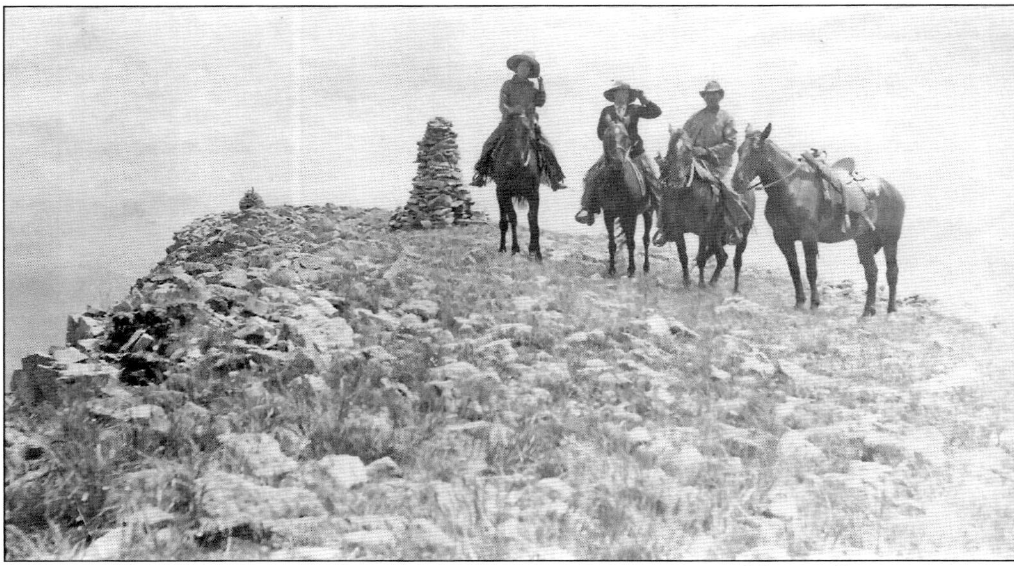

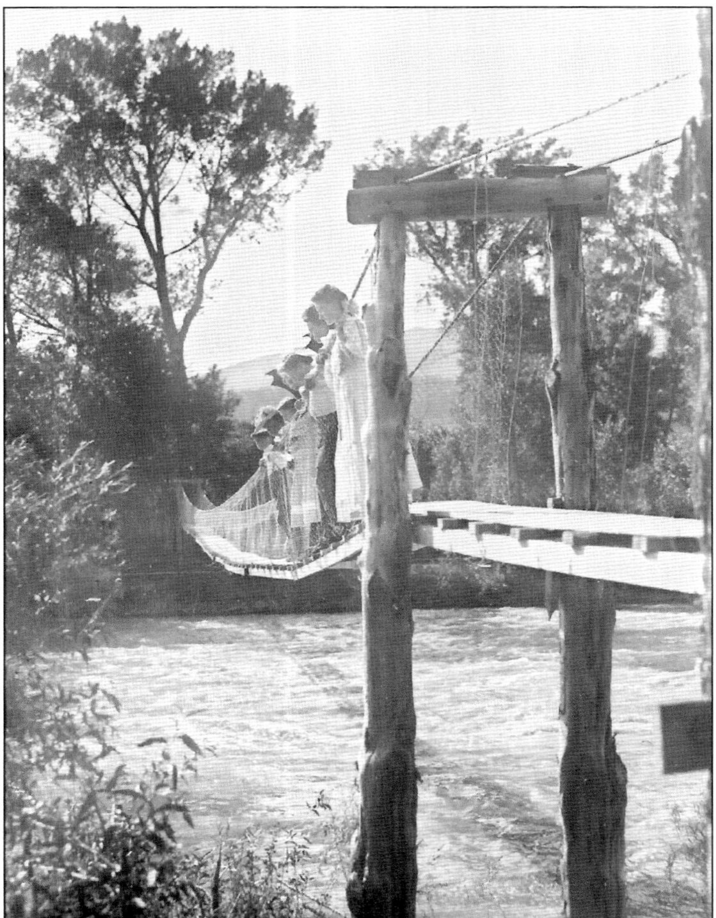

Mount Gunnison Horseback Ride, 1913. Anna Beezley (left) and Emma and John F. Taylor have ascended Mount Gunnison on horseback, except for some very steep places where the horses were led. Horses and riders proudly stand at the summit. John Beezley took the photograph. An article in the August 28, 1913, *Paonian* newspaper calls this the first ascent by two couples on horseback. (Marilyn Bruce Tate.)

Suspended Bridge Holiday, c. 1910. The view from the Stephen's Grove swinging bridge over the North Fork does not look dangerous. However, in high water, this would not be a good afternoon plan. The bridge was located near the site of the Heddles Bridge, so it predates 1912. (NFHS.)

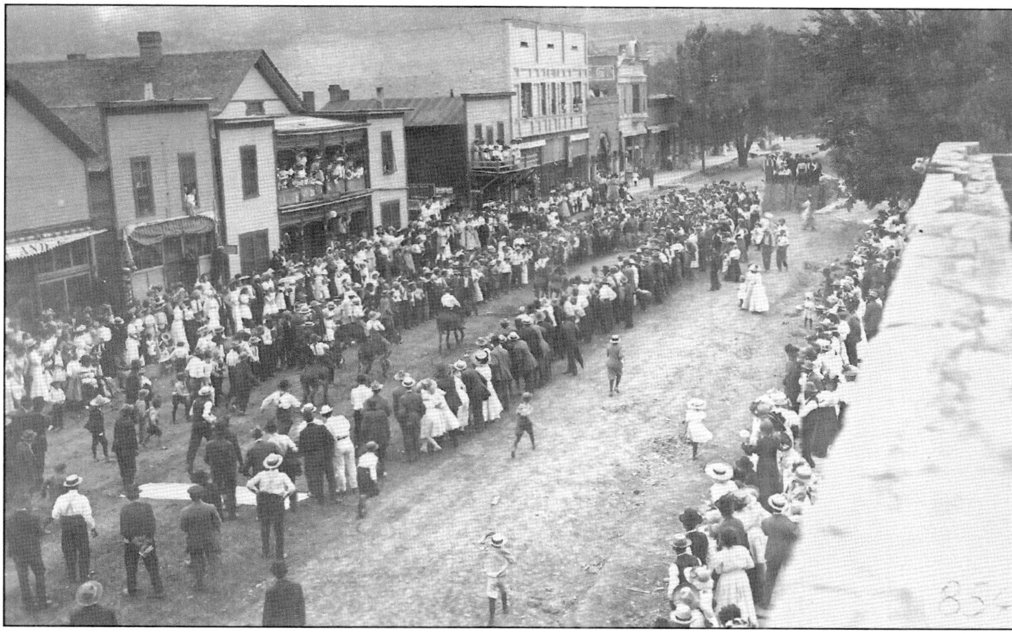

IOWA DAYS. A 1910 burro race brought out a huge crowd in downtown Paonia. Many of the early Paonia settlers were Quakers from Earlham, Iowa. By 1909, there were seven celebrations held at different places, among them Midway, Allen's Grove, and William Clarke's lawn. (NFHS.)

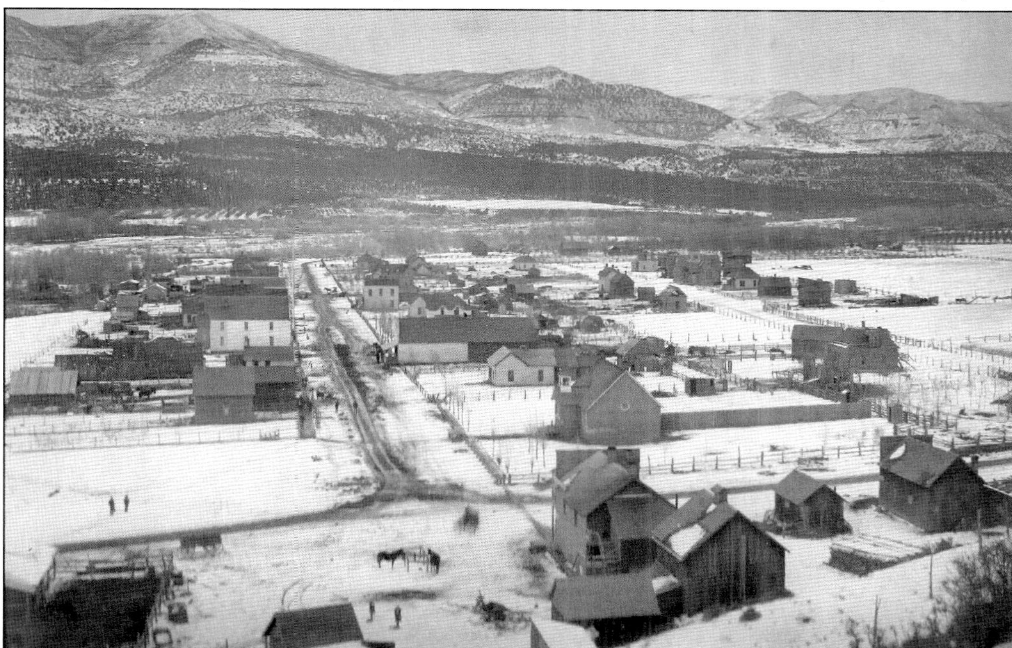

WINTER IN PAONIA, 1899. In this photograph, the steeple of the Methodist church can be seen. It is often used to date old pictures. After winter, the streets were described as muddy. Work resumed on sidewalks in the spring of 1911. In summer, when the streets were dusty, the town hired a man and team to sprinkle the streets for $100 per month. (NFHS.)

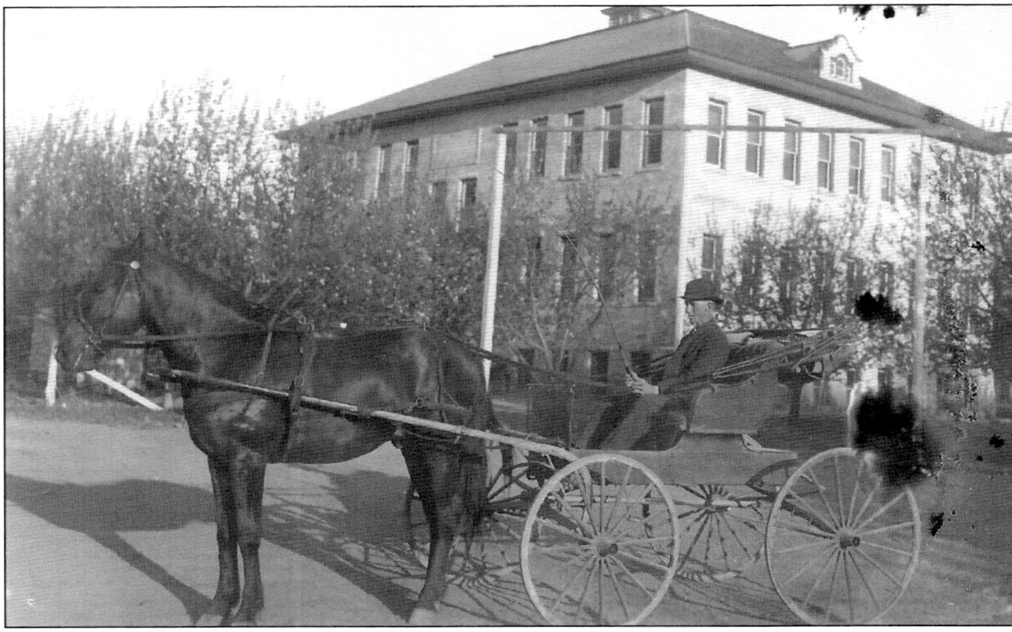

Paonia High School, 1912. Contractors for the building were E.S. Cady, woodwork, Thomas Edwards, concrete, and Dwight Bennett, masonry. The building was constructed in two sections. Blooming fruit trees were replaced by blue spruce. In a middle window on the second story was the motto: "Time flies over us, but leaves its shadow behind." Early principal Horace Wubben became president of Mesa College, now Colorado Mesa University, in Grand Junction. (NFHS.)

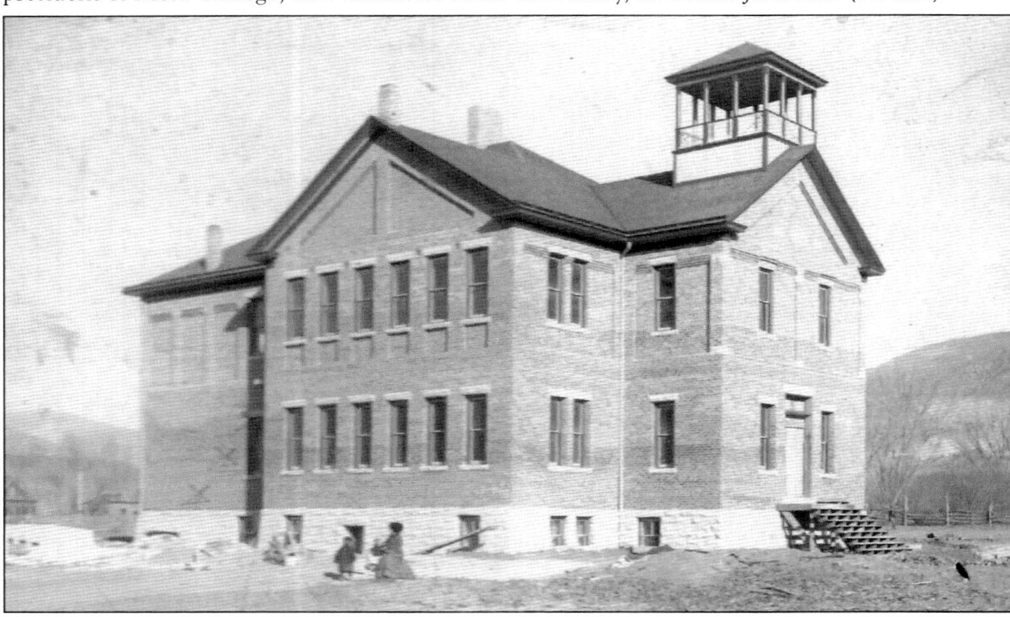

Paonia School, 1903. This brick building with 12 grades cost $17,000. In 1905, sixteen students were in high school. There were many schools in early times on both sides of the river. Bethlehem and Midway were on the north side; Dry Gulch, Minnesota, Lamborn, and Bigelow (1897) were on the south side. (NFHS.)

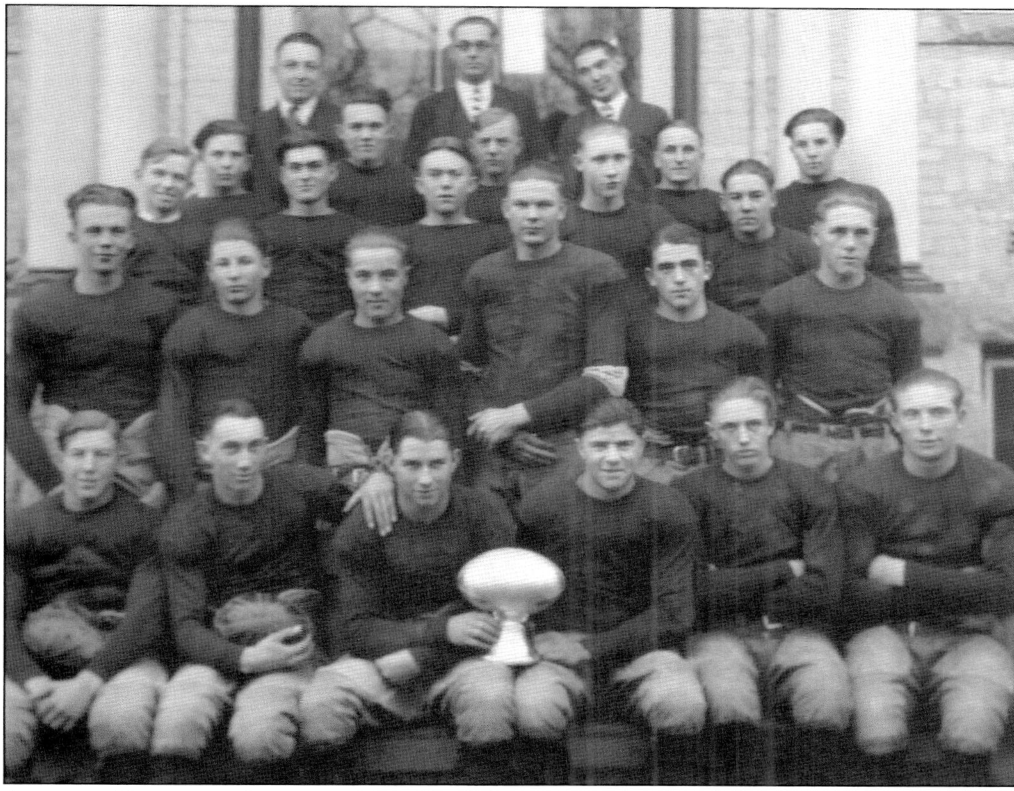

REGIONAL FOOTBALL CHAMPS, 1926. The Western Slope regional championship resulted in a three-way tie between Grand Junction, Delta, and Paonia. Therefore, another game at Grand Junction was scheduled to decide the outcome. Excited Paonia fans arrived by train. Each team was given two quarters of play. Grand Junction beat Delta 32-0; Paonia beat Grand Junction 6-0; and Paonia defeated Delta 13-0 to be named champions. Paonia High School coach was Dan Lawrence. The playing field at the Paonia Park is named for him. (NFHS.)

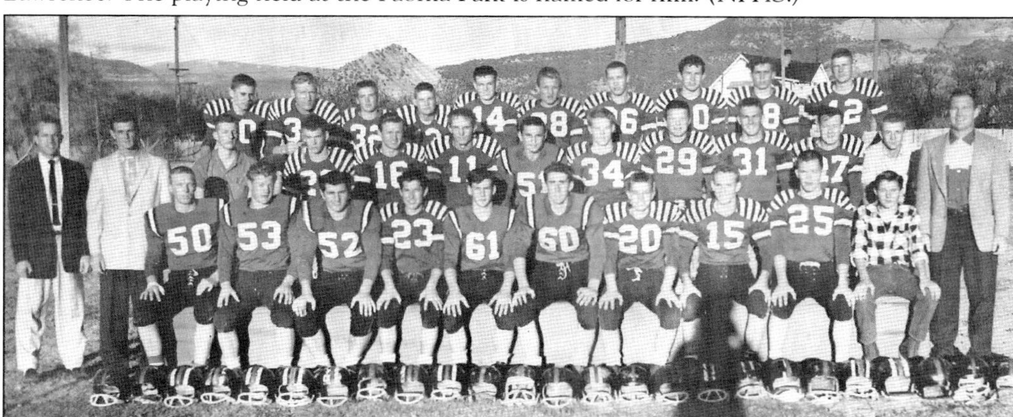

STATE FOOTBALL CHAMPIONS, 1959. Another big win for the Paonia High School Eagles was the Colorado Class A football championship in 1959. The score was Paonia 7, Windsor 0. In the semifinals, Paonia defeated Alamosa 16-14 in a sudden-death playoff. Coaching staff included head coach Granville King, Gary Noddings, Leon Shell, and Calvin Campbell. (Tyler Studio.)

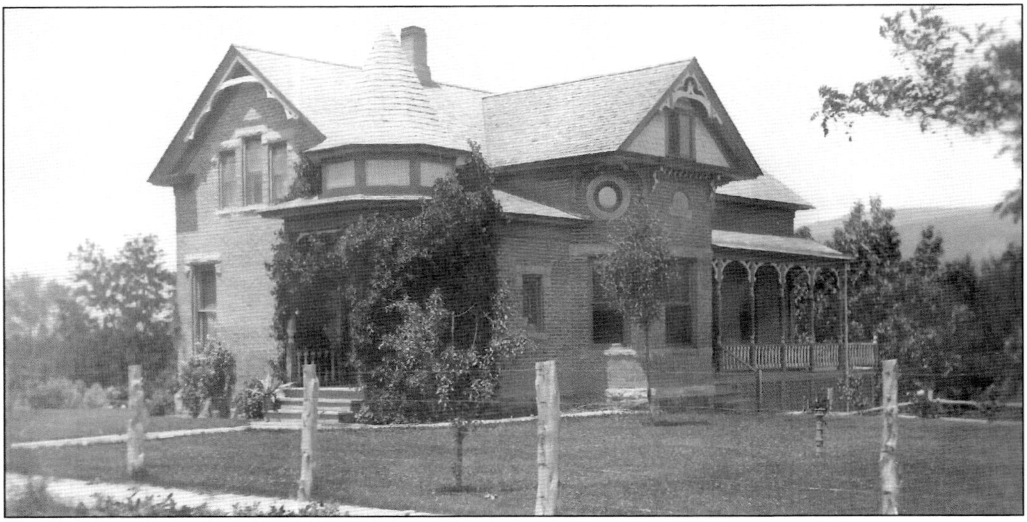

E.J. Mathews Home, 1905. Mathews bought the Samuel Wade homestead in 1894, building the home with bricks fired on site. When he was elected mayor (1908–1910), the property was incorporated into Paonia. Mathews Lane was named in his honor. The Mathews family sold the house to Paul Berg in 1943. On June 10, 1909, actors are seen dancing to "Take a Little Walk" from *Florodora* on E.J. Mathew's lawn. As for Samuel Wade, seven generations of his direct descendants have lived in Paonia. (Both, NFHS.)

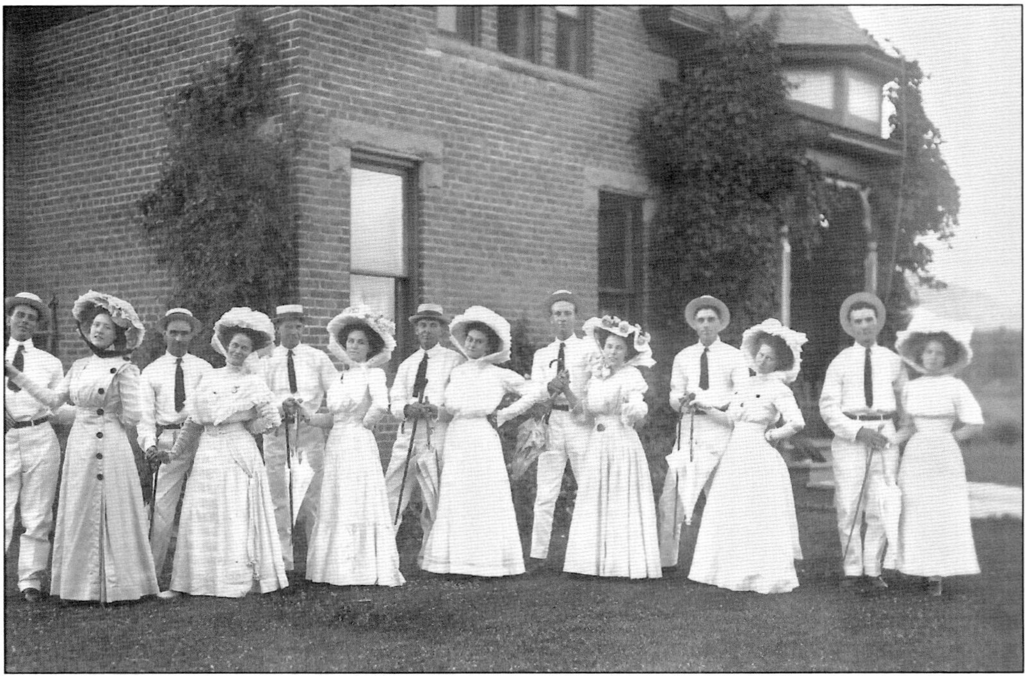

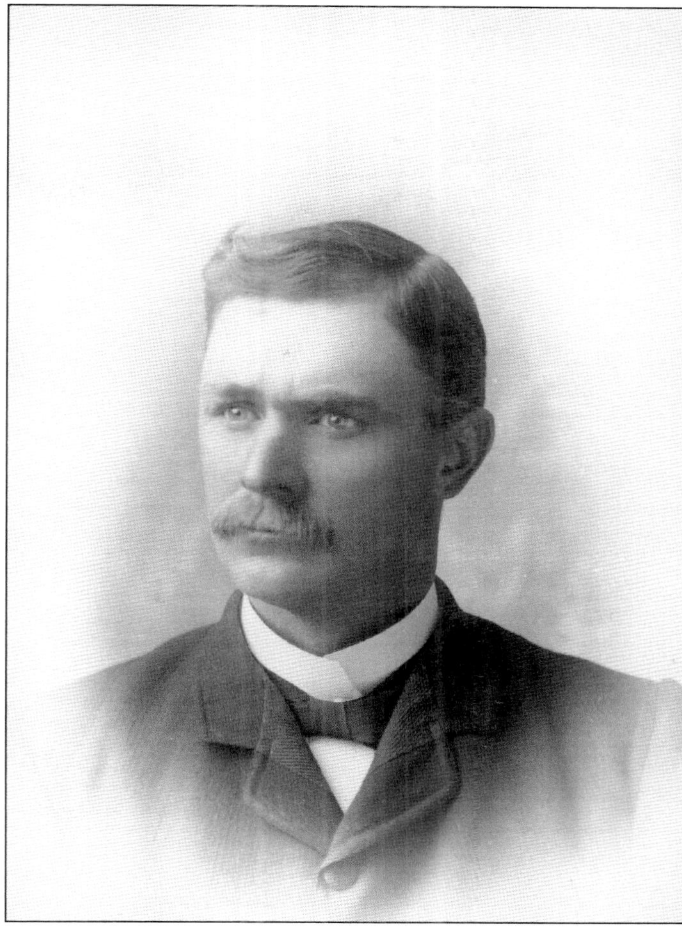

WILLIAM ALLEN CLARKE. In 1881, Clarke's claim was divided from Samuel Wade's at the current Grand Avenue. The Clarke claim extended east to encompass most of present Paonia. In 1892, he lived in this new brick home with his wife and, later, children Olive and Harold. Clarke gave land for the Paonia Park and Methodist Church. In 1905, forty boxes of apples were picked from one tree on his property. This illustrates the productivity of the fertile soil in the North Fork. Paonia fruit became well known after it won six awards at the Chicago World's Fair in 1893. Also, gold medals were received at the 1898 Trans-Mississippi Exposition in Omaha, attracting more attention to the area. (Right, A.J. Stephens; below, NFHS.)

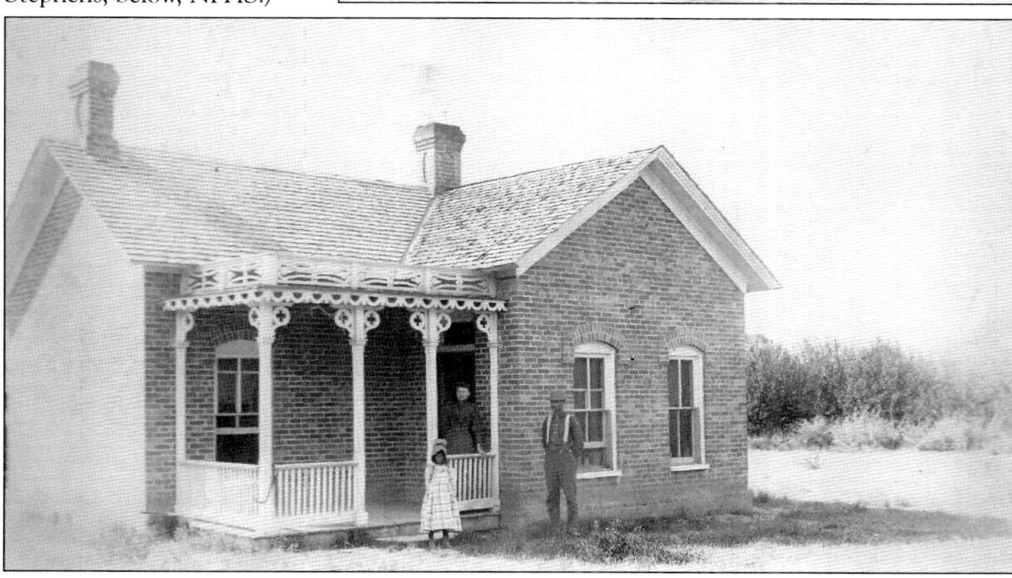

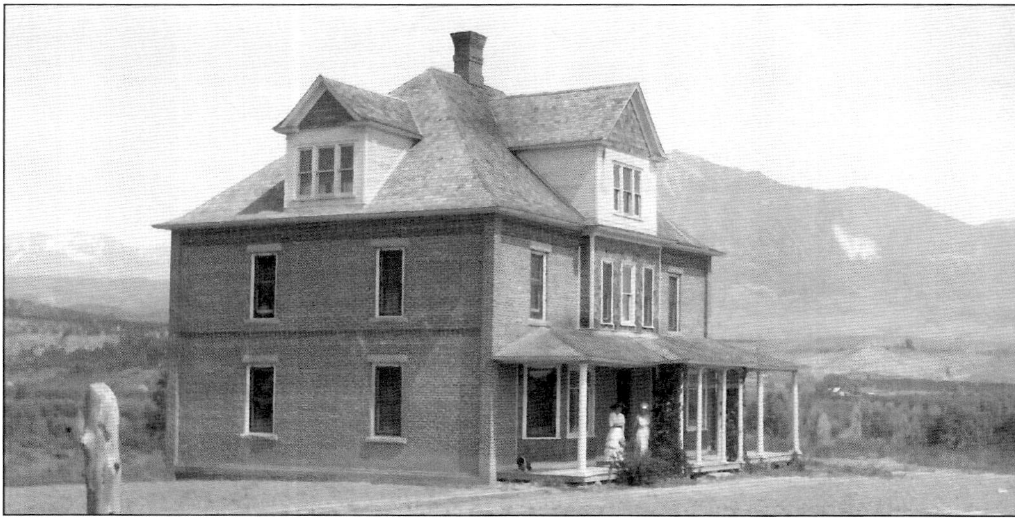

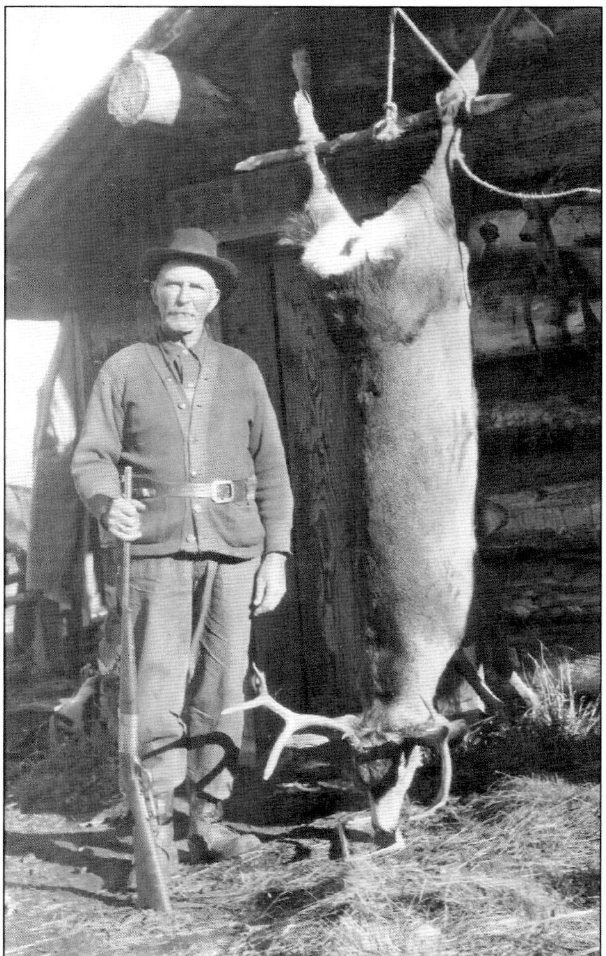

RAY BRUCE HOME, 1909. Angus R. Bruce from Nova Scotia settled first on what became Bruce Mesa (Garvin Mesa) in 1886. He later established the Riverside Ranch, building the 1905 home, shown above, with brick fired on the property. A fall from a cherry tree in 1922 resulted in his death. His son Raymond (1900–1989) and wife, Laura Taylor, remained on the ranch until Ray's death in 1989. Angus' brother John Bruce was a mover and shaker in Paonia. At left, Laura Taylor's father, cattle rancher John Taylor, is pictured with a trophy deer that provided venison for his wife, Emma Ballard, and eight children. The valley had bountiful game. Taylor was from Earlham, Iowa, and came to Paonia in 1905. (Both, Marilyn Bruce Tate.)

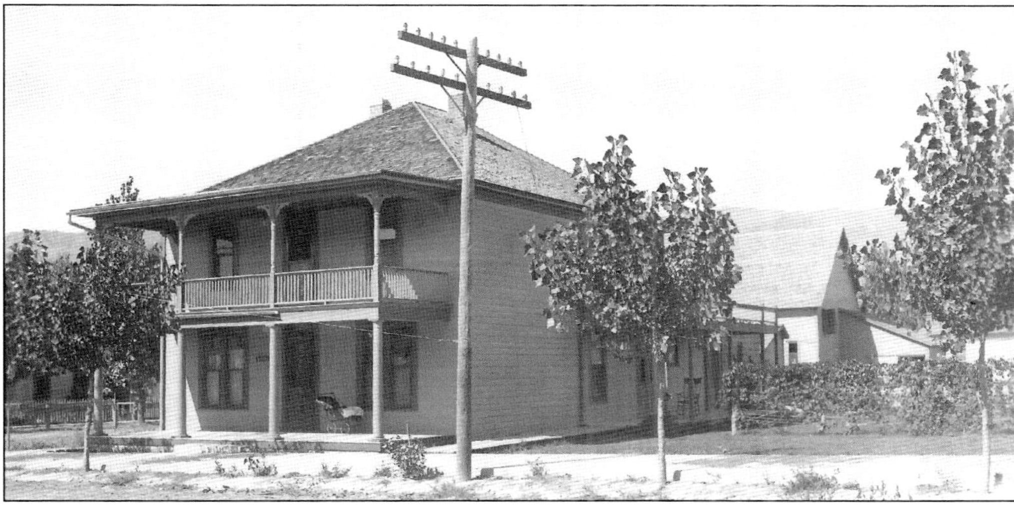

Dr. H.W. Hazlett's Home and Office, 1905. In 1908, David Beezley was attacked by a wild boar in his alfalfa field. It took 20 stitches by the doctor to sew him up. Typhoid, measles, grippe, diphtheria, pneumonia, smallpox, and scarlet fever were prevalent. Although there were quarantines, many died. (NFHS.)

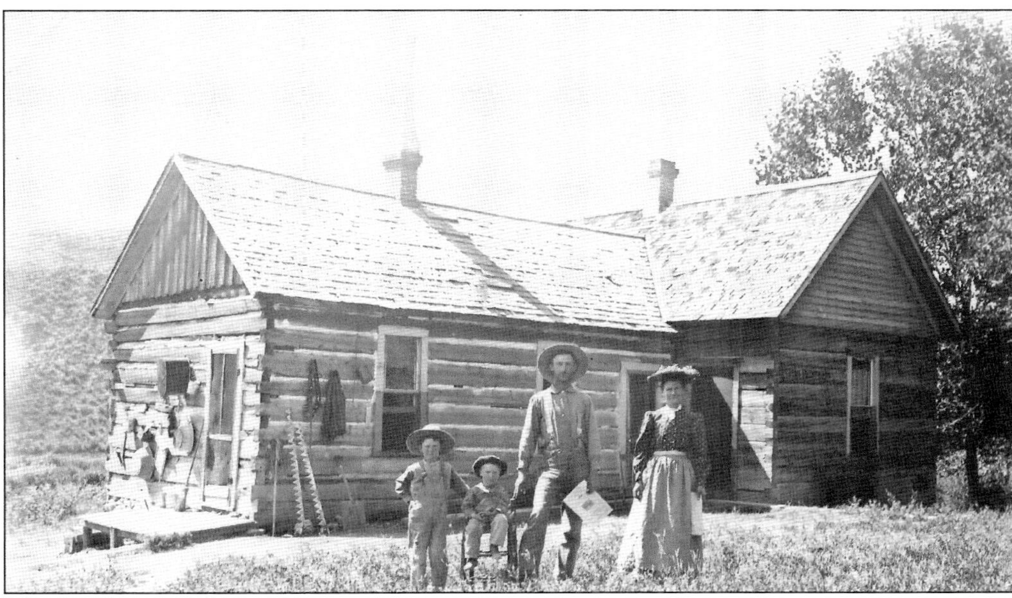

Log Cabin, 1906. Cowpuncher Lee Young and his wife and family lived in this cabin. One day, when Young was riding with Guy Hammond, Ed Sherwood, and George Newman, they killed a huge bear near Bowie. (NFHS.)

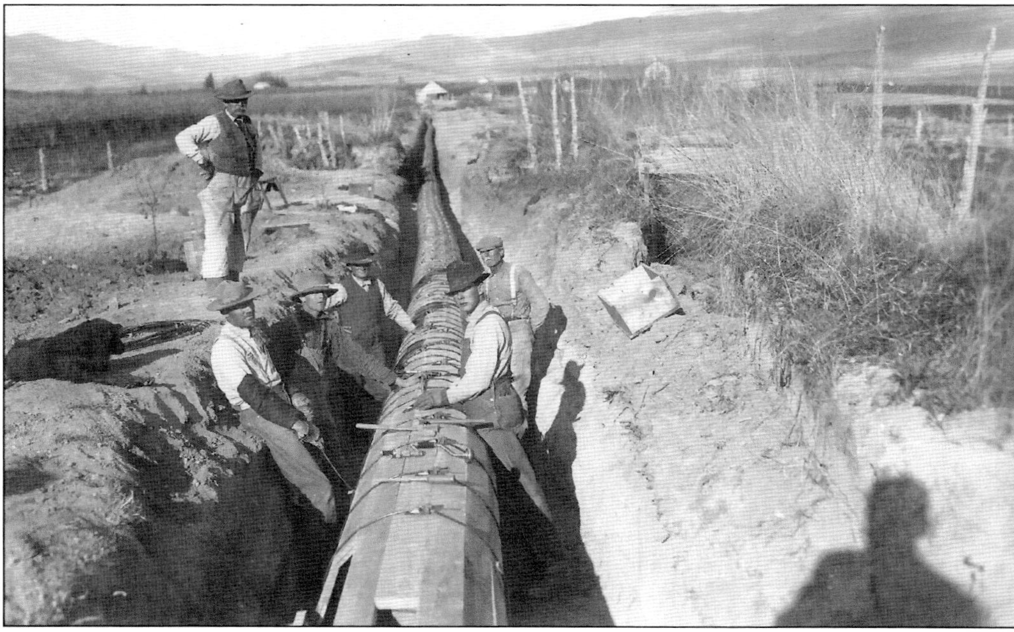

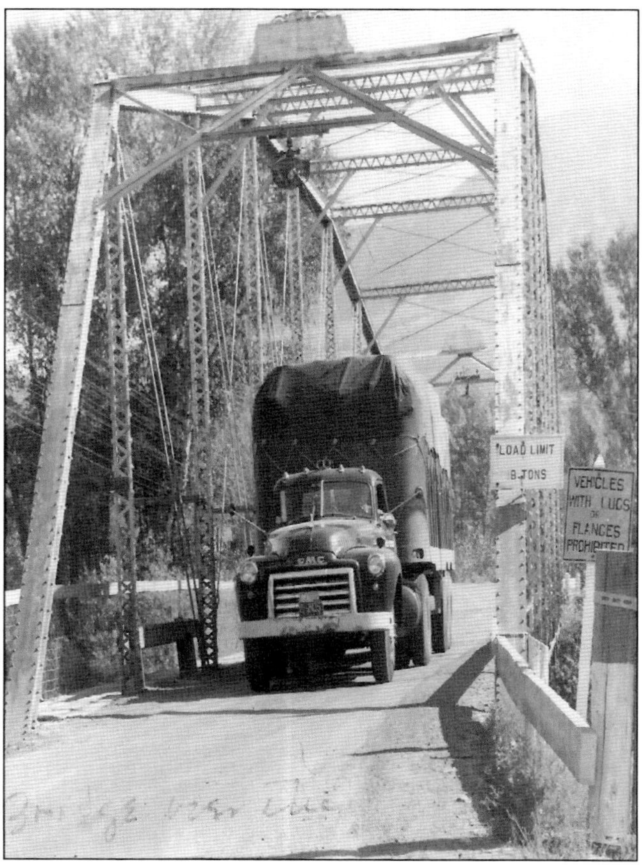

Cady's Pipeline. Building a canal was an arduous task. Picks and shovels were used, and many young boys lost their health from the work. The whole valley was honeycombed with ditches and canals. The most famous was the Fire Mountain Canal. Started in 1896 and taking five years to build, the 32-mile canal carried water all the way from Somerset to Paonia to Hotchkiss for thirsty fruit trees. (NFHS.)

Heddle's Bridge. Today, this 1912 bridge is the only one remaining of three girder bridges once in the Paonia area. When West Third Street Bridge washed out in 1907, a cable across the river with a basket transported people from bank to bank for a short time. Midway Elberta Bridge, washed out in 1912, was never rebuilt. In the summertime, fruit was moved across the river with a temporary bridge at the Elberta crossing connecting the orchards to the fruit. (NFHS.)

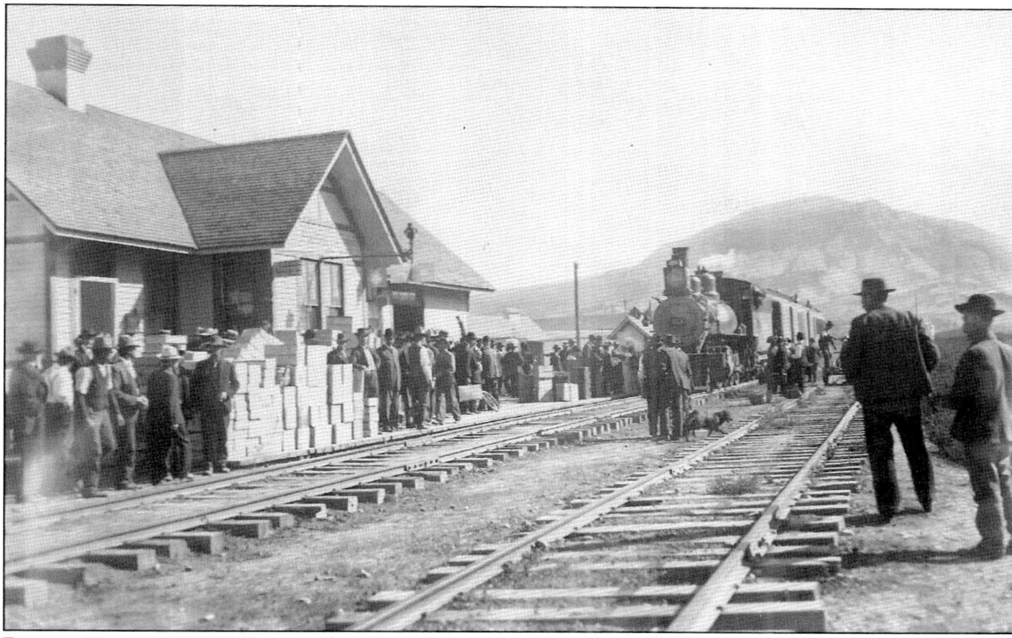

PAONIA DEPOT, 1908. Denver Rio Grande came to Paonia in 1902, providing a means to transport fruit. Until 1906, narrow-gauge cars had to be reloaded to broad-gauge cars at Delta. Previously, fruit was taken in wagons to Delta, the closest railhead. Passenger trains ran from Somerset to Delta in early morning, returning in the evening. Many fruit workers came by train to the harvest. (NFHS.)

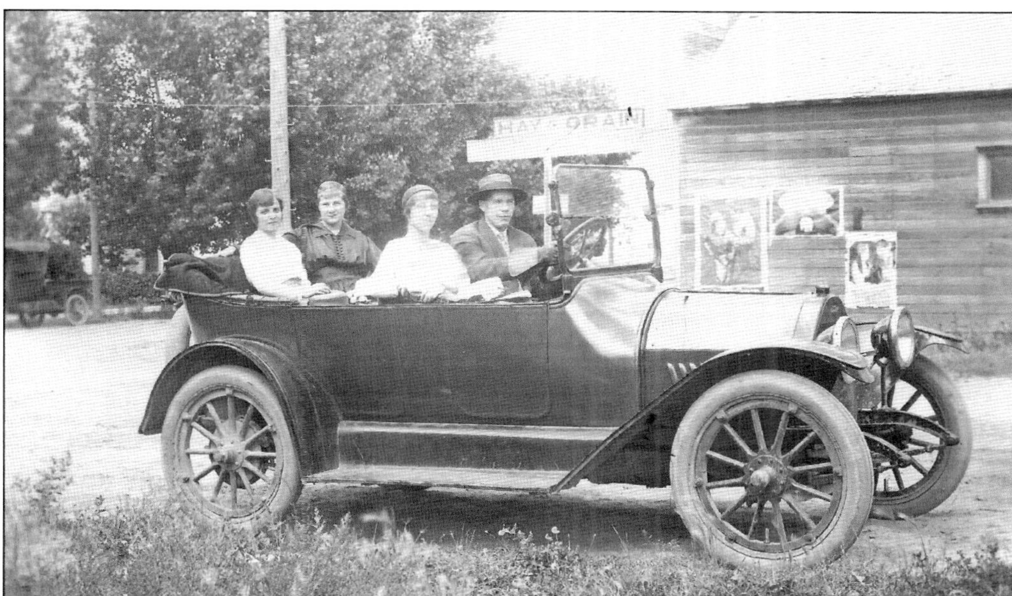

CAR, 1920S. The 1920s were the decade of the automobile. Even by 1912, six firms were selling cars. The trip by car from Paonia to Delta took two hours. Automobiles were bumping into things, going off the road, frightening horses, and forcing buggies to the ditch. One doctor preferred his buggy for house calls because of terrible road conditions. (NFHS.)

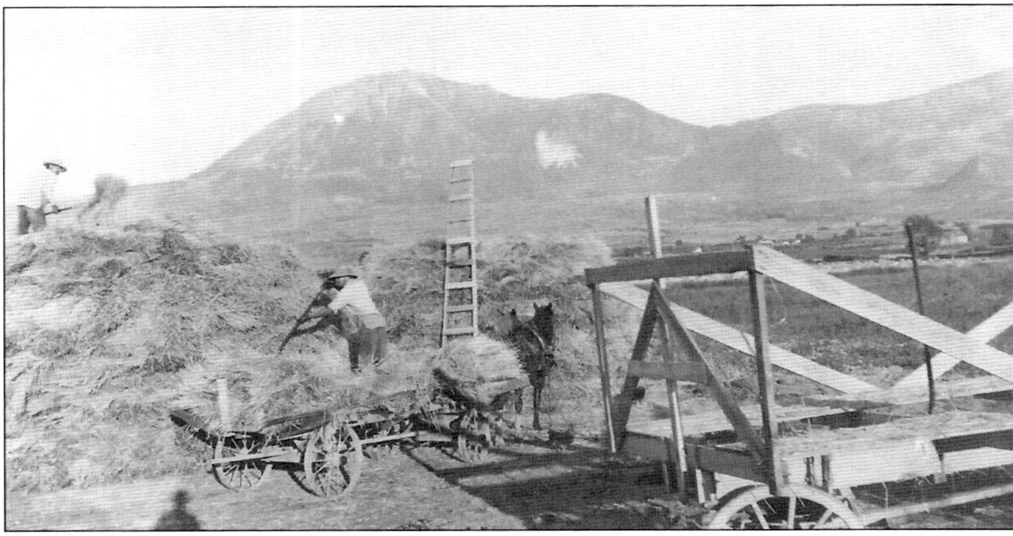

Chinn Land and Livestock Corporation. The ranch was a part of the Sam Angevine claim. In 1909, proprietors W.H. Garvin and E.W. Mouty announced they were only hiring white laborers for harvest even though Hotchkiss was employing Japanese. Besides fruit, the ranch had hot spring baths, cattle fed with ranch hay, and natural gas discovered at 1,800 feet. (Marilyn Bruce Tate.)

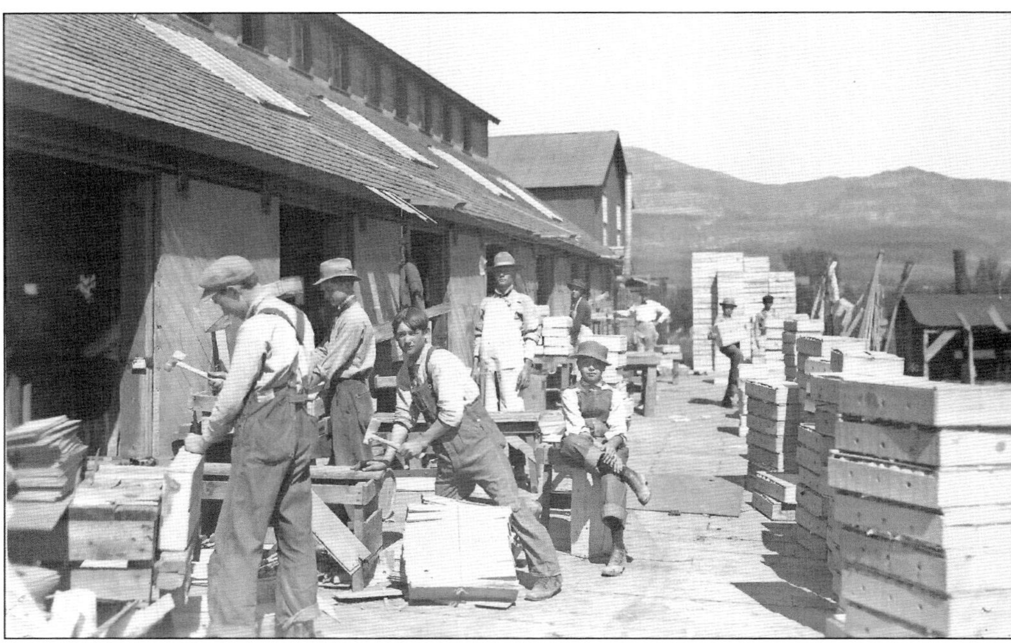

Association Nailers. This group is making boxes for the North Fork Fruit Growers Association. Boxes were also assembled at the Nelson Brothers Box Mill on Hubbard Creek and taken by wagon to Bowie to be loaded on a train bound for Paonia. After a fire at the box mill, the operation moved to Paonia in 1913. (NFHS.)

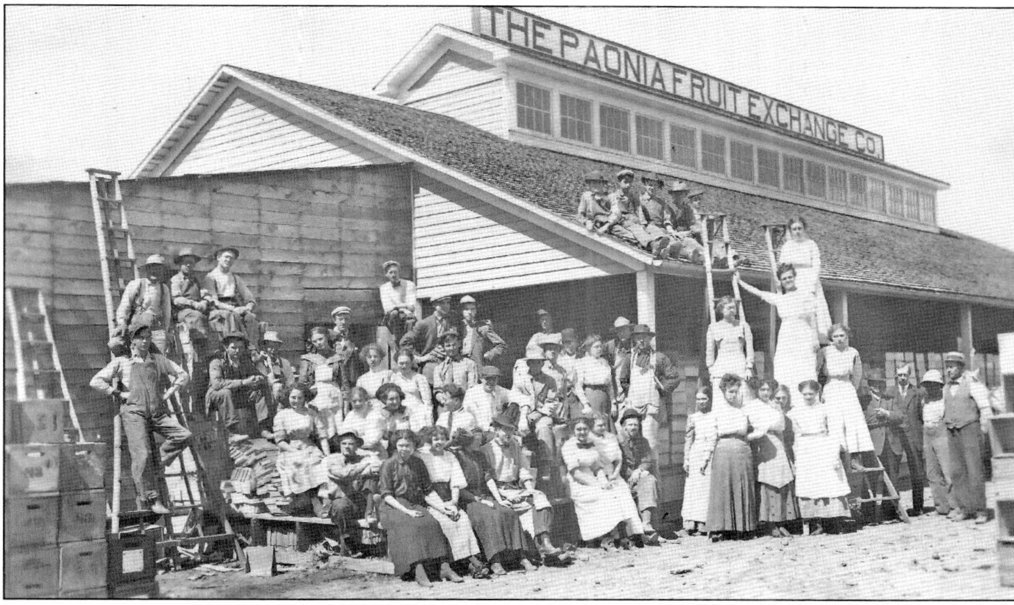

Paonia Fruit Exchange. This shed was built at Coburn switch. L.S. Cofield managed the packinghouse, cannery, and evaporator. Tragically, the businesses were sold out in 1916 because of two poor crop years. Cofield died of appendicitis in 1917 at age 40. (NFHS.)

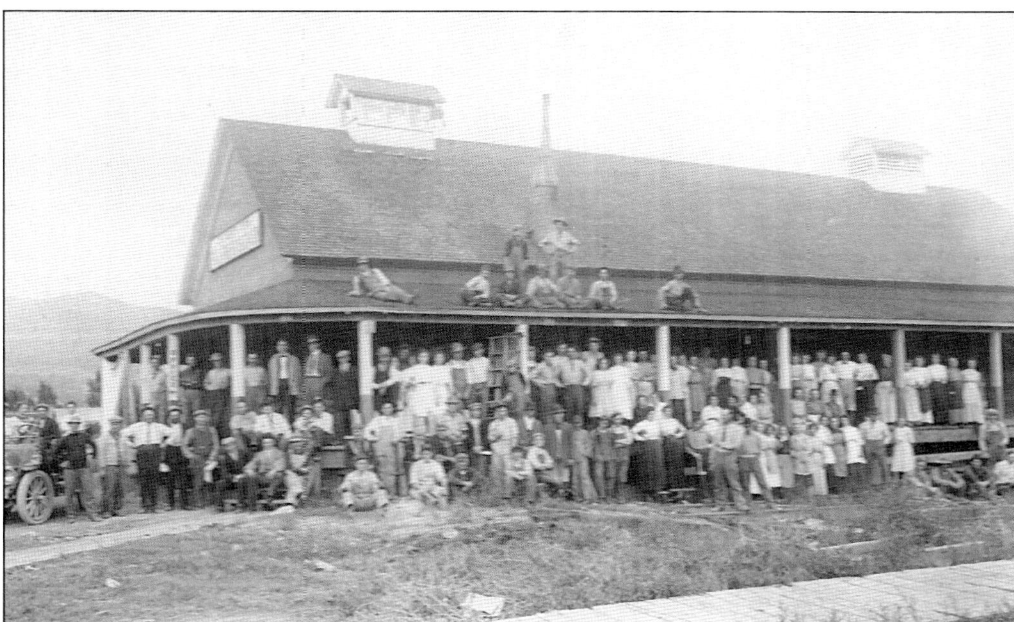

North Fork Fruit Growers Association. There were five North Fork Fruit Growers packing sheds in the area. The railroad switches were Roberts, Paonia, Elberta (Midway), Hotchkiss, and Coburn. This building remains in Paonia in 2012. From 1935 until 1967, it was Palmer and Company, managed by Harry Palmer's partner, Rea Sutliff. (NFHS.)

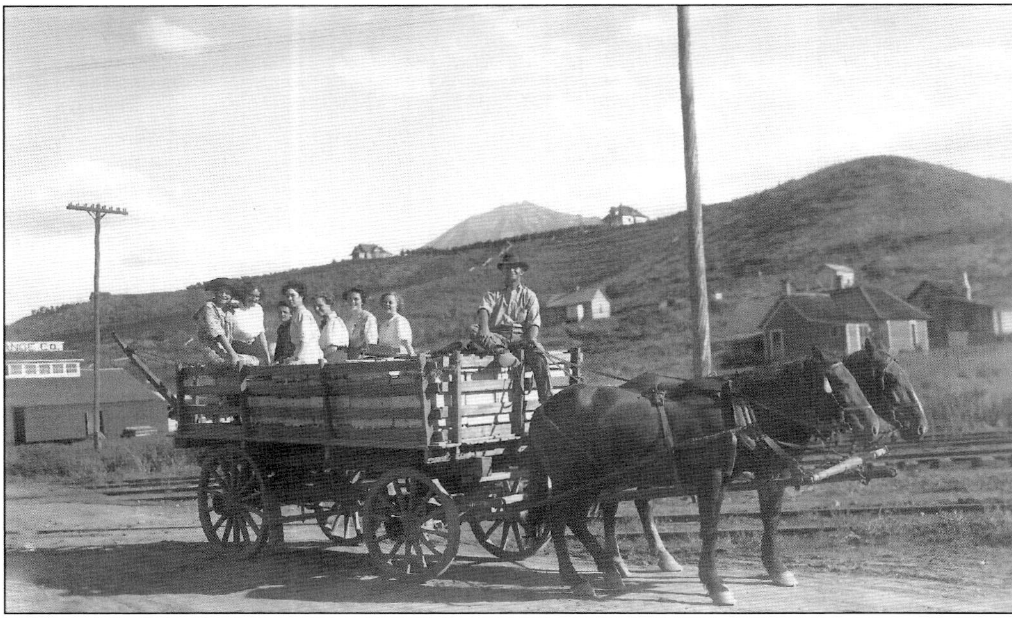

Union Fruit Company, 1911. A crew wagon is going to the Union Fruit Company pictured below. In 1913, some 24 carloads of peaches, 116 carloads of apples, and 27 carloads of bulk apples were shipped. In 1914, prices for fancy-grade apples were Jonathan, $1.21; Grimes Golden, $1.61; Rome Beauty, $1.22; and Winesap, $1.19. The newer, three-story 1917 co-op located at the end of Grand Avenue had an 84-foot north-facing front with railroad tracks to the south. It played a prominent role in fruit history. Gilbert Wilson's High Country Fruit was a more recent fruit house. Total shipments for all of Paonia in 1917 in number of carloads were 300 of apples, 400 of peaches, 14 of potatoes, 2 of apricots, 3 of prunes, 1 of onions, 1 of hay, 2 of oats, 2 of wool, and 19 of stock. (Both, NFHS.)

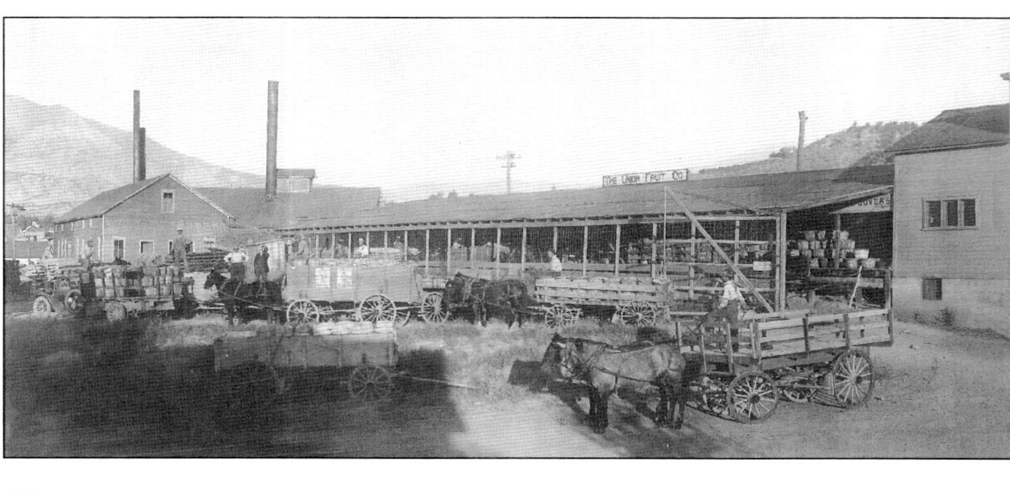

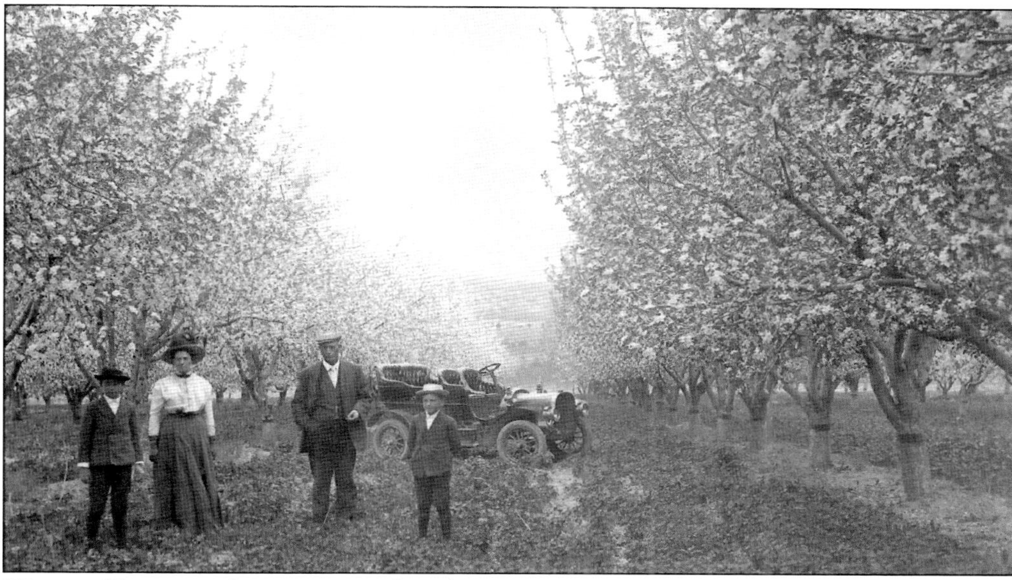

WELDON HAMMOND ORCHARD. North Fork Fruit Growers Association elected him 1907 director, 1909 treasurer, and 1910 president. Hammond, president of Fruit Exchange Bank, owned the first automobile in Paonia, a two-cylinder Rambler. Pictured with him are his children Floyd (right) and Harold and wife, Mittie. His fruit ranch was claimed originally by George Root. (NFHS.)

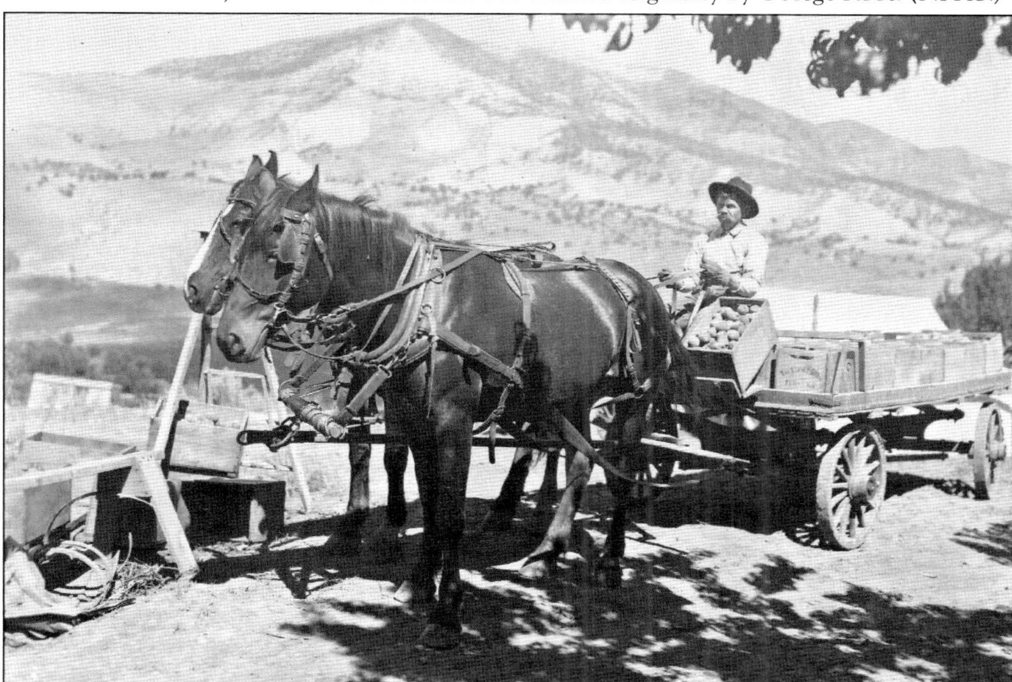

EXCELSIOR FRUIT RANCH WAGON, 1911. This ranch east of Paonia boasted one of the largest peach orchards. It was owned by brothers Charles and Frank Van Deren. The crop projected for 1912 was 45,000 boxes of peaches. Later, the Wades and Paonia Marketing were associated with this orchard. (NFHS.)

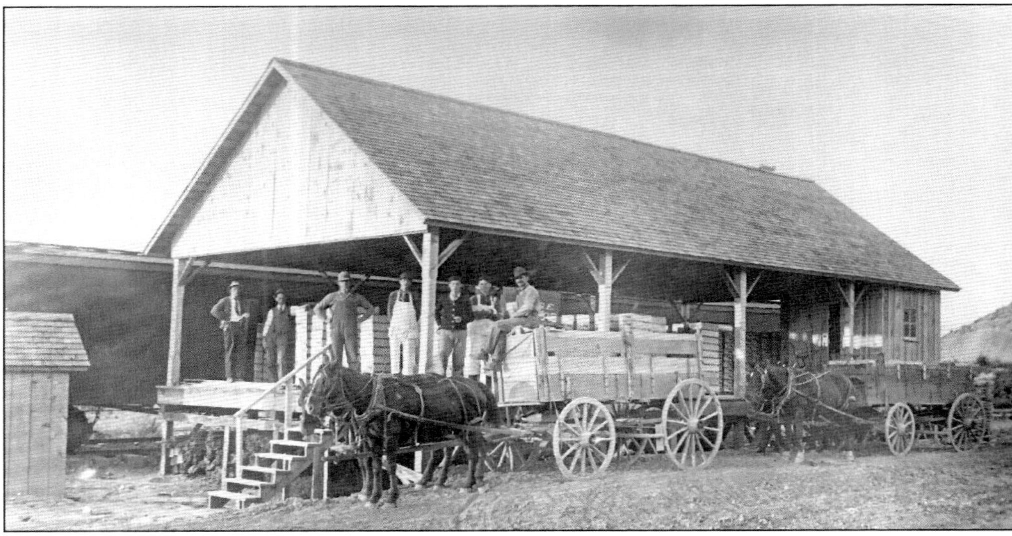

Bell Creek Dance Hall. Originally a fruit-loading dock, Bell Creek was a private dance club in the 1930s for families living on Stewart and Bone Mesa. Later, the club sponsored a public dance, but it continued to have private gatherings for its members. Referred to as the Saturday night "Hoorah" dance, the inside was supervised, but outside there was alcohol and wild behavior. (HCHS.)

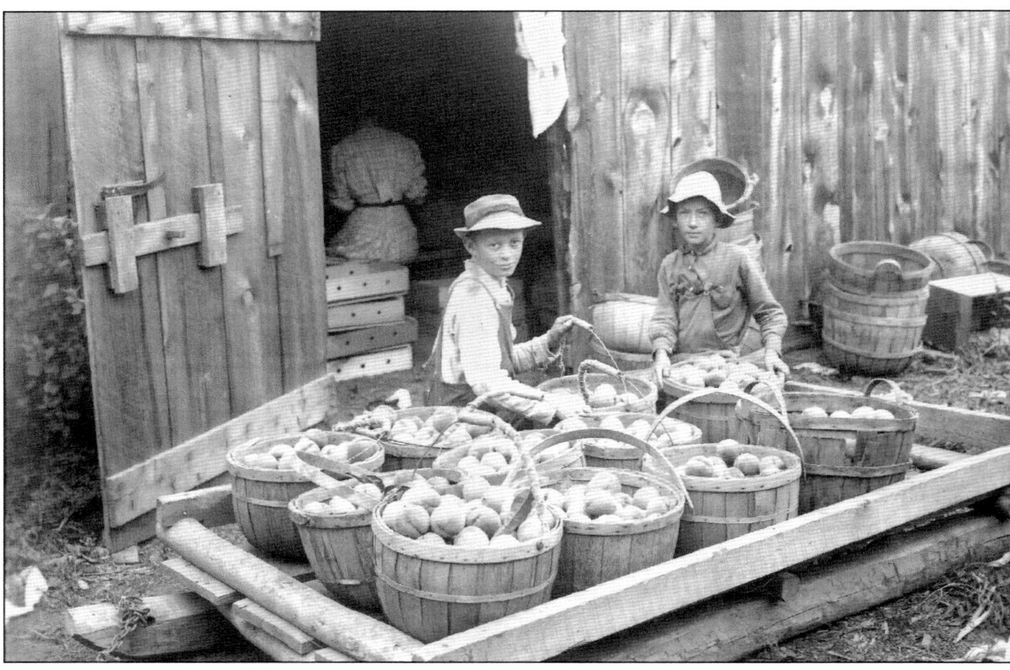

John Beezley Shed, 1911. Peaches are still available in 2012, just 130 years after fruit trees were introduced to the North Fork Valley. Imagine the pleasure of biting into these juicy Elberta peaches. The Beezley family continues to live in the North Fork Valley. Along with the many tourists visiting Paonia, they still enjoy Paonia fruit. (NFHS.)

Five

Bowie

The mountain valleys east of Paonia have produced coal for over a century. Dinosaur tracks in mines gives a hint that the seams of "black gold" (coal) have been waiting to be found for centuries. Millions of years ago, dinosaurs were roaming the North Fork Valley that consisted of rivers, swamps, lagoons, and the like. At the same time, dense forests deposited peat in fresh water, and this was the beginning of the coal formation. The first mine west of Bowie actually began on a small scale until the arrival of Alexander Bowie in 1906. Bowie was born in Scotland, where he began working in coal mines at the age of 10. After immigrating to Nova Scotia in 1866, he landed in Pennsylvania, studied engineering, and became the first mine inspector in Pennsylvania. He then began his trek west to New Mexico and then to Colorado.

He came to what became the Bowie area to supervise the growth of the new mine location. Bowie proved to be a successful businessman and public servant, having been in the New Mexico State Legislature and other organizations. Just as his dream of a perfect coal town was coming to reality, he died in 1917. But his family had the fortitude to carry on the company and town the way he had wanted.

Instead of a long, winding road to access the portal, a gravity tram was installed to transport coal and miners up and down the steep hillside. New cottages sprang up to accommodate the miners and their families. There were privately owned stores, a post office, a school, and neat cottages. As the automobile became popular and the roads improved, the miners began living in neighboring communities.

The railroad passed close by to pick up the coal that was not sold locally. The valley was dotted with varied orchards. Life was good in this little community even though at times the coal industry was not profitable.

The story of the Bowie family and coal mine will persevere, even though today the town has been torn down and the original mine has been sold. A few of the buildings have been utilized in the North Fork Valley, and the general manager's house was actually torn down piece by piece and reassembled at a new location.

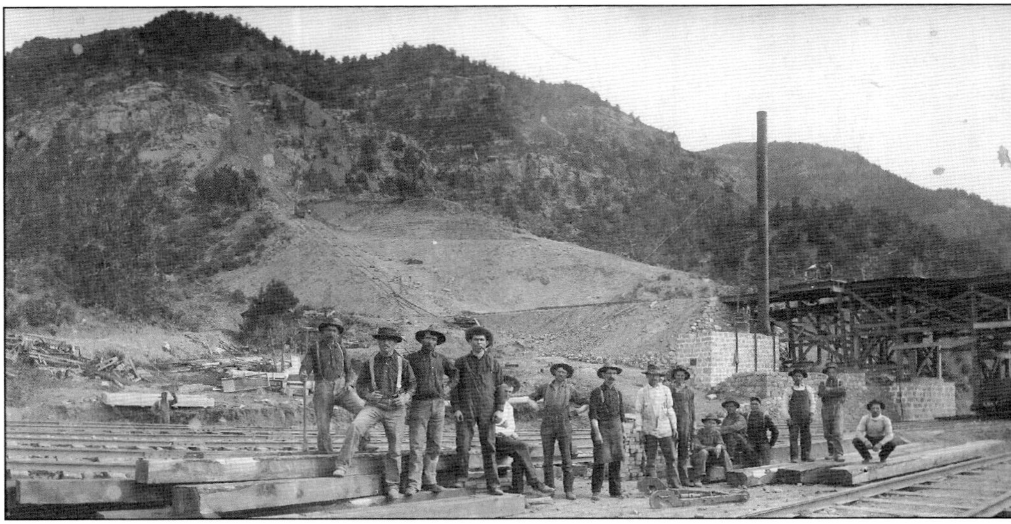

The Beginning. The Juanita Coal and Coke Company was incorporated in 1902 in Pueblo. C.M. Morris was elected president, and Dr. A.T. King was the vice president. The mine was six miles east of Paonia. Morris was the first general manager, followed by H.B. King. Harry Mallot was the first mine superintendent. Most stockholders were from Pueblo, and among them was Mahlon Thatcher. When Alexander Bowie was employed at Rockvale, Colorado, Thatcher met up with him. In 1906, Bowie was hired as general manager. A post office was named Bowie after the first two names, Reading and Juanita, were rejected. A new portal began, and the first coal was delivered to the tipple in 1907. Now, the railroad had coal to transport as well as the booming fruit crops in the North Fork Valley. (Both, Bowie Collection.)

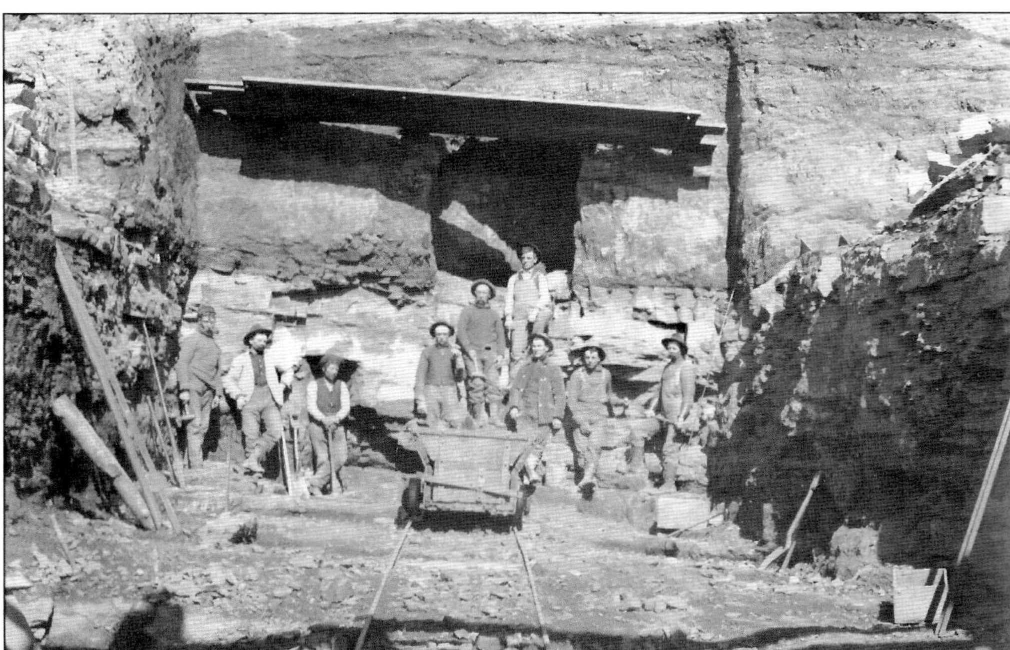

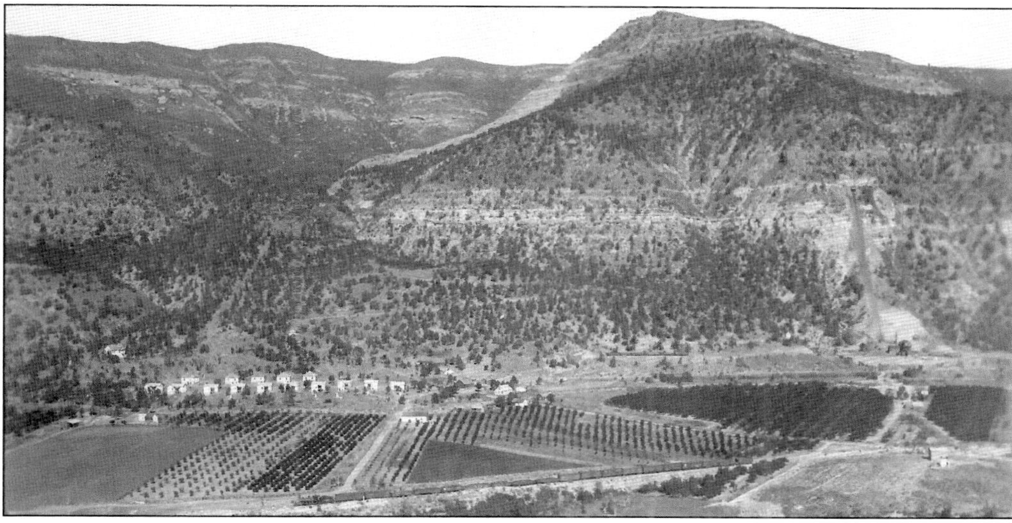

THE TOWN. Boardinghouses, bunkhouses, an office (below), and the mine manager's home were built. Employees could live in the cottage houses also being constructed. The quaint coal town was like no other community; Bowie did not allow a company store or a saloon. In 1913, three new cottages with six rooms, one cottage with four rooms, four cottages with three rooms, and a brick house for the mine owners were constructed. Independent Lumber supplied the building materials. By 1915, all houses had electric power provided by a mine generator. The Bowie mine paid the miners with $2 bills to illustrate how much money was being poured into the North Fork economy. A large amount was spent in Paonia. (Both, Bowie Collection.)

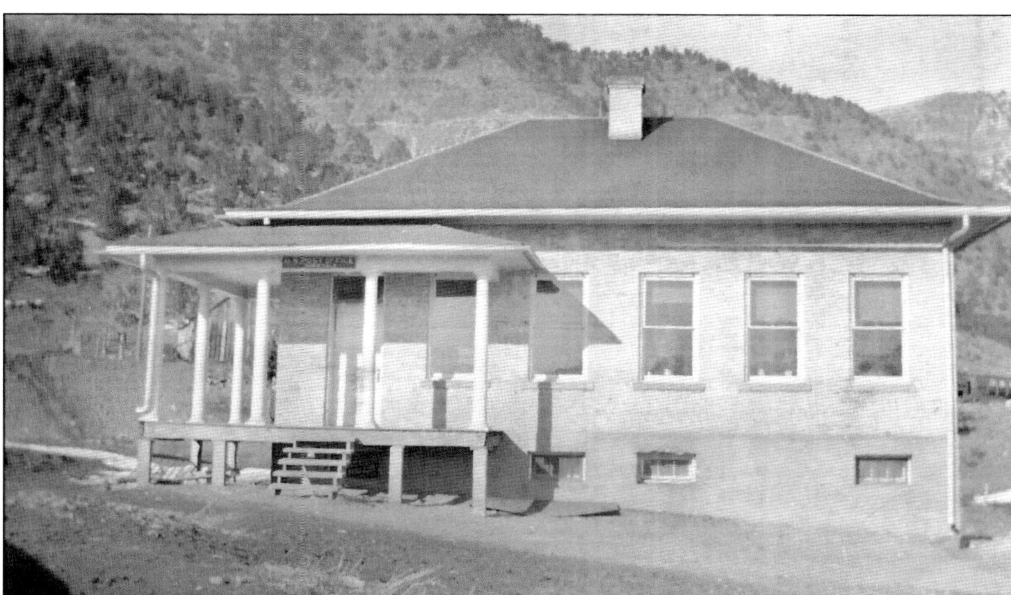

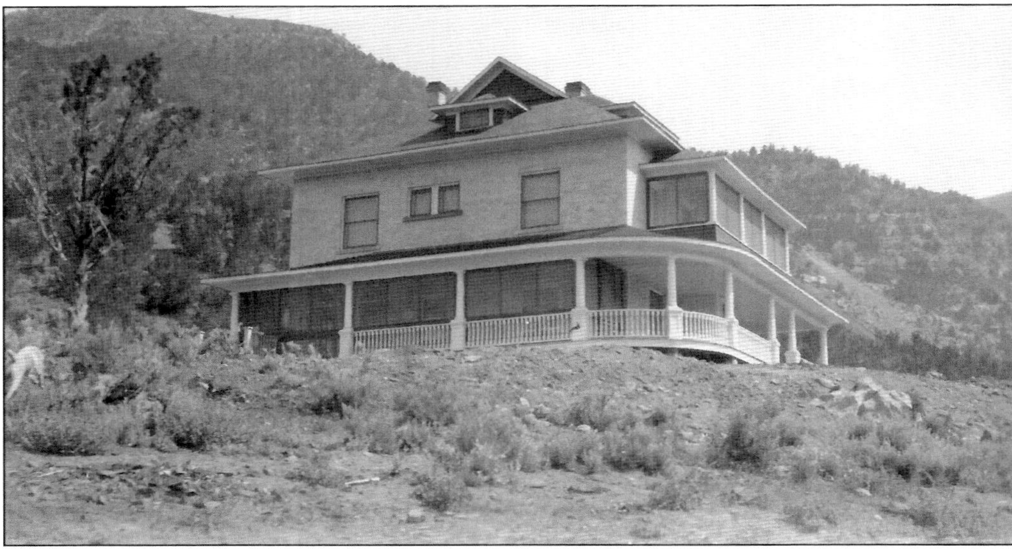

The General Manager's House. This house looks out over the rest of the town and the valley below. It was three stories tall and had 10 large rooms and 2 baths. Three of Bowie's sons—John, Alex, and William—lived in ordinary miner's houses (below). Wallace, who never married, lived in the big house. When the mine was sold to Coors in 1974, most of the buildings were torn down. Steve and Lisa West had fallen in love with this house and wanted to move it to their property, which was not possible. So they tore it down, labeling every single piece as they took it apart, and now the house sits on Stewart Mesa. It took them over seven months to tear down, and they stored it all in a log house. (Both, Bowie Collection.)

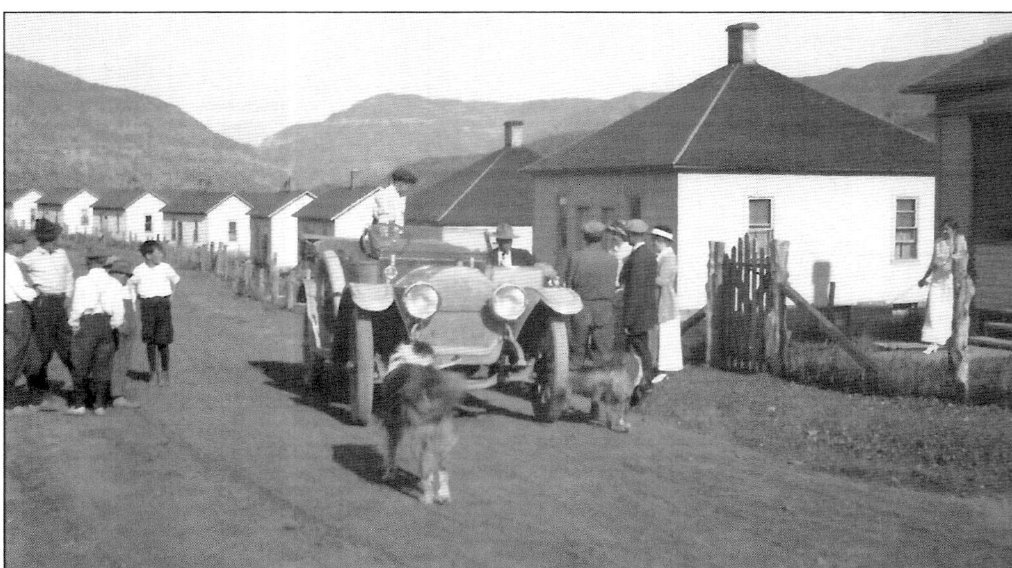

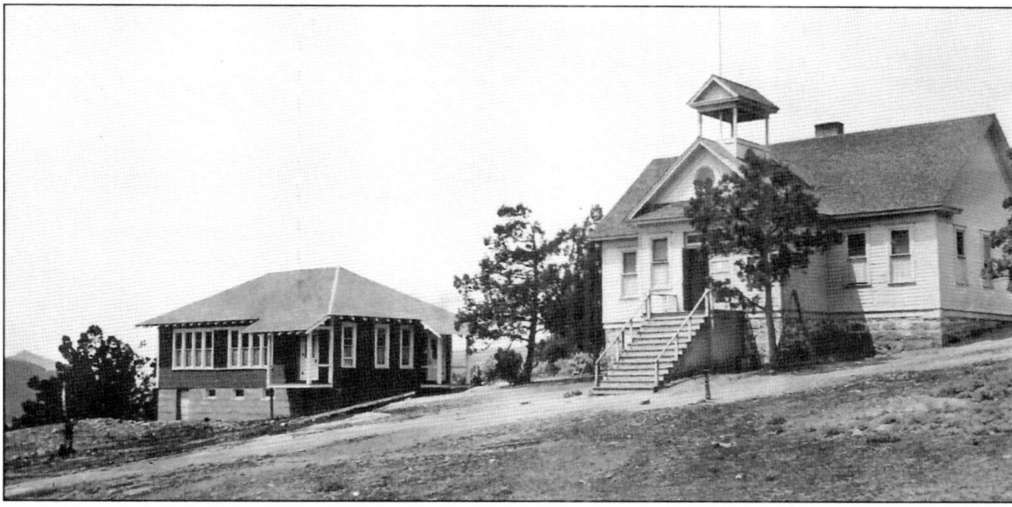

Bowie School. Built in 1907, the first school (right) was a one-room cabin for all eight grades. In 1914, the school had an enrollment of 69. The second school (left) was built in 1920 to accommodate the higher grades. The final class was in the 1950 school year, when the school district was consolidated. The building was moved to Paonia to become part of the museum complex. (Bowie Collection.)

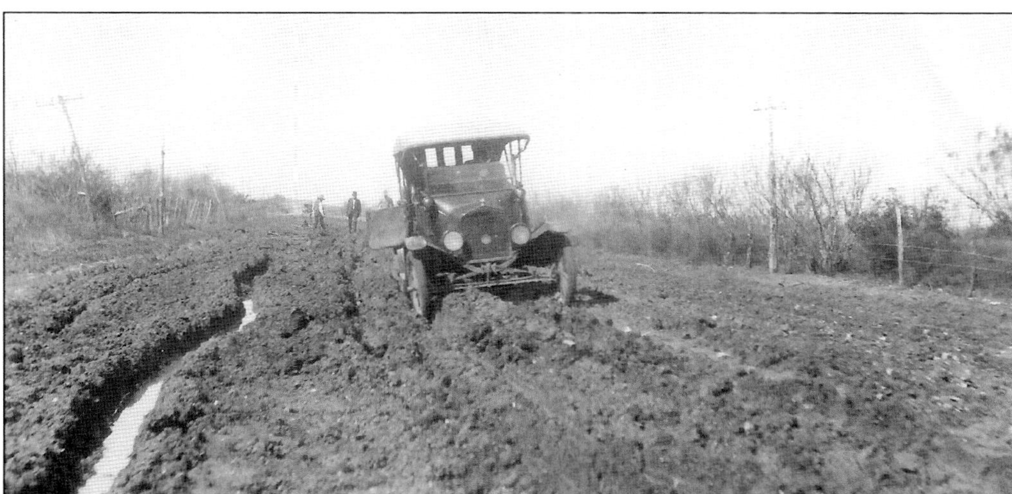

Driving to Bowie. One problem about the road to Bowie in 1914 was that the autos had to back up on turns to let wagons by. Six men and teams were sent to make turnouts as requested by Alex Bowie, who owned a car. In 1917, the road to Bowie was washed out because of a break in the Fire Mountain Canal. (Bowie Collection.)

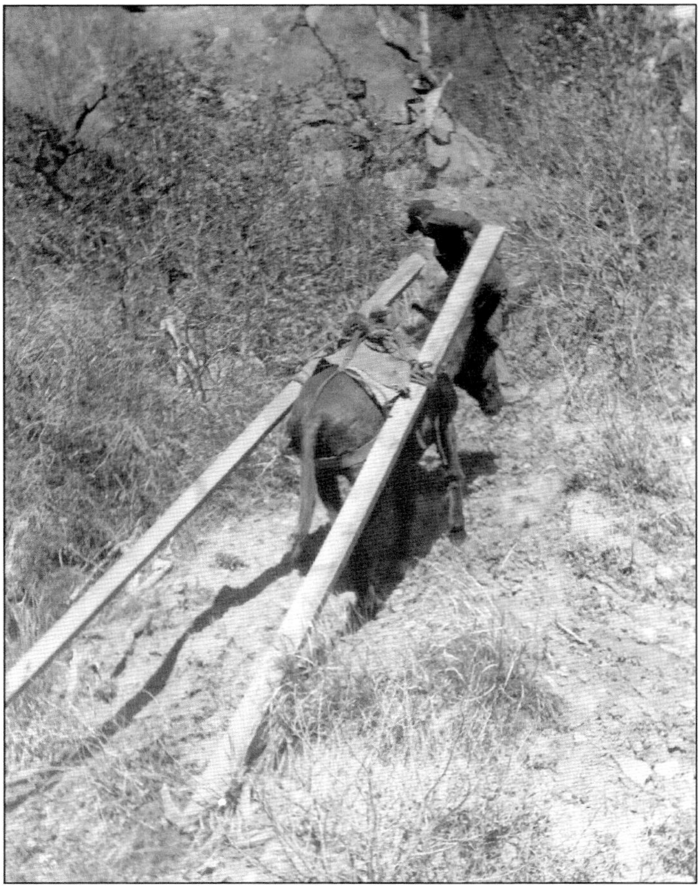

The Mules. Mules played an important role in the Bowie mine history. They were used inside and out. Hauling lumber up the hill was not unusual for them. They were used in all types of ways, such as pulling a boxcar, with young lads watching. At Bowie, they were not allowed to spend the whole time in the mine, as was the case at other mines. If that happened, the mules usually were blind when they came out, as they would not be accustomed to the light. They had weekends off and a nice stall area to rest. One day, Elizabeth Bowie was missing some scissors and found that her husband was trimming the mules' tails. With new mining equipment appearing, the day came when they were not used anymore and retired. (Both, Bowie Collection.)

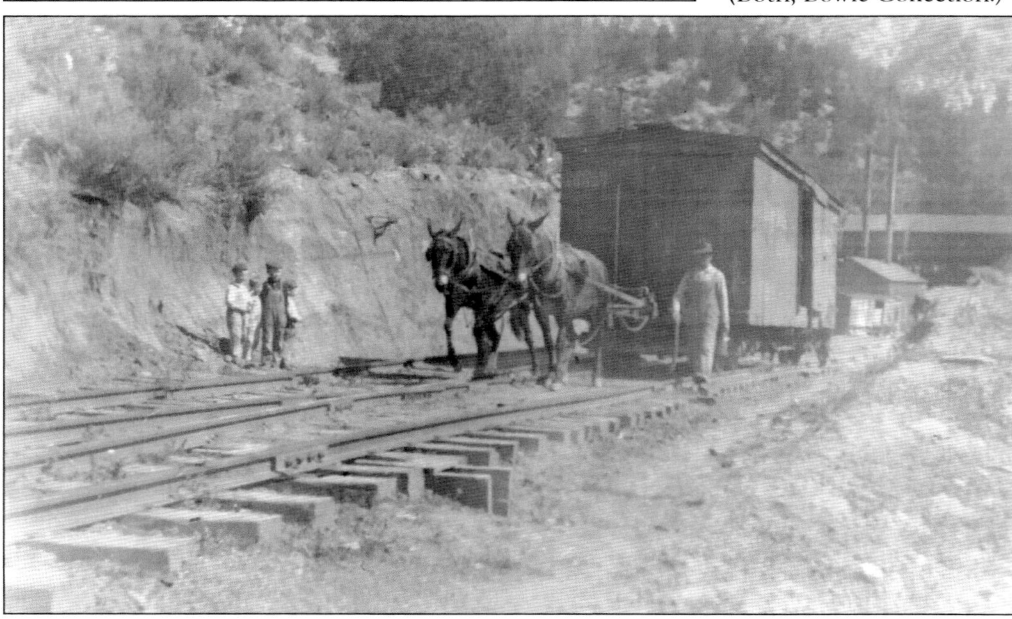

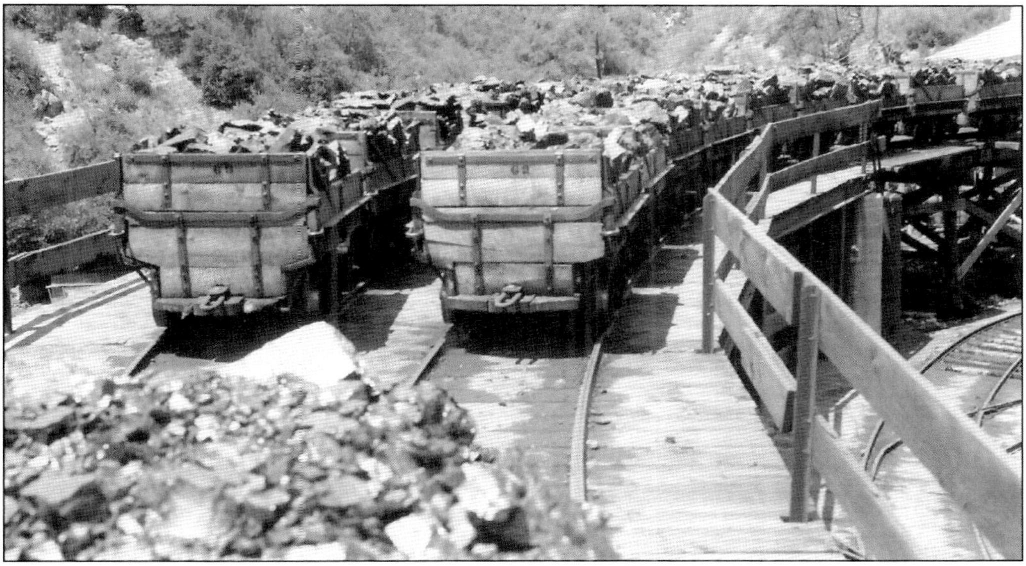

The Mine Cars. The cars that transported coal from the mine were higher on the front end so coal would not spill out going down the incline. As the car approached the bottom, coal was weighed at the tipple, dumped into a storage hopper, screened, and loaded into railroad cars. Mine cars were also used to haul the miners up to the mine. Going down, they utilized a device called a boat, consisting of wood with one side grooved the full length to fit on the rail, a metal plate curved up on the front, and a rubber air hose squeezed on the back for a brake. The miner would sit cross-legged and use his left hand to squeeze the brake and his right hand to hold a piece of coal for balance. (Both, Bowie Collection.)

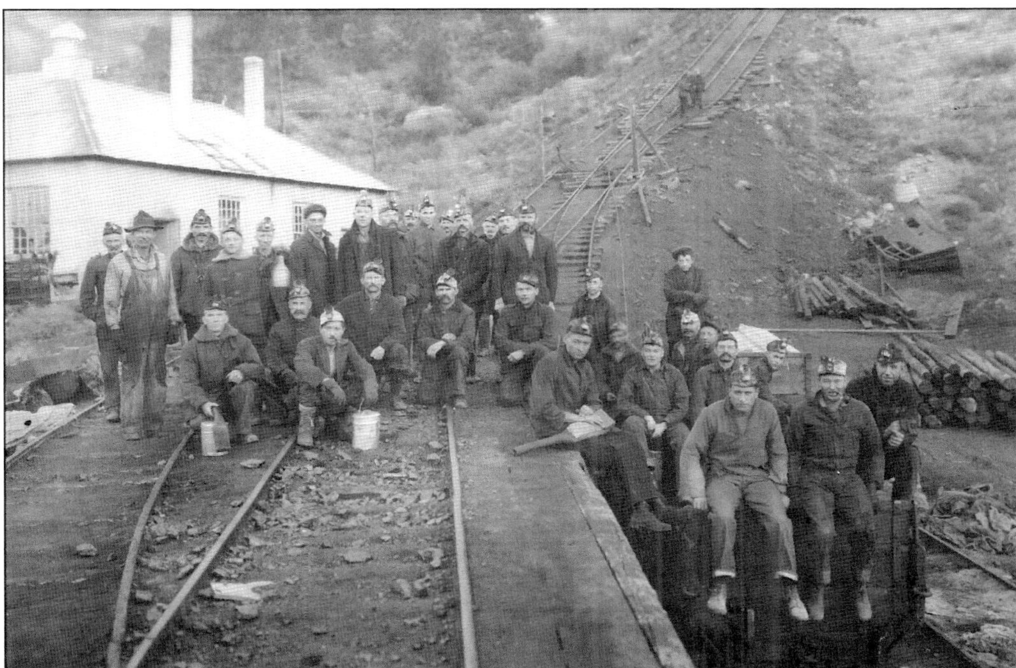

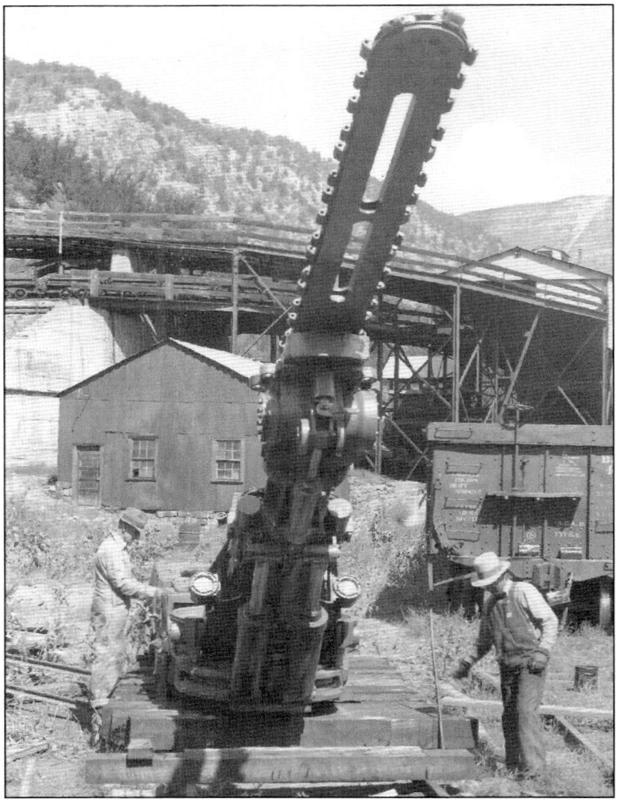

Cutter Arrives. In 1937, mining at Bowie would change forever the day the Seven A.U. Sullivan hydraulic cutting machine came to town by rail. After it was unloaded, the slow trek up the hill began. The men who had used the old methods of mining would remember how they mined coal. They worked in pairs and used a pick to undercut an entry. Holes were then drilled by hand. Black powder cartridges were made up, and one cartridge was placed in the hole and tamped. Then a rod would be forced in, and when pulled out, a fuse would be added to the charge. When all holes were loaded, the fuses were lit. Then, the loose coal (extracted by the blast) was shoveled into mine cars and sent outside. (Both, Bowie Collection.)

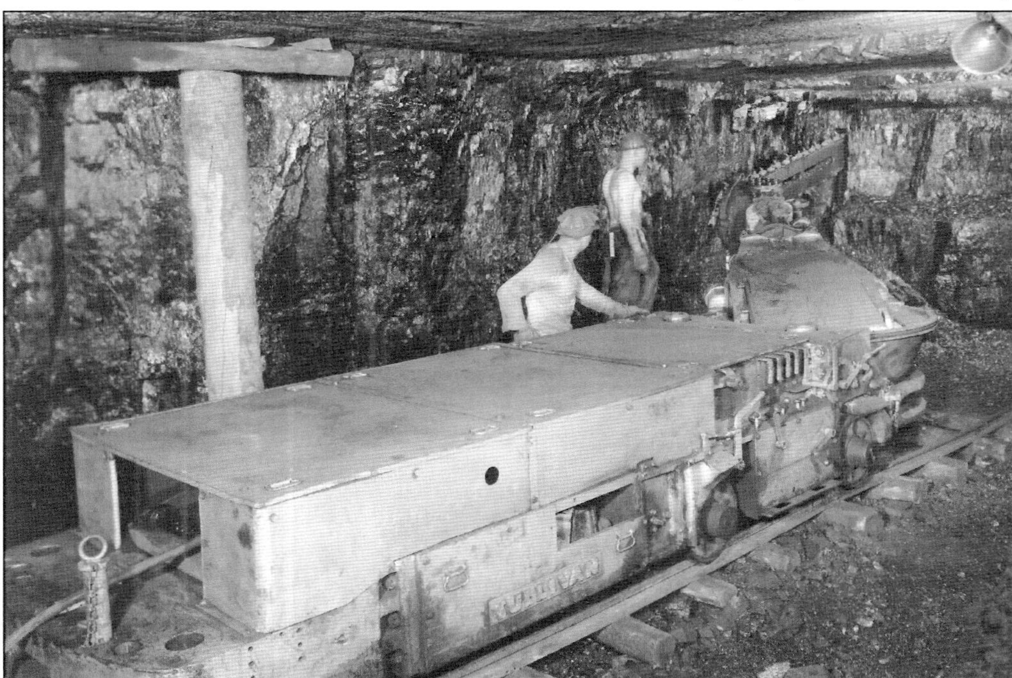

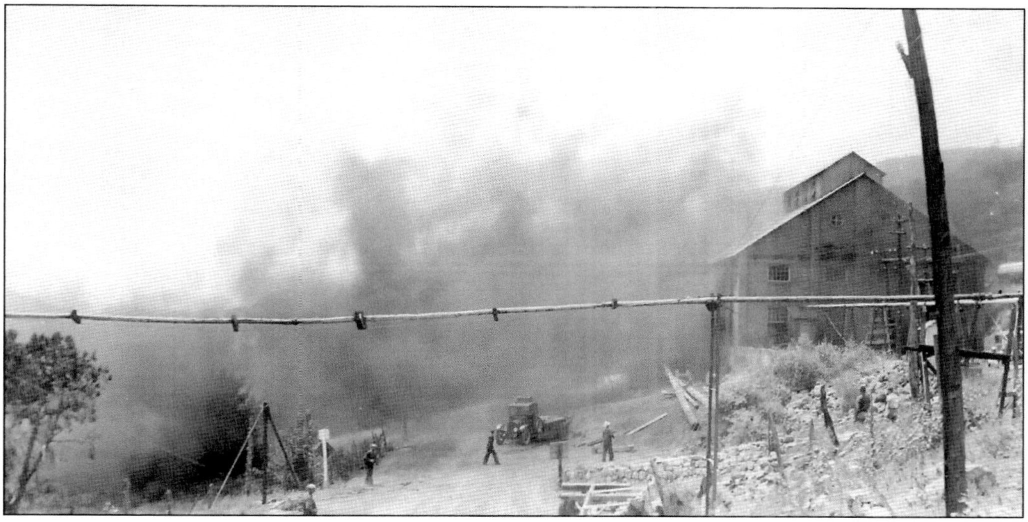

Dropped Stack. Noticing that the stack was rusting out at the bottom, mine owners made the decision to replace it. The old one had to be torn down first. This was done much like cutting down a tree, with guy ropes or wires. Once the dust cloud cleared, people came to examine the fallen stack. The children climbed on it and walked around like gymnasts trying to balance themselves. A new stack was built, section by section, a couple of days later. A winch was used until all sections were pieced together and became one. No one was hurt during the process. (Both, Bowie Collection.)

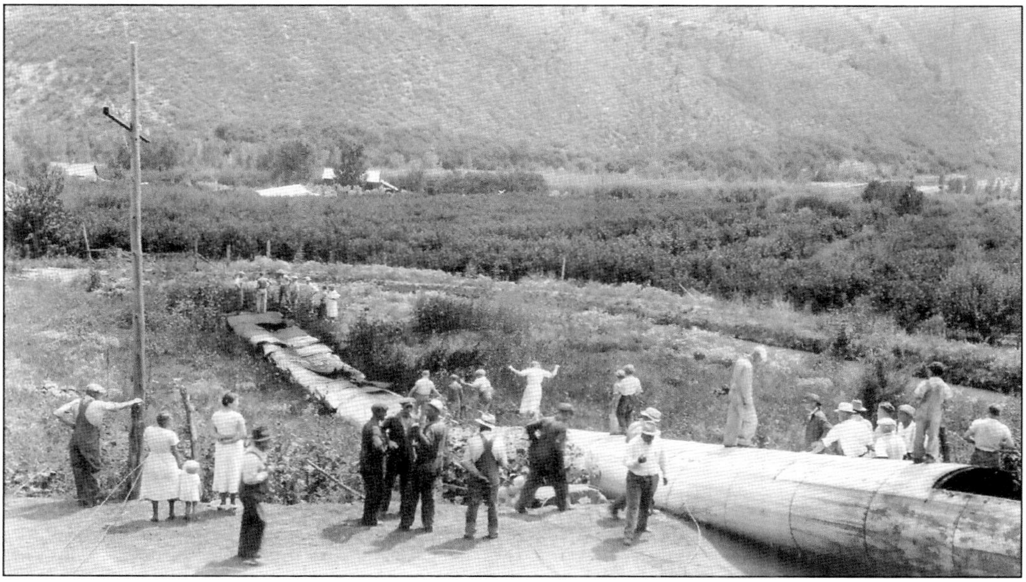

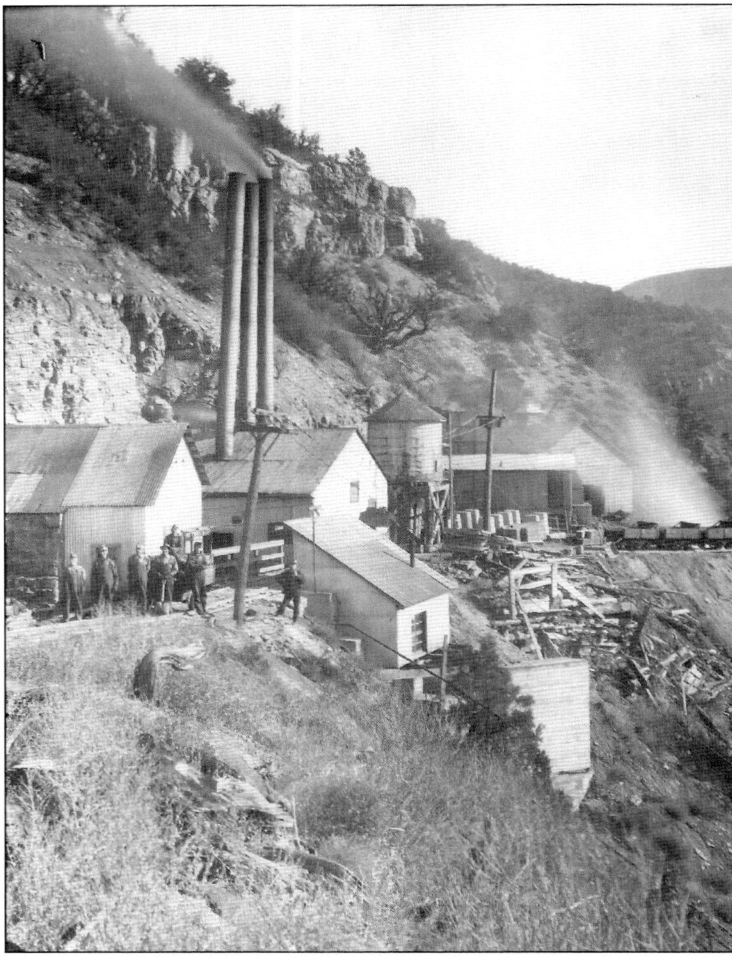

Equipment at the Mine. The tram used to run by a cable system, with each cable going back into the mine attached to a drum. Controlled by a wheelman at the pilothouse, one cable was unwinding as the cars descended, and the winding cable was used as the cars came up. In 1909, a steam-powered hoist was installed to pull loaded cars out of steep areas of the mine that the mules could not handle. Ventilation was provided by a furnace and stack. In 1911, a steam-powered fan was installed. In 1915, there was a generating plant built, but it was replaced by a power plant in 1922. And finally, in 1928, a new steel tipple was built to replace the old one. (Both, Bowie Collection.)

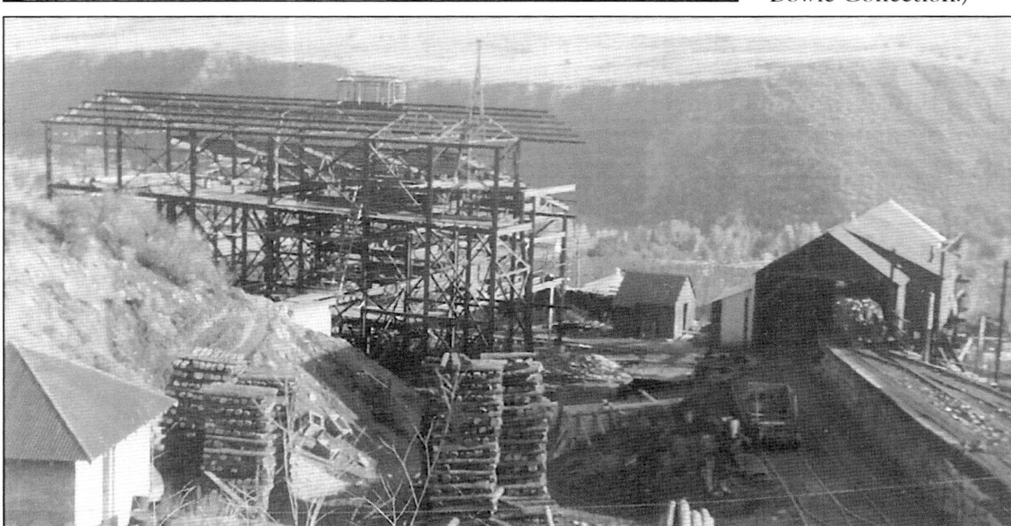

Six

Somerset and Nearby Mines

Settlers to the North Fork placed their hope in fruit. Little did they know that coal would be the driving economic force in later years. There were many mines near Somerset. Some were Bear, Oliver, and Hawk's Nest.

Somerset, named after Somersetshire, England, would play a major role in the development of "black gold" (coal). Early Somerset was settled when miners from Crested Butte came by an old Indian trail to the area. Even today, Somerset residents have close ties to relatives in Crested Butte. Geologist Ira. Q. Sanborn discovered a vein of coal in 1883 near present Somerset. During the Panic of 1893, Sanborn had to abandon his claim. Ed Hanson accumulated a number of claims around Somerset that he sold to Utah Fuel Company.

Of greatest importance was the arrival of the narrow-gauge Denver & Rio Grande Railroad in 1902. That same year, Utah Fuel opened a portal, shipping out its first commercial coal New Year's Day, 1903.

In 1904, miners were paid $6.30 for a 10-hour shift. Their pay was in gold or silver. Seventy to 80 men produced 450 tons of coal a day. As Somerset grew, houses replaced tents. The company houses were four-sided, boxlike structures. One of the first buildings was a saloon with a community center on the second story. Added to the mix were a company store, a boardinghouse (provided by the mine for young, single men), a schoolhouse, and, later, a hospital, in 1913.

In 1910, the population was estimated at 600, with 85 company houses. The miners came from many places. Some languages listed in the 1910 census are Finnish, Greek, Italian, Slovak, English, French, German, and Polish. Although Somerset was a melting pot, residents got along remarkably well in a close-knit and caring town. The 10-hour days in the mine were grueling, but Somerset was known for its hospitality, including popular polka dances.

Economic times in 1915 were difficult. Only 30 tons of coal a day—half the normal output—were produced by 206 miners. Many miners farmed when the mine was not working. From 1902 until the present, good and bad times in the North Fork Valley were tied the economic ups and downs of the energy industry.

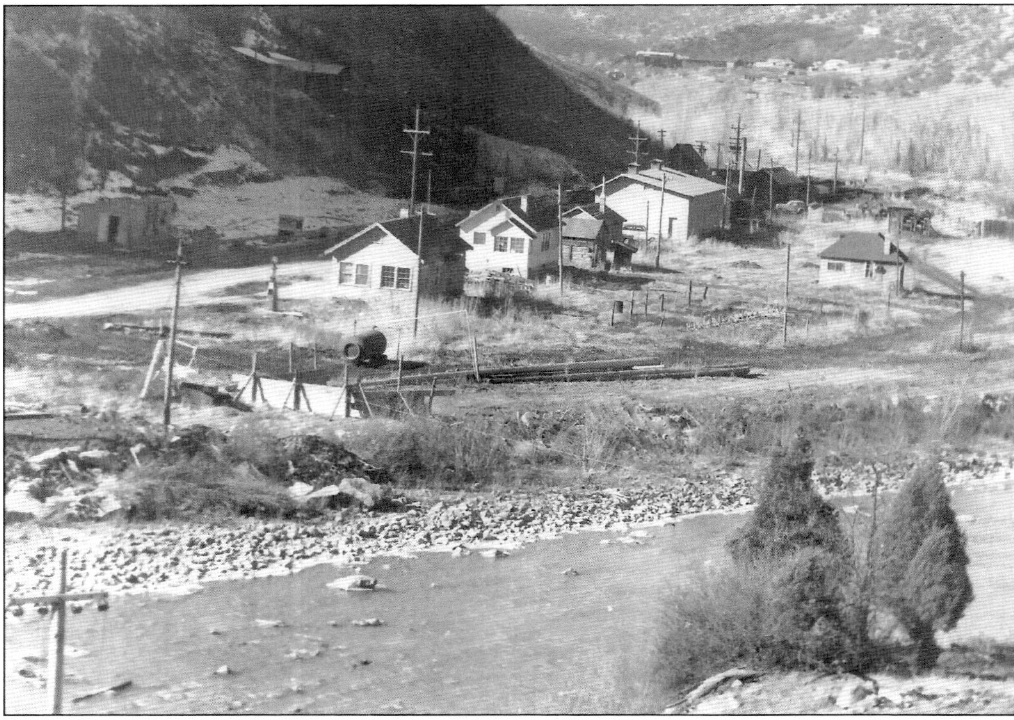

Bear Coal Mine. Tony Bear and Virginia Marta met in Bowie and were married in 1914. The coal story begins after they purchased 160 acres near Somerset. In 1935, they bought their first permit to mine coal in Colorado for $50. A survey located the mine and underground works. After World War II, there was a decline in the coal market, especially with the switch in domestic use from coal to natural gas. When Tony died in 1959, Virginia and sons Charles, William, and James continued to operate the mine. In 1970, Bear Coal Company sold the property to Atlantic Richfield, which operated the mine in 1981. The Bears purchased the Clark Mine west of the original mine and continued to mine coal. Bill Bear Sr. and sons operated that mine until 1996. (Both, Bill and Terrie Bear.)

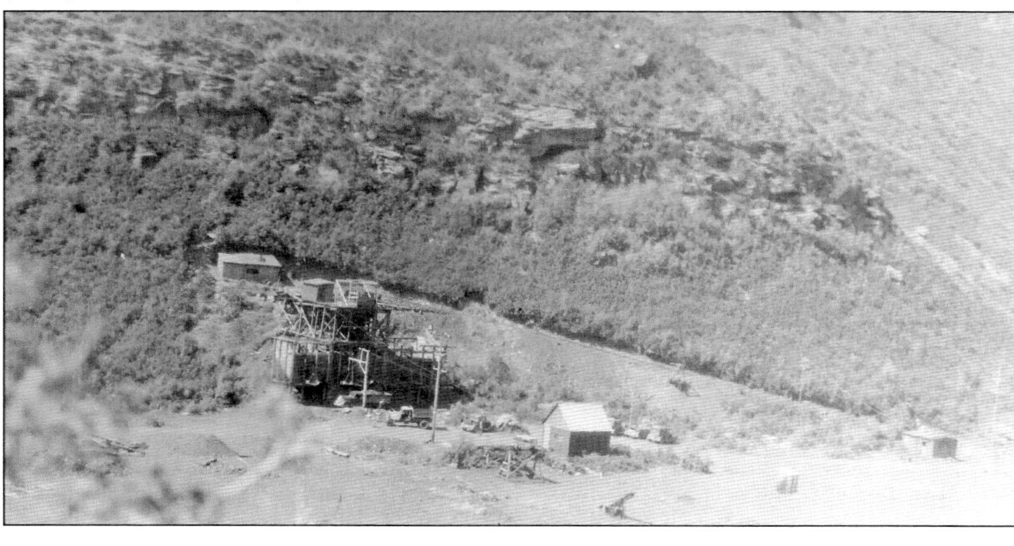

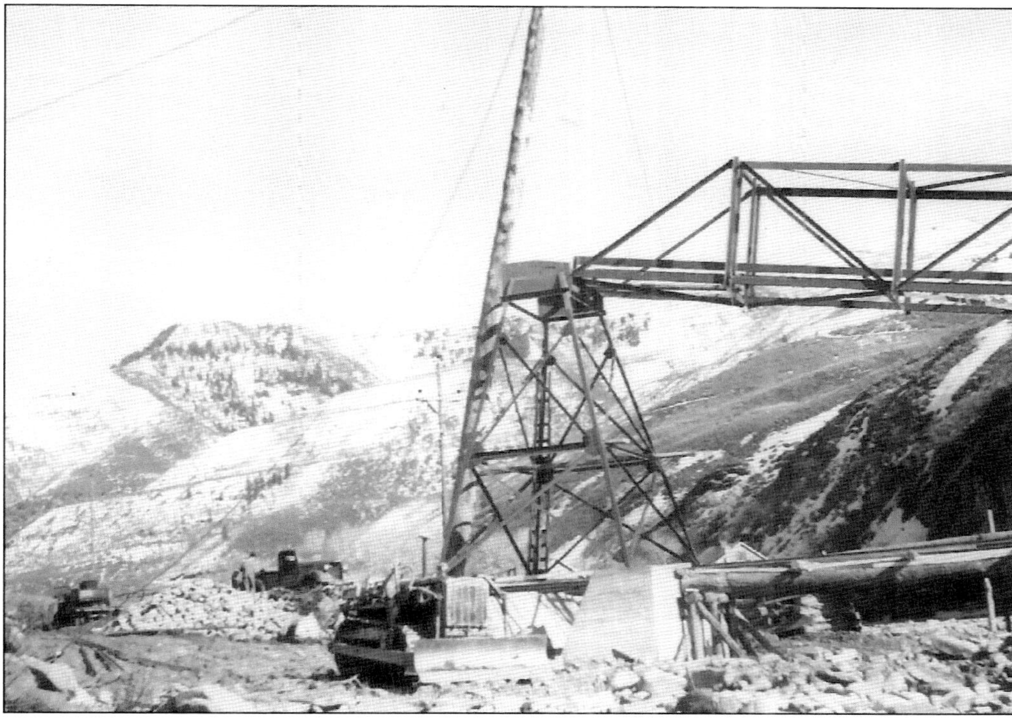

Bear Coal Mine Equipment and Structures. In 1933, Tony Bear lost his job at Somerset. He and Virginia searched for coal on their property for their own use. They discovered a seam of coal that was mined with a pick, shovel, and wheelbarrow. The Bears were able to mine coal for neighbors also. Later, the mining equipment consisted of a mine car, a mule, and some used mine rail. As the small venture turned into a family business, the equipment had to be updated. In 1961, a complete unit of conventional equipment was purchased. In 1963, a continuous miner replaced the conventional equipment. Above is a conveyor dump station to the tipple crossing the North Fork River in 1940s. Below is a completed structure for the conveyor. (Both, Bill and Terrie Bear.)

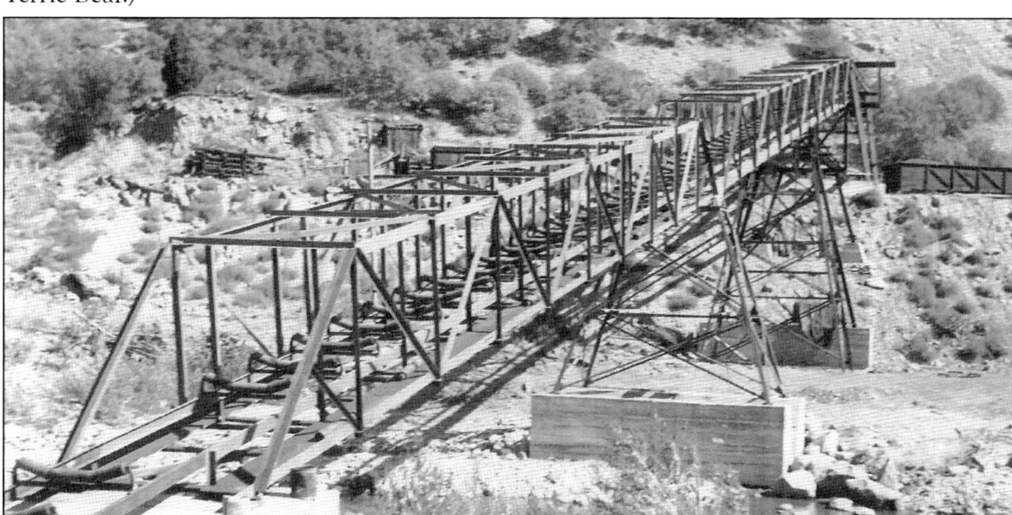

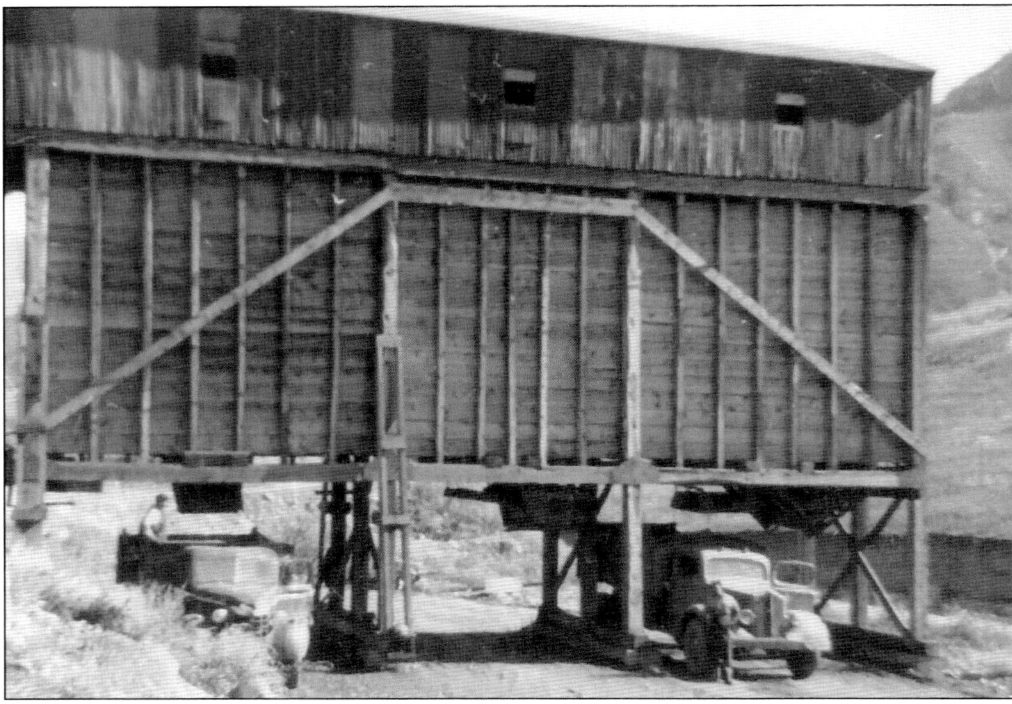

Hawk's Nest Tipple, 1947. In 1903, Clement Audin Sr. (1881–1957) immigrated to the United States from Belgium. His highest wage, after 12 years in a Belgium mine, was 70¢ a day. He began mining on his property in 1932, first subleasing the mine popularly called Hawk's Nest and later, in 1938, leasing it directly. In 1943, he became superintendent of Champion Coal Mining Company (Hawk's Nest). Pictured below, from left to right, are Audin's sons Abel Audin, Ralph Audin, and Clement Audin Jr. and Alvin Axelson (clerk). (Both, Ralph Audin Jr.)

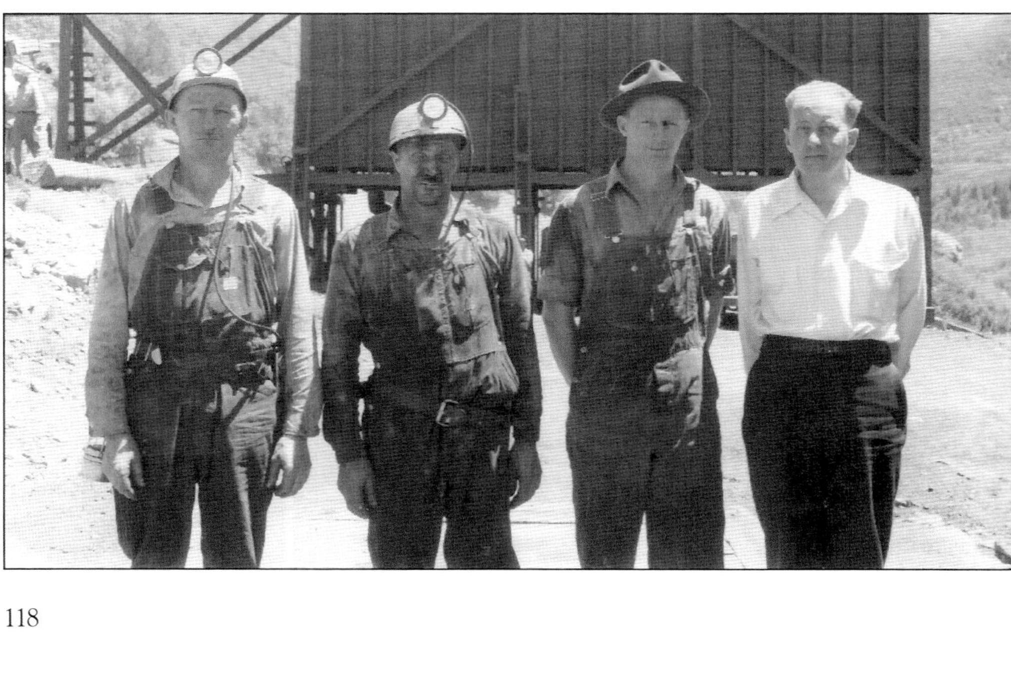

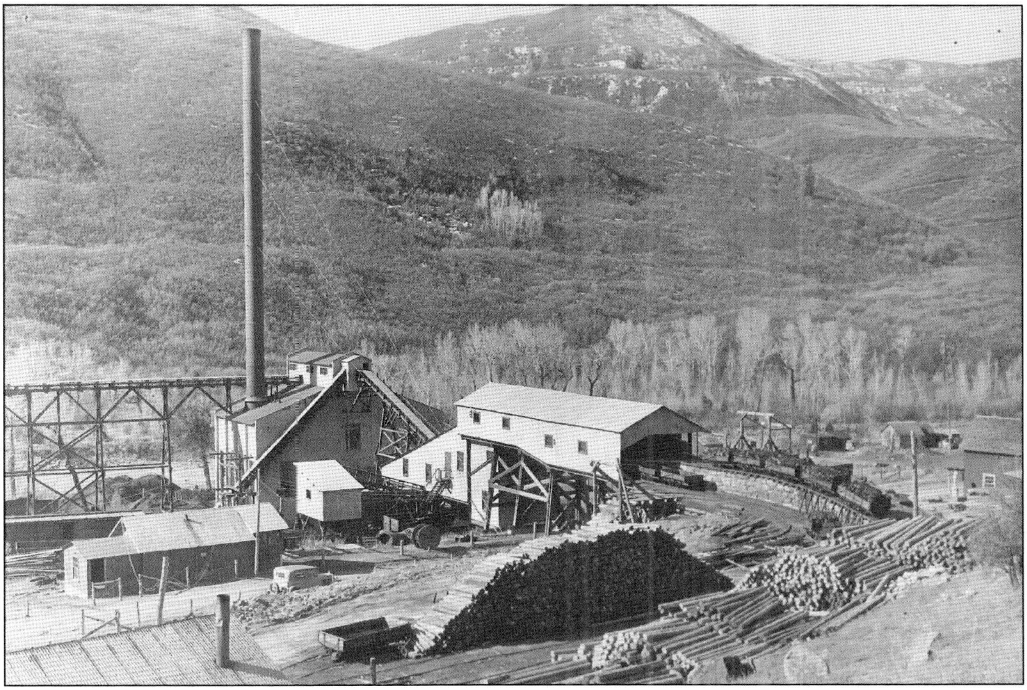

Oliver Mine. The mine began in 1926 on the north side of the river, 12 miles above Paonia. Coal was marketed under the brand name Red Glow. General manager Charles Oliver lived in Paonia. When Charles died in 1927, stepson Clinton Oliver (1884–1934) became manager. The mine supplied coal from the tipple to the 1930 Oliver Power Plant, later Western Colorado Power. Also, coal was hauled to Somerset for loading on the train; but in 1928 a connecting railway was built, referred to as the Oliver Short Line. After Clinton Oliver's death, mine operations were continued by Ronald and Edwin Oliver. In 1949, the mine was sold to Calumet Fuel. (Above, NFHS; below, Bowie Collection.)

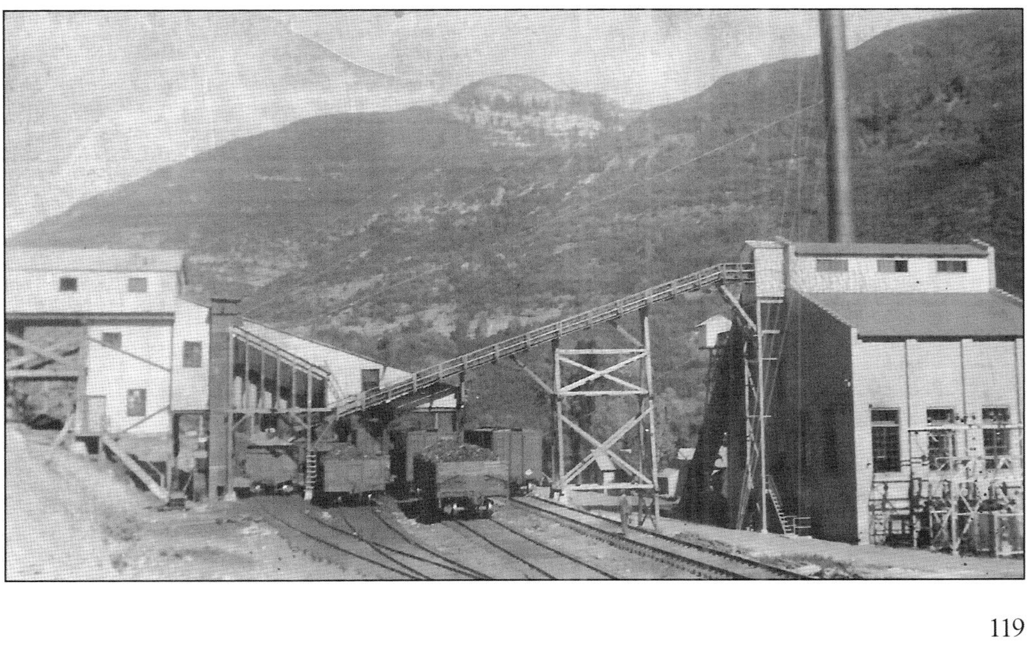

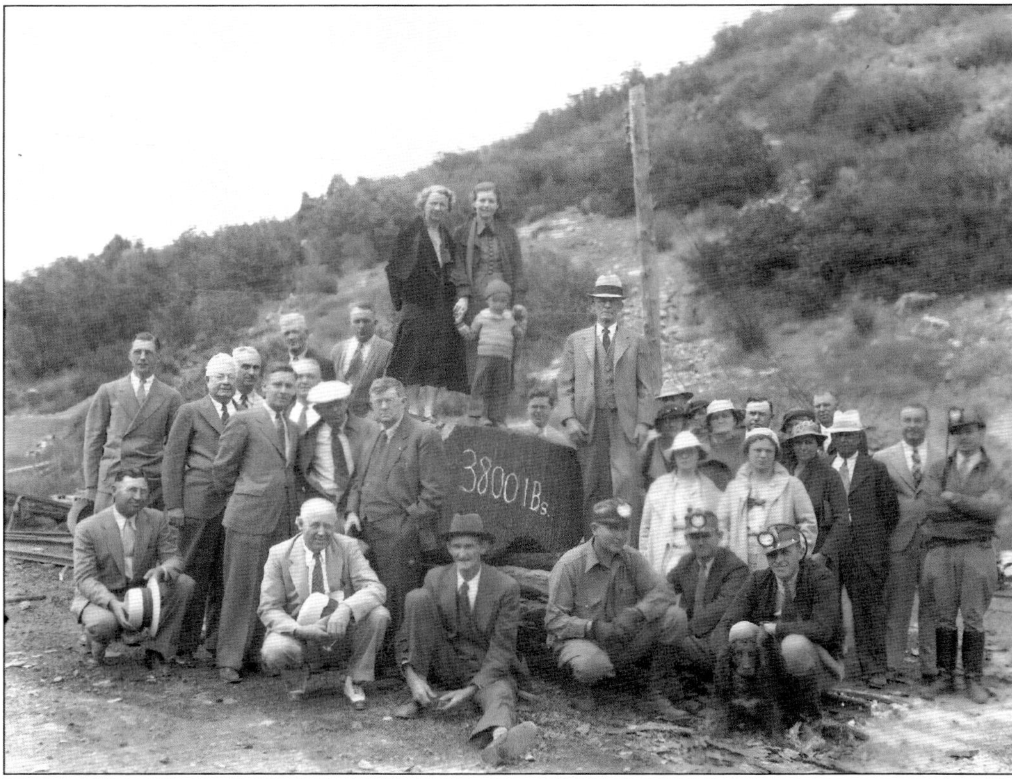

OLIVER MINE TOUR, 1937. Likely, this is a group of Paonia Rotarians and wives invited to the Oliver Mine by Ronald Oliver. Edwin Oliver was general manager, and John Hovgaard was sales manager. The group gathered at the mine in July 1937 for a tour and pictures. (Perhaps the individuals saw a dinosaur track; tracks were common in all mines.) Pictured second on the left on top of a large chunk of coal is Mayme Kemp, Oliver Mine secretary, with an unidentified woman. Mayme Kemp Abseck (1914–2012) was born in Paonia and remained in the community all her life. She married a handsome miner, Joseph Abseck. In 1941, twins Judy (Livingston) and Jody (Mead) were born. After World War II, brothers Joseph and George Abseck established A & M Electric in Paonia. (Above, NFHS; below, Bowie Collection.)

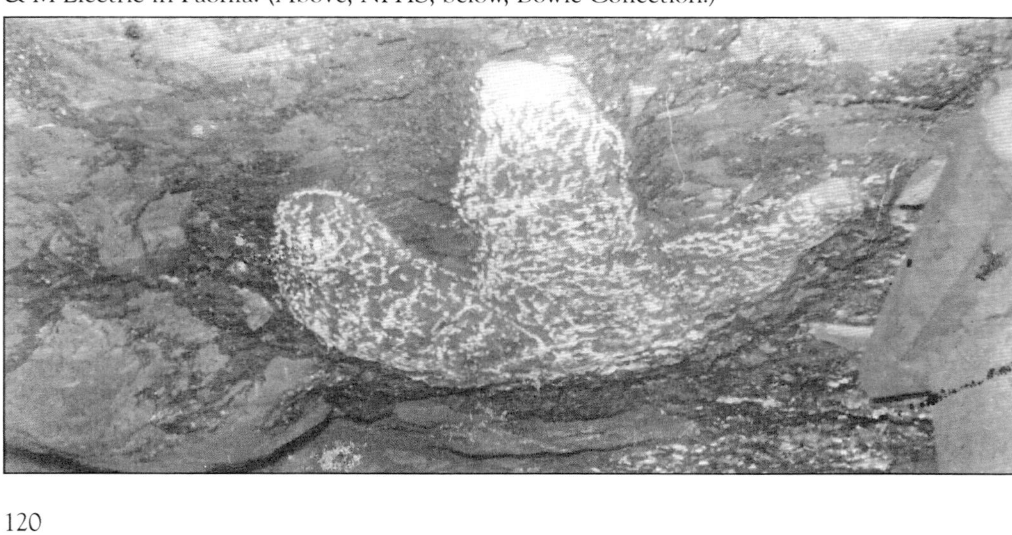

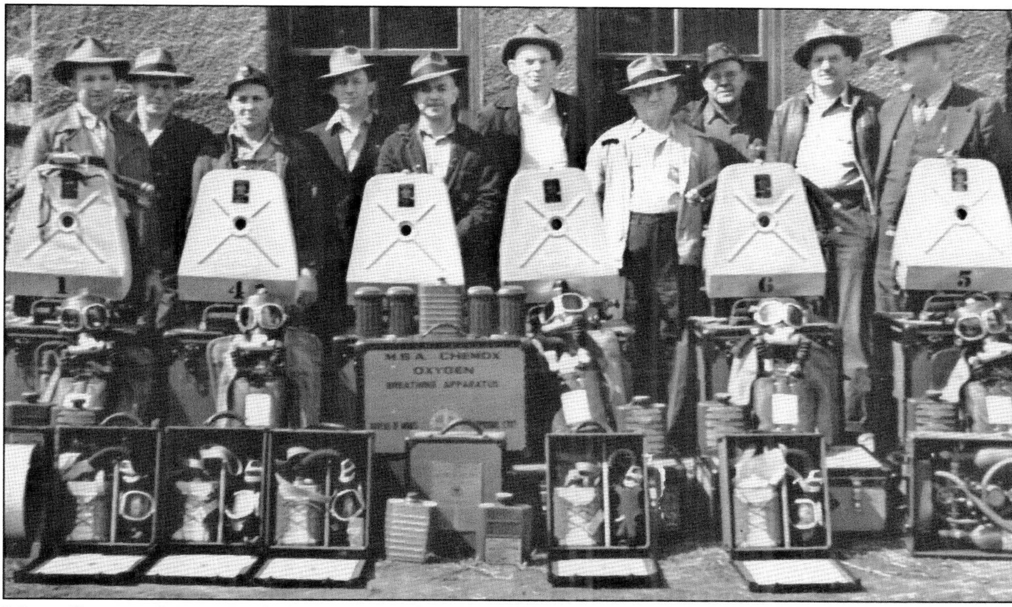

Mine Safety. Mines such as Bowie and Somerset shared in their information and equipment for making mine rescues. In 1913, Roger Payne, age 27, was killed by a powder blast at the Somerset mine when he cut the fuse too short. Oddly, his father had been killed in England in a similar accident. In later years, mine safety was emphasized with classes designed to keep miners aware of dangerous situations that could arise in the mines. In early times, miners worked with a partner who knew mining safety. Often, sons worked with their fathers, as several generations became miners. Both fire and floods were dangers, and tunnel collapses often led to death. The oxygen tanks, part of the mine rescue equipment shown, would last about 12 hours. (Above, Bowie Collection; below, Ralph Audin Jr.)

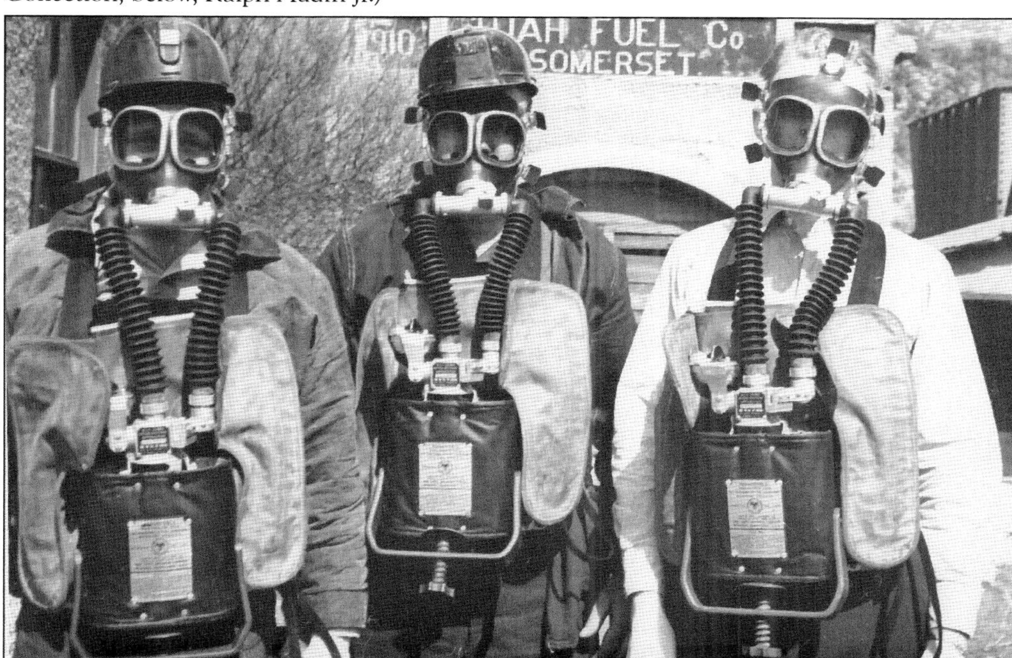

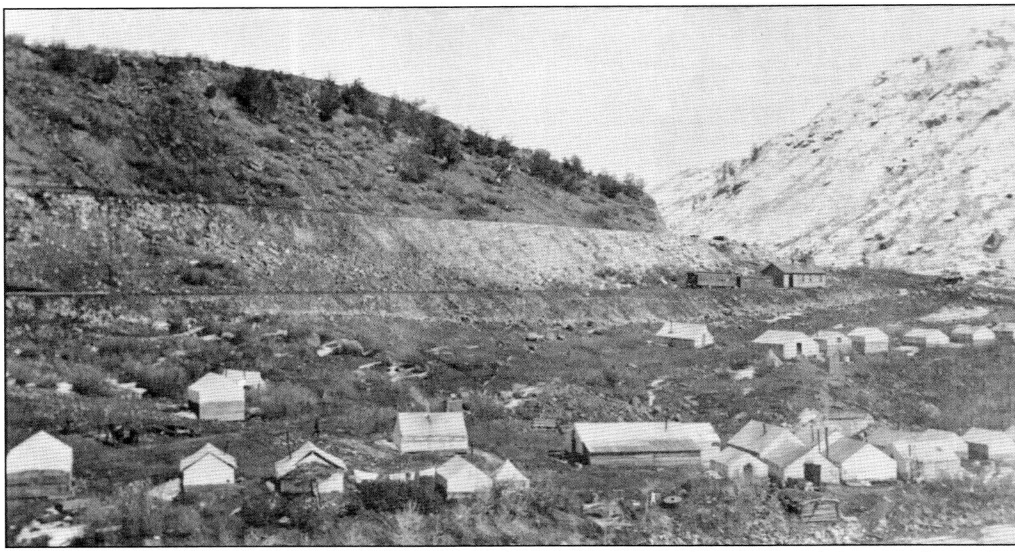

Tent Town to Company Houses. Many of the miners came from Crested Butte, where they had strong ties. At first, Somerset was a town of tents, typical of most early mining camps. Board floors and board sides were covered with tarps. Somerset soon had company houses and a company store. Its saloon was owned by colorful Jim Smith. In January 1916, Somerset Social Club charged dues of 75¢ for use of three pool tables, a reading room, and a game room. The club was open from 9:00 a.m. to 10:00 p.m., and drinking and gambling were banned. Early membership totaled 179 men. A boardinghouse nicknamed "The Beanery" provided lodging for single mine workers. Because of so many single men, a girl who attended Somerset dances said she never sat out a dance. (Both, DCHS.)

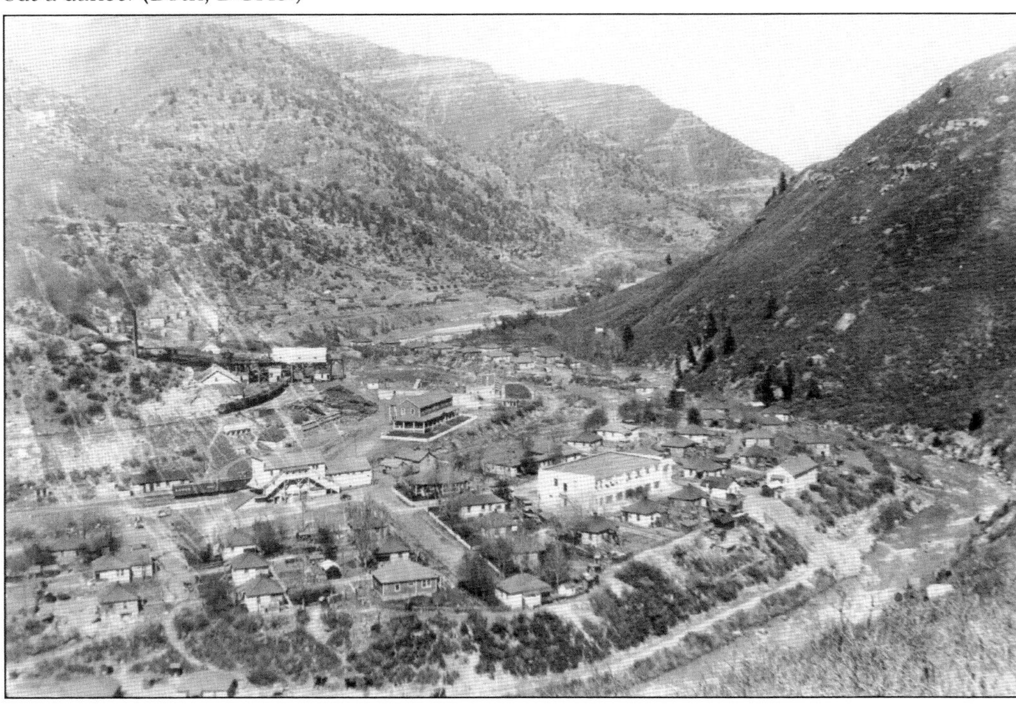

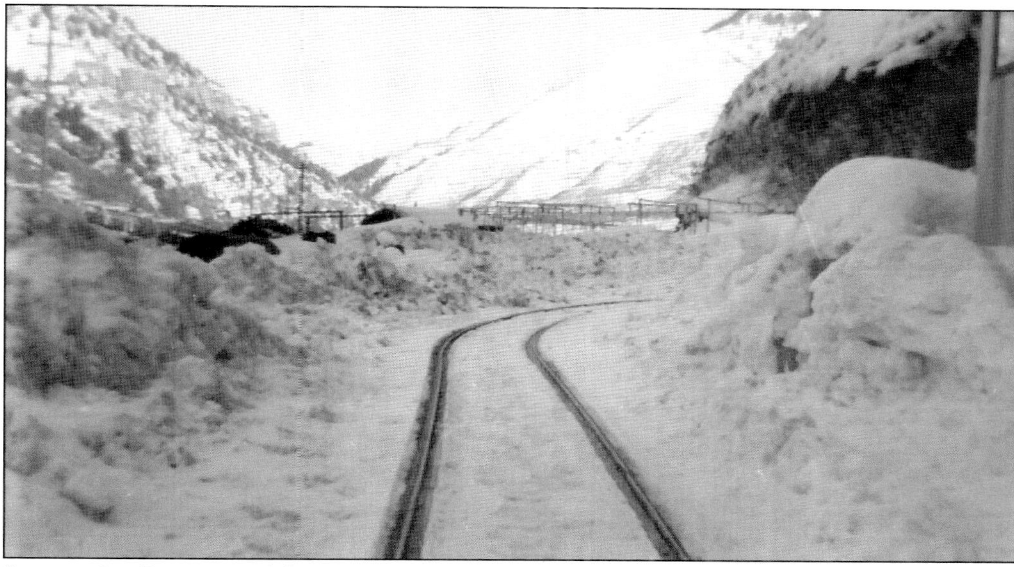

SNOWED IN. Deep snow fell in early February 1916, and the coal train from Somerset was unable to pull the train through drifts. Another engine was drafted to push from the back. The only problem was that the back engine kept pushing when the front engine had run into a large rock. The men in the front engine jumped, and four cars of coal turned over. (Bill and Terrie Bear.)

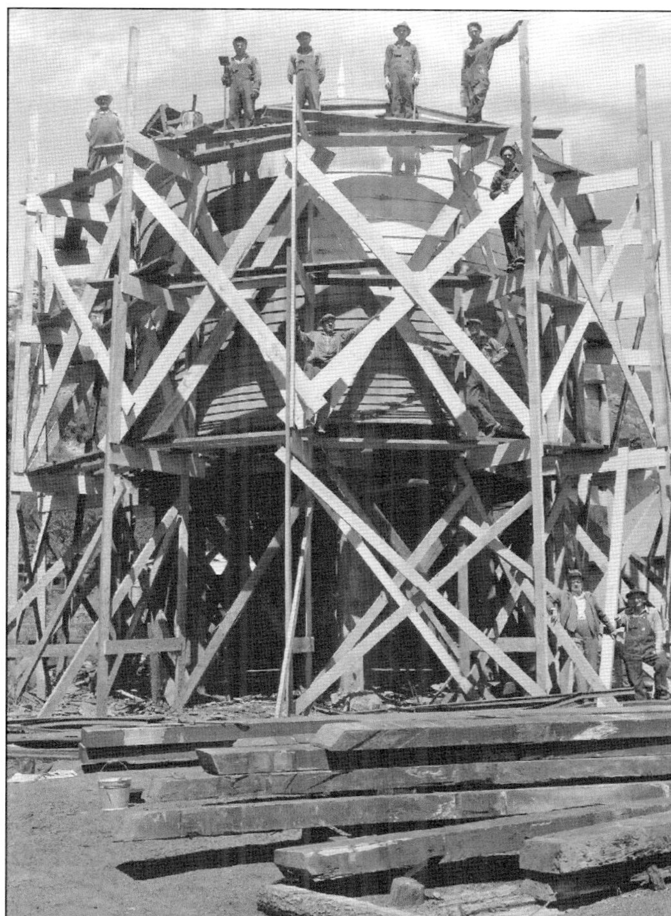

WATER TOWER. This tower provided water for the steam engine. The train carried drinking water from Paonia to Somerset when Somerset's muddy water was undrinkable. Mail was delivered by the train. In 1911, the Post Office Department said that Somerset was the only post office not connected to the outside by wagon. In 1915, the first automobile arrived. Otto Bross had the first car accident. (NFHS.)

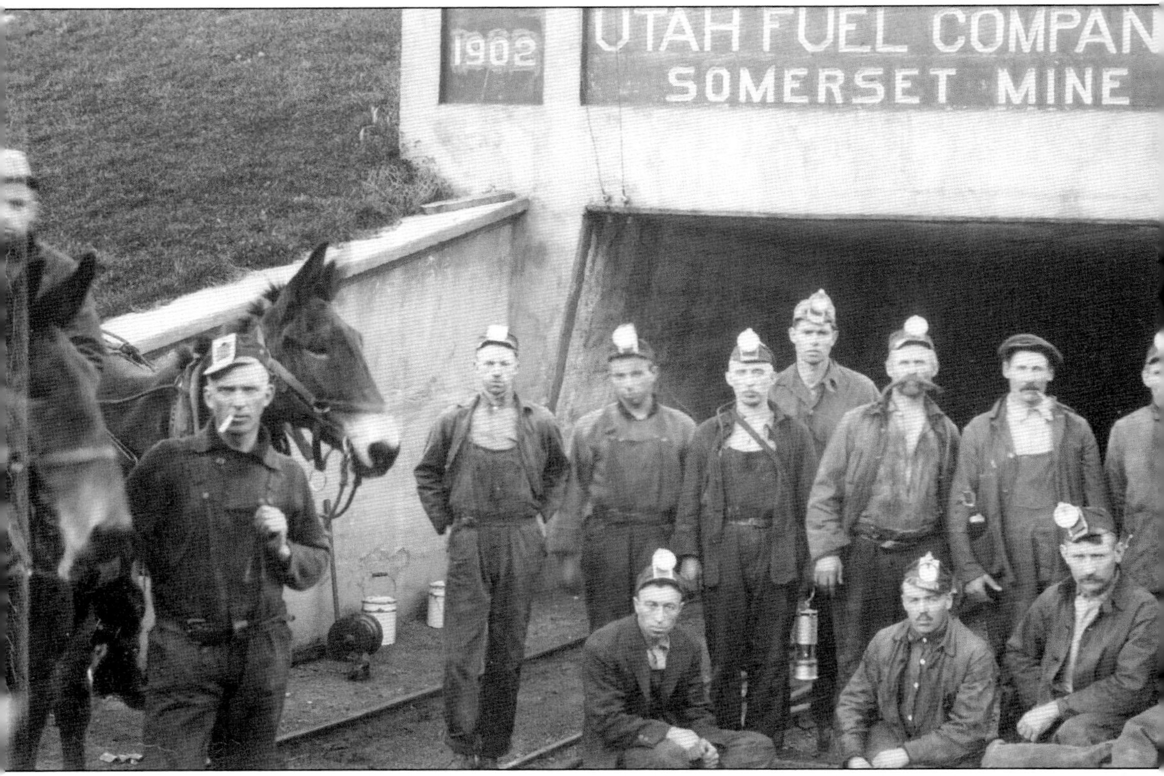

Somerset Portal. Miners are pictured at the 1902 portal of Utah Fuel. Somerset miners joined the United Mine Workers of America in 1933. Published in *Coal Age* magazine in 1939 are the names of miners who had worked for 20 years at Somerset. Listed are S. Turcsanski, W.H. Long, F. Tullio, H. Evans, R. Williams Jr., H. Nies, V. Luoma, T. Zakely Sr., J. Abseck Sr., A. Kocjancic, J. Kralj, C. Bartolo, T. Plute Jr., V. Maki, M. Karnely Sr., J.H. Cowan, M. Plute, D.E. Schmidt, O. Saari, I. Sanborn Sr., J. Delost, E. Dolgan, A. Penko, B. Charlesworth, T. Morgan, H. Mraule, L. Greenamyer, M. Mlaker, J. Payne, B. Poletta, L. Ungaro, A. Delost, J. Fatur, F. Daschner, I.J. Gaddis, M. Pagotto, S. Bohnet, G. Palmer, J. Rametti, A. Justin, and A. Kovacic. (Both, DCHS.)

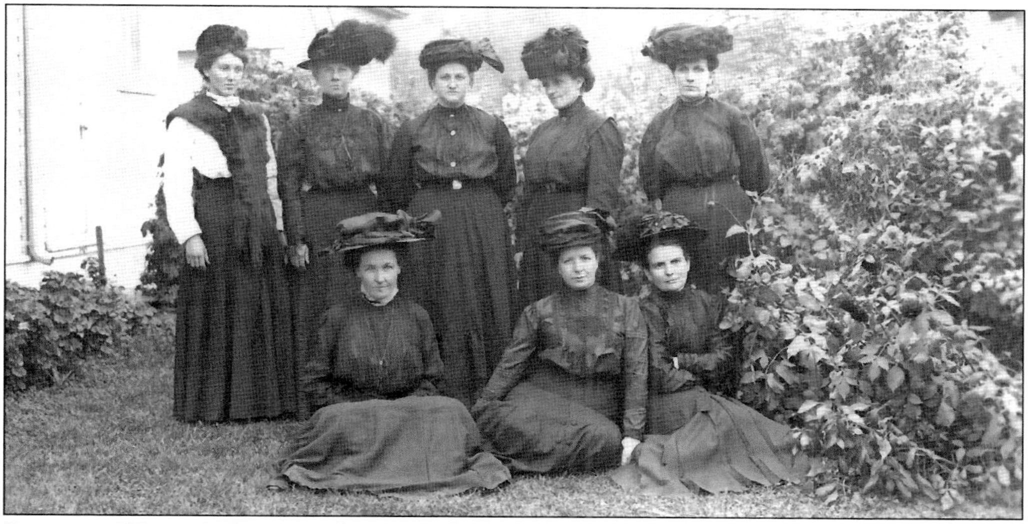

Somerset Women's Club. In this image from the early days, ladies are dressed beautifully for a club event. Perhaps this was an afternoon of sipping tea from cups that were family heirlooms from Europe. Some of the events enjoyed in the years 1938 to 1948 were roundtable discussions, a literary meeting, Scotch bridge, a social hour of cards, and being guests of the Paonia Woman's Club, which was noted for elegant tables with silver service for tea or coffee. Somerset had many musical groups that provided entertainment for the town, including Somerset Cowgirl Band, a girls' violin group, and Somerset Brass Band. An early band director was Paul Hunten. His wife, Augusta, was a member of the Woman's Club. (Above, Bill and Terrie Bear; below, NFHS.)

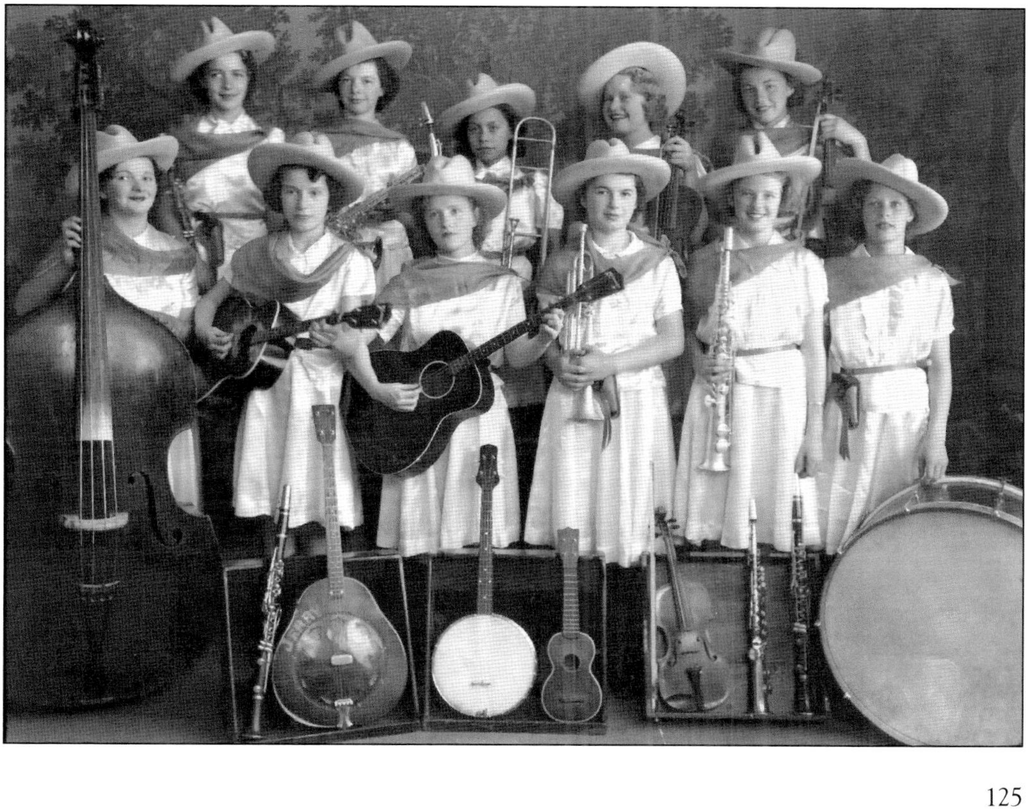

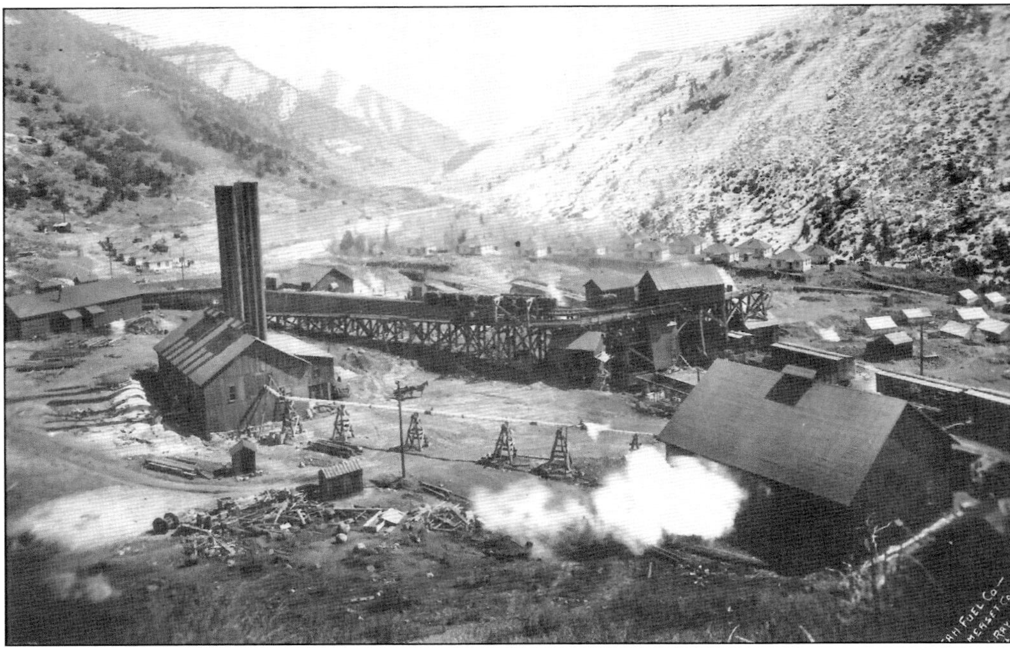

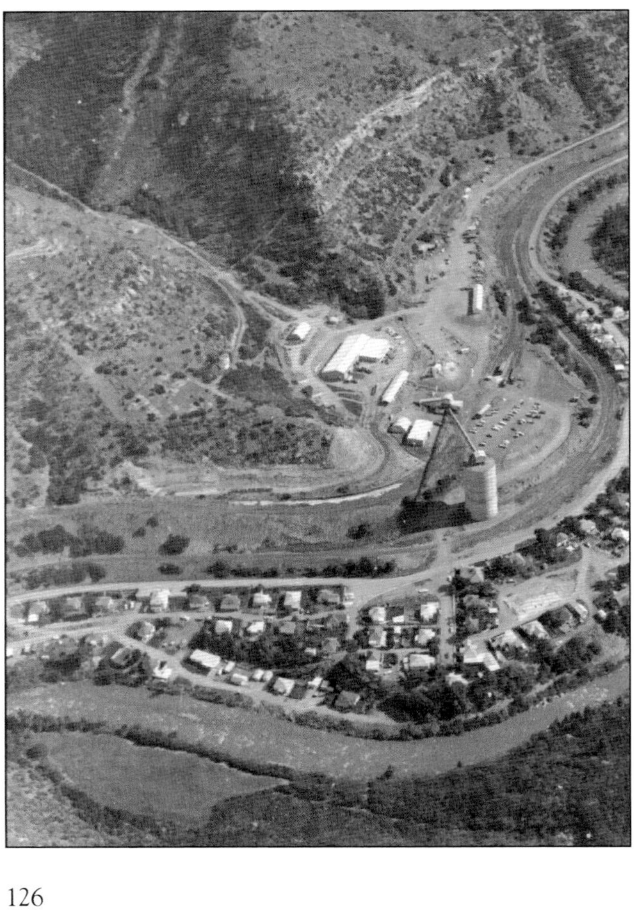

Pastimes in a Mining Town. A popular sport in early times was baseball. Even to this day, Somerset miners are avid sports fans. The Somerset baseball team was outstanding and feared by other teams it played. In the 1940s, a favorite pastime of Somerset kids was paddling in the swimming hole by the big rock. Many children lived all summer in swimsuits. Those brave enough to dive could paint their initials on the rock. One great hike was to the "Palace Hotel," a large rock formation above Somerset. A forbidden sport was climbing on the turnstile, a big track on a circular bed, which turned the train engine around to face back down the canyon. (Above, Bill and Terrie Bear; left, DCHS.)

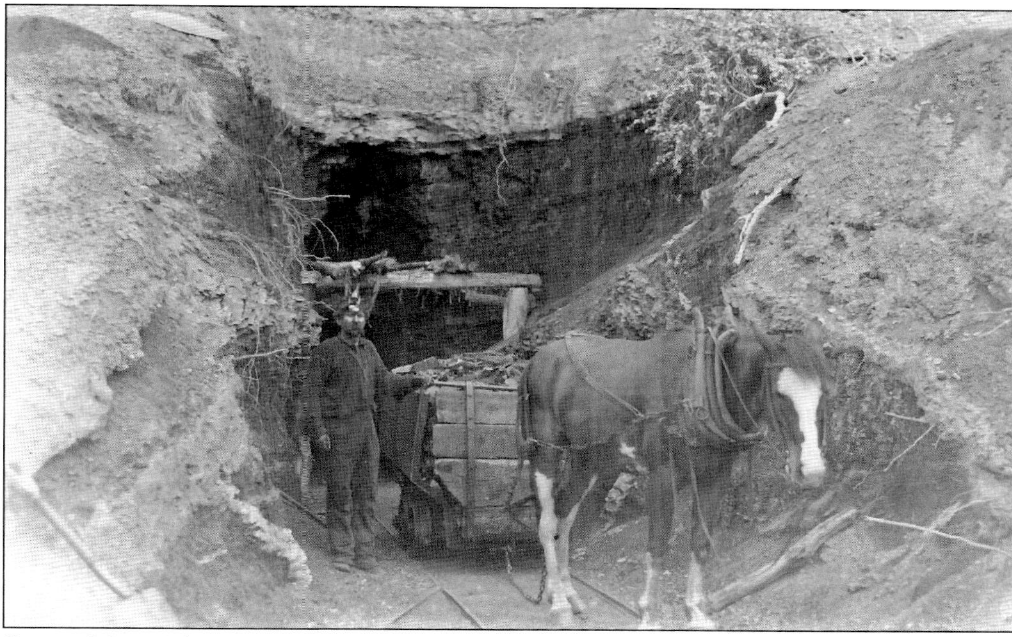

Cowan Mine. There were many small mines in the hills around Paonia. In early times, most of these mines supplied coal to blacksmiths. Many settlers just gathered cottonwood on the river bottom to burn for heat. Mercantile owner Milton Spencer estimated that the cost of coal for heating per year would only be $10. Some small mines to the north of Paonia were the Dorrance, Converse, Conine, and Cowan Mines. Westmoreland's presence in Paonia began in 1976 with Converse. Later, all these mines became Westmoreland mines. Pictured at the Black Diamond portal of the Cowan mine is Charles Cowan Sr. He lost his life when an empty coal car he was riding across the trestle tipped over, throwing him into the deep gully. (Both, Cowan family.)

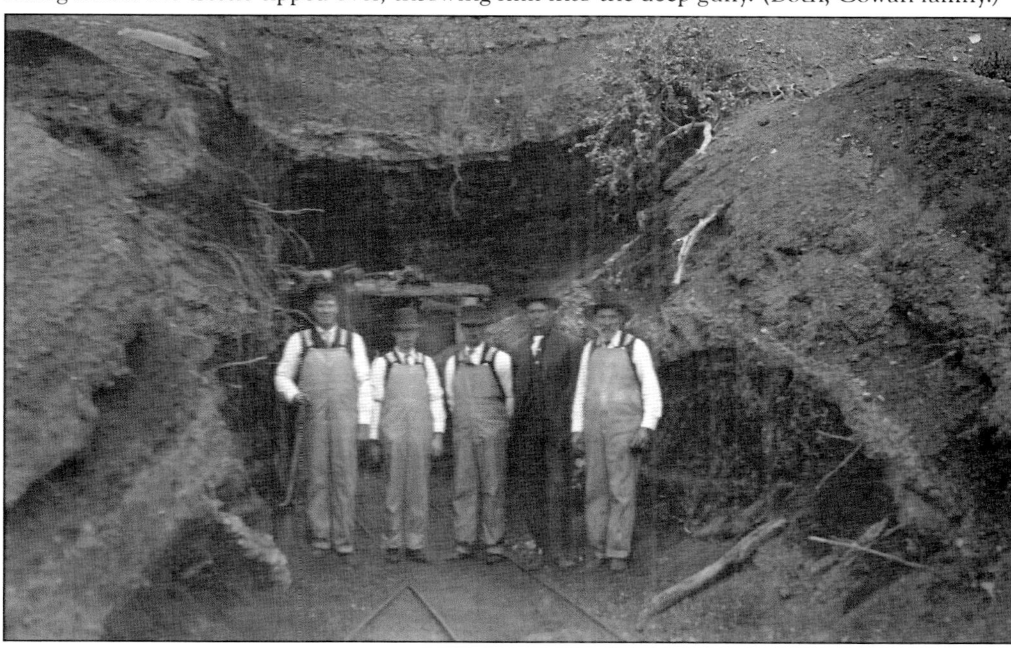